CHRISTMAS CLASSICS

CHRISTMAS CLASSICS

A TREASURY FOR LATTER-DAY SAINTS

DESERET BOOK COMPANY, SALT LAKE CITY, UTAH

Library of Congress Catalog Card Number 95-78852

ISBN 1-57345-089-8

Printed in the United States of America

10 9 8 7 6 5 4 3 2 1

CONTENTS

CHAPTER ONE
The Christ Child

Ancient Prophets Speak—The Coming of Our Lord	*Selected Scriptural Passages*	3
A God Is Born	*Bruce R. McConkie*	10
For All Mankind	*Mabel Jones Gabbott*	16
On the Morning of Christ's Nativity	*John Milton*	17
Remembering Jesus	*Harold B. Lee, N. Eldon Tanner, and*	
	Marion G. Romney	18
"The Birth of Jesus Christ Was on This Wise"	*Gerald N. Lund*	19
You, Simeon, Spirit-filled	*Jay A. Parry*	27
The Wonder of the Story	*Charles Irvin Junkin*	27
His Gift	*Giles H. Florence, Jr.*	28
The Mary-Song	*Betty W. Madsen*	28
Thoughts on Christmas	*Hugh B. Brown*	29
Keeping Christ in Christmas	*Ezra Taft Benson*	30
Looking for a King	*George MacDonald*	33
Mary and Her Son	*Margery S. Stewart*	33
A Christmas Carol	*Gilbert K. Chesterton*	34
As Joseph Was A-Walking	*Old English Carol*	34

CHAPTER TWO
Faith & Testimony

The Wondrous Gift	*Spencer W. Kimball*	37
Let Every Heart Keep	*Phillips Brooks*	40
That Holy Star	*William Cullen Bryant*	40
O Holy Child	*Phillips Brooks*	40
Time for Hope	*Joann Jensen McGrath*	41
In Temptation	*Weiss Wenig*	42

Pilgrimage to Christmas	*Dorothy J. Roberts*	50
The Little Match Girl	*Hans Christian Andersen*	51
Winter Quarters	*Berta Huish Christensen*	53
Yuletide in a Younger World	*Thomas Hardy*	54
Three Levels of Christmas	*William B. Smart*	54

CHAPTER THREE
Shepherds & Wise Men

The Three Kings	*Henry Wadsworth Longfellow*	59
The Miracle	*Claire S. Boyer*	60
Good Tidings of Great Joy	*David O. McKay*	61
How Simple	*Angelus Silesius*	62
Dividers of the Stars	*Vesta P. Crawford*	62
When the Wise Man Appeared	*William Ashley Anderson*	63
The Shepherds and the Magi	*Young Men's Mutual Improvement Association Manual, 1897–98*	65
A Hymn on the Nativity of My Saviour	*Ben Jonson*	66
We Three Kings of Orient Are	*John Henry Hopkins, Jr.*	66
From a Far Country	*Vesta P. Crawford*	67
The Song of a Shepherd-boy at Bethlehem	*Josephine Preston Peabody*	68
The Holy Night	*Elizabeth Barrett Browning*	69

CHAPTER FOUR
Love & Sharing

Food for Santa	*Anna Marie Scow, as told to Jack M. Lyon*	73
Most Gentle Love	*Anonymous*	73
Christmas Is for Sharing	*Richard Warner, as told to Emma Lou Warner Thayne*	74
The Gift	*Elaine Reiser Alder*	75
The Visit of the King	*Bertha Irvine*	78
A Christmas Hymn	*Christina Georgina Rossetti*	84
I Think You Have a Fire at Your Store	*LaRue H. Soelberg*	84
Gifts for the Poor	*Shirley G. Finlinson*	86

Trouble at the Inn	Dina Donohue	88
Loving Father, Help Us	Robert Louis Stevenson	90

CHAPTER FIVE
Blessing Others

Are You Ready for Christmas?	Harold B. Lee	93
For Them	Eleanor Farjeon	94
Three Christmas Gifts	Mildred Goff	95
The Joy of Giving	John Greenleaf Whittier	96
On the Night of the Nativity	Anonymous	96
Harry's Carol	Lisa Dahlgren	97
On Another Street	Berta Huish Christensen	99

CHAPTER SIX
Giving & Receiving

Charity Christmas	Alma J. Yates	103
The Snow Is on the Land	S. Dilworth Young	110
Unto the Least of These	Marilyn McMeen Miller Brown	111
To Springvale for Christmas	Zona Gale	112
Nearest and Dearest	Ruth Moench Bell	117
A Christmas Thought	James Russell Lowell	121

CHAPTER SEVEN
Service & Sacrifice

Our Pickle-Jar Christmas	Wilma M. Rich	125
Keeping Christmas	Henry Van Dyke	128
The Year of the Flexible Flyers	Aney B. Chatterton	129
The Christmas We Gave Away	Marilyn Ellsworth Swinyard	131
The Christmas Letter	Charles M. Manwaring	134
Mom's Vacation	Elsie C. Carroll	136
A Special Christmas	S. Dilworth Young	143

The Joy They Shared	*Juanita Sadler*	144
Christmas, Second Time Around	*Steve D. Hanson*	145
The Gift of the Magi	*O. Henry*	147

CHAPTER EIGHT
Worship & Joy

Christmas Legends	*Denis A. McCarthy*	153
All Are Vocal with His Name	*Phillips Brooks*	153
The Joys of Christmas	*Ezra Taft Benson*	154
There's a Song in the Air	*Josiah G. Holland*	160
In the Bleak Mid-Winter	*Christina Georgina Rossetti*	160
Friend to Friend	*S. Dilworth Young*	161
Brightest and Best of the Sons of the Morning	*A. C. Smyth*	161
Uncle Kees' Christmas Rebellion	*Pierre Van Paassen*	162
The Oxen	*Thomas Hardy*	163
A Christmas Carol	*Christina Georgina Rossetti*	164
The Joy of Christmas	*Charles Dickens*	164
A Warm and Gracious Christmas	*Marion D. Hanks*	165
My Gift	*Eugene Field*	172
The Earth Has Grown Old	*Phillips Brooks*	172
Thou Whose Birth	*A. C. Swinburne*	173
The Christmas Peace	*F. H. Sweet*	173
Ever 'gainst That Season	*William Shakespeare*	174
Holiday on the Bus	*Tracine Hales Parkinson*	174

CHAPTER NINE
Home & Family

The Old Blue Bike	*Joel R. Bryan*	179
Christmas Reminiscences	*Joseph F. Smith, from a letter to a son*	180
A Family Affair	*Lucy Parr*	182
Christmas at Sea	*Robert Louis Stevenson*	186
The Year We Discovered Tradition	*Jay A. Parry*	188

CHAPTER TEN
Celebration & Fun

Christmas Every Day	*William Dean Howells*	195
The Ghost of Christmas Present	*Charles Dickens*	200
At Christmas Be Merry	*Thomas Tusser*	203
Christmas Time	*From an 18th-Century Ballad*	203
The Christmas Miracle	*Robert Keith Leavitt*	204
A Christmas Eve Thought	*Harriet Brewer Sterling*	205
The Night Before Christmas	*Clement C. Moore*	206
Is There a Santa Claus?	*Francis P. Church*	207
Index of Titles		209
Index of Authors		211

Appreciation is expressed for permission to use the following:

"For All Mankind," by Mabel Jones Gabbott, from the *Relief Society Magazine,* Dec. 1965.

"The Birth of Jesus Christ Was on This Wise," by Gerald N. Lund, from *Jesus Christ, Key to the Plan of Salvation,* Deseret Book Company, 1991.

"His Gift," by Giles H. Florence, Jr., from the *Ensign,* Dec. 1987.

"The Mary-Song," by Betty W. Madsen, from the Christmas News section of the *Deseret News,* no date, reprinted in Berta H. Christensen, *Christmas Is for You,* Deseret Book 1968.

The Wondrous Gift by Spencer W. Kimball, booklet from Deseret Book, 1978.

"Time for Hope," by Joann Jensen McGrath, from the *Ensign,* Dec. 1991.

"Winter Quarters," by Berta Huish Christensen, from *Christmas Is for You,* Deseret Book Company, 1968.

"Three Levels of Christmas," by William B. Smart, from *Messages for a Happier Life,* Deseret Book Company, 1989.

"Food for Santa," by Anna Marie Scow, as told to Jack M. Lyon.

"The Gift," by Elaine Reiser Alder, from the *Ensign,* Dec. 1983.

"I Think You Have a Fire at Your Store," by LaRue H. Soelberg, from the *Deseret News,* Dec. 21, 1970.

"Gifts for the Poor," by Shirley G. Finlinson, from the *Friend,* Dec. 1993.

"Are You Ready for Christmas?" by Harold B. Lee, from the *Improvement Era,* Dec. 1968.

"Harry's Carol," by Lisa Dahlgren, from the *New Era,* Dec. 1991.

"On Another Street," by Berta Huish Christensen, from *Christmas Is for You,* Deseret Book, 1968.

"Charity Christmas," by Alma J. Yates, from the *New Era,* Dec. 1984.

"The Snow Is on the Land," by S. Dilworth Young, from the *Improvement Era,* Dec. 1970.

"Unto the Least of These," by Marilyn McMeen Miller Brown, from the *Ensign,* Dec. 1976.

"Our Pickle-Jar Christmas," by Wilma M. Rich, from the *Ensign,* Dec. 1993.

"The Year of the Flexible Flyers," by Aney B. Chatterton, from the *Ensign,* Dec. 1984.

"The Christmas We Gave Away," by Marilyn Ellsworth Swinyard, from the *Deseret News,* Dec. 24, 1971.

"The Christmas Letter," by Charles M. Manwaring, from the *New Era,* Dec. 1982.

"The Joy They Shared," by Juanita Sadler, from the *New Era,* Dec. 1993.

"Christmas, Second Time Around," by Steve D. Hanson, from the *Ensign,* Dec. 1979.

"Friend to Friend," by S. Dilworth Young, from the *Friend,* Dec. 1972.

A Warm and Gracious Christmas, by Marion D. Hanks, booklet from Deseret Book Company, 1991.

"Holiday on the Bus," by Tracine Hales Parkinson, from the *New Era,* Dec. 1990.

"The Old Blue Bike," by Joel R. Bryan, from the *New Era,* Dec. 1984.

"The Year We Discovered Tradition," by Jay A. Parry, from the *Ensign,* Dec. 1977.

Appreciation is expressed to The Church of Jesus Christ of Latter-day Saints for the use of the following:

"The Miracle," by Claire S. Boyer, from the *Relief Society Magazine,* Dec. 1928.

"Good Tidings of Great Joy," by David O. McKay, from the *Improvement Era,* Dec. 1958.

"Dividers of the Stars," by Vesta P. Crawford, from the *Relief Society Magazine,* Dec. 1959.

"From a Far Country," by Vesta P. Crawford, from the *Relief Society Magazine,* Dec. 1952.

"Christmas Is for Sharing," by Richard Warner as told to Emma Lou Warner Thayne, from the *Improvement Era,* Dec. 1964.

"Three Christmas Gifts," by Mildred Goff, from the *Improvement Era,* Dec. 1957.

"Mom's Vacation," by Elsie C. Carroll, from the *Relief Society Magazine,* Dec. 1930.

We acknowledge copyright holders whose material we may have included but with whom we were unable to make personal contact. Other works are in public domain.

Thanks to the following, who made this book possible:

Cindy L. DeYoung, typist
Michelle Eckersley, art director and designer
Scott Greer, illustrator
Devan Jensen, proofreading coordinator
Camille Lots, permissions coordinator
Jack M. Lyon, production coordinator
Patricia J. Parkinson, initial researcher and typographer
Jay A. Parry, editor and compiler
Ida M. Robinson, typist
Andrea I. Smith, researcher
Elsha Ulberg, permissions coordinator
Alden L. Weight, researcher

And special thanks to the dozens of authors who shared their talent and insight on the many aspects of the wonderful season of Christmas.

CHAPTER ONE

The Christ Child

Ancient Prophets Speak—The Coming of Our Lord

Part 1:
What the Seers Saw

Therefore the Lord himself shall give you a sign;
Behold, a virgin shall conceive, and bear a son,
And shall call his name Immanuel. . . .
[And ye shall say:]
For unto us a child is born,
Unto us a son is given:
And the government shall be upon his shoulder:
And his name shall be called Wonderful, Counseller,
The mighty God, The everlasting Father, The
   Prince of Peace.
Of the increase of his government and peace
There shall be no end,
Upon the throne of David, and upon his kingdom,
To order it, and to establish it with judgment and
   with justice
From henceforth even for ever.
The zeal of the LORD of hosts will perform this. . . .
[Yea,] behold, the time cometh, and is not far dis-
   tant,
That with power,
The Lord Omnipotent
Who reigneth, who was, and is from all eternity to
   all eternity,
Shall come down from heaven among the children
   of men,
And shall dwell in a tabernacle of clay,
And shall go forth amongst men, working mighty
   miracles,

Such as healing the sick,
Raising the dead,
Causing the lame to walk,
The blind to receive their sight,
And the deaf to hear,
And curing all manner of diseases.
And he shall cast out devils,
Or the evil spirits
Which dwell in the hearts of the children of men.
And lo, he shall suffer temptations,
And pain of body, hunger, thirst, and fatigue,
Even more than man can suffer, except it be unto
   death;
For behold, blood cometh from every pore,
So great shall be his anguish for the wickedness
And the abominations of his people.
And he shall be called Jesus Christ,
The Son of God,
The Father of heaven and earth,
The Creator of all things from the beginning;
And his mother shall be called Mary.
And lo, he cometh unto his own,
That salvation might come unto the children of
   men
Even through faith on his name;
And even after all this they shall consider him a
   man,
And say that he hath a devil,
And shall scourge him,
And shall crucify him.
And he shall rise the third day from the dead;
And behold, he standeth to judge the world;
And behold, all these things are done
That a righteous judgment might come
Upon the children of men. . . .
[Yea,] behold, he shall be born of Mary,
At Jerusalem which is the land of our forefathers,
She being a virgin, a precious and chosen vessel,

Who shall be overshadowed
And conceive by the power of the Holy Ghost,
And bring forth a son, yea, even the Son of God.
And he shall go forth,
Suffering pains and afflictions and temptations of
    every kind;
And this that the word might be fulfilled
Which saith he will take upon him
The pains and the sicknesses of his people.
And he will take upon him death,
That he may loose the bands of death which bind
    his people;
And he will take upon him their infirmities,
That his bowels may be filled with mercy, according
    to the flesh,
That he may know according to the flesh
How to succor his people according to their infirmi-
    ties. . . .
And behold, this will I give unto you
For a sign at the time of his coming;
For behold, there shall be great lights in heaven,
Insomuch that in the night before he cometh
There shall be no darkness,
Insomuch that it shall appear unto man as if it was
    day.
Therefore, there shall be one day and a night and a
    day,
As if it were one day and there were no night;
And this shall be unto you for a sign;
For ye shall know of the rising of the sun
And also of its setting;
Therefore they shall know of a surety
That there shall be two days and a night;
Nevertheless the night shall not be darkened;
And it shall be the night before he is born.
And behold, there shall a new star arise,
Such an one as ye never have beheld;
And this also shall be a sign unto you.

And behold this is not all,
There shall be many signs and wonders in heaven.
And it shall come to pass that ye shall all be amazed,
And wonder, insomuch that ye shall fall to the
    earth.
And it shall come to pass that whosoever shall
    believe
On the Son of God,
The same shall have everlasting life.
(Isaiah 7:14, 9:6–7; Mosiah 3:5–10; Alma 7:10–12;
    Helaman 14:1–8)

Part 2:
The Birth of Jesus Christ

Now the birth of Jesus Christ was on this wise: . . .
The angel Gabriel was sent from God
Unto a city of Galilee, named Nazareth,
To a virgin espoused to a man whose name was
    Joseph,
Of the house of David;
And the virgin's name was Mary.
And the angel came in unto her, and said,
Hail, thou that art highly favoured,
The Lord is with thee:
Blessed art thou among women.
And when she saw him, she was troubled at his say-
    ing,
And cast in her mind what manner of salutation this
    should be.
And the angel said unto her,
Fear not, Mary: for thou hast found favour with
    God.
And, behold, thou shalt conceive in thy womb,
And bring forth a son, and shalt call his name
    JESUS.
He shall be great,
And shall be called the Son of the Highest:

And the Lord God shall give unto him
The throne of his father David:
And he shall reign over the house of Jacob for ever;
And of his kingdom there shall be no end.
Then said Mary unto the angel,
How shall this be, seeing I know not a man?
And the angel answered and said unto her,
The Holy Ghost shall come upon thee,
And the power of the Highest shall overshadow
    thee:
Therefore also that holy thing which shall be born
    of thee
Shall be called the Son of God.
And, behold, thy cousin Elisabeth,
She hath also conceived a son in her old age:
And this is the sixth month with her, who was called
    barren.
For with God nothing shall be impossible.
And Mary said, Behold the handmaid of the Lord;
Be it unto me according to thy word.
And the angel departed from her.
And Mary arose in those days,
And went into the hill country with haste, into a
    city of Juda;
And entered into the house of Zacharias,
And saluted Elisabeth.
And it came to pass, that,
When Elisabeth heard the salutation of Mary,
The babe leaped in her womb;
And Elisabeth was filled with the Holy Ghost:
And she spake out with a loud voice, and said,
Blessed art thou among women,
And blessed is the fruit of thy womb.
And whence is this to me,
That the mother of my Lord should come to me?
For, lo, as soon as the voice of thy salutation
Sounded in mine ears,
The babe leaped in my womb for joy.

And blessed is she that believed:
For there shall be a performance of those things
Which were told her from the Lord.
And Mary said, My soul doth magnify the Lord,
And my spirit hath rejoiced in God my Saviour.
For he hath regarded the low estate of his hand-
    maiden:
For, behold, from henceforth all generations shall
    call me blessed.
For he that is mighty hath done to me great things;
And holy is his name.
And his mercy is on them that fear him
From generation to generation.
He hath shewed strength with his arm;
He hath scattered the proud in the imagination of
    their hearts.
He hath put down the mighty from their seats,
And exalted them of low degree.
He hath filled the hungry with good things;
And the rich he hath sent empty away.
He hath holpen his servant Israel, in remembrance
    of his mercy;
As he spake to our fathers, to Abraham, and to his
    seed for ever.
And Mary abode with her about three months,
And returned to her own house. . . .
[Now] Mary was espoused to Joseph,
[And] before they came together,
She was found with child of the Holy Ghost.
Then Joseph her husband, being a just man,
And not willing to make her a publick example,
Was minded to put her away privily.
But while he thought on these things, behold,
The angel of the Lord appeared unto him in a
    dream,
Saying, Joseph, thou son of David,
Fear not to take unto thee Mary thy wife:

For that which is conceived in her is of the Holy
　　Ghost.
And she shall bring forth a son,
And thou shalt call his name JESUS:
For he shall save his people from their sins.
Now all this was done, that it might be fulfilled
Which was spoken of the Lord by the prophet, saying,
Behold, a virgin shall be with child,
And shall bring forth a son,
And they shall call his name Emmanuel,
Which being interpreted is, God with us.
Then Joseph being raised from sleep
Did as the angel of the Lord had bidden him,
And took unto him his wife. . . .
And it came to pass in those days,
That there went out a decree from Caesar Augustus,
That all the world should be taxed. . . .
And all went to be taxed, every one into his own city.
And Joseph also went up from Galilee, out of the
　　city of Nazareth,
Into Judaea, unto the city of David, which is called
　　Bethlehem;
(Because he was of the house and lineage of David:)
To be taxed with Mary his espoused wife,
Being great with child.
And so it was, that, while they were there,
The days were accomplished that she should be
　　delivered.
And she brought forth her firstborn son,
And wrapped him in swaddling clothes,
And laid him in a manger;
Because there was no room for them in the inn. . . .
And [Joseph] knew her not till she had brought
　　forth
Her firstborn son:
And he called his name JESUS.
(Matt. 1:18; Luke 1:26–56; Matt. 1:18–22; Luke
　　2:1–7; Matt. 1:25)

Part 3:
The Witnesses

And there were in the same country
Shepherds abiding in the field,
Keeping watch over their flock by night.
And, lo, the angel of the Lord came upon them,
And the glory of the Lord shone round about them:
And they were sore afraid.
And the angel said unto them,
Fear not: for, behold, I bring you good tidings of
　　great joy,
Which shall be to all people.
For unto you is born this day in the city of David
A Saviour, which is Christ the Lord.
And this shall be a sign unto you;
Ye shall find the babe wrapped in swaddling clothes,
Lying in a manger.
And suddenly there was with the angel
A multitude of the heavenly host praising God, and
　　saying,
Glory to God in the highest,
And on earth peace, good will toward men.
And it came to pass,
As the angels were gone away from them into
　　heaven,
The shepherds said one to another,
Let us now go even unto Bethlehem,
And see this thing which is come to pass,
Which the Lord hath made known unto us.
And they came with haste,
And found Mary, and Joseph,
And the babe lying in a manger.
And when they had seen it, they made known
　　abroad
The saying which was told them concerning this
　　child.
And all they that heard it

Wondered at those things which were told them by
the shepherds.
But Mary kept all these things, and pondered them
in her heart.
And the shepherds returned,
Glorifying and praising God for all the things
That they had heard and seen, as it was told unto
them. . . .
And it came to pass that in the [promised land of
America], . . .
Behold, the prophecies of the prophets
Began to be fulfilled more fully;
For there began to be greater signs
And greater miracles wrought among the people.
But there were some who began to say
That the time was past for the words to be ful-
filled, . . .
And it came to pass that they did make
A great uproar throughout the land;
[But] the people who believed . . . did watch stead-
fastly
For that day and that night and that day
Which should be as one day as if there were no
night,
That they might know that their faith had not been
vain.
Now . . . there was a day set apart by the unbelievers,
That all those who believed in those traditions
Should be put to death except the sign should come
to pass. . . .
[Wherefore,] Nephi . . . bowed himself down upon
the earth,
And cried mightily to his God in behalf of his
people. . . .
And it came to pass that he cried mightily unto the
Lord, all that day;
And behold, the voice of the Lord came unto him,
saying:

Lift up your head and be of good cheer;
For behold, the time is at hand,
And on this night shall the sign be given,
And on the morrow come I into the world. . . .
Behold, I come unto my own,
To fulfill all things which I have made known
Unto the children of men from the foundation of
the world,
And to do the will, both of the Father and of the
Son—
Of the Father because of me, and of the Son
because of my flesh.
And behold, the time is at hand,
And this night shall the sign be given.
And it came to pass
That the words which came unto Nephi were ful-
filled, . . .
For behold, at the going down of the sun there was
no darkness;
And the people began to be astonished . . .
Yea, . . . all the people upon the face of the whole
earth
From the west to the east,
Both in the land north and in the land south,
Were so exceedingly astonished that they fell to the
earth.
And it came to pass that there was no darkness in all
that night,
But it was as light as though it was mid-day.
And it came to pass that the sun did rise in the
morning again,
According to its proper order;
And they knew that it was the day that the Lord
should be born,
Because of the sign which had been given.
And it had come to pass, yea, all things, every whit,
According to the words of the prophets.
And it came to pass also that a new star did appear,

According to the word. . . .
And when eight days were accomplished
For the circumcising of the child,
His name was called JESUS,
Which was so named of the angel
Before he was conceived in the womb.
And . . . they brought him to Jerusalem,
To present him to the Lord; . . .
And to offer a sacrifice
According to that which is said in the law of the
    Lord,
A pair of turtledoves, or two young pigeons.
And, behold, there was a man in Jerusalem,
Whose name was Simeon;
And the same man was just and devout,
Waiting for the consolation of Israel:
And the Holy Ghost was upon him.
And it was revealed unto him by the Holy Ghost,
That he should not see death,
Before he had seen the Lord's Christ.
And he came by the Spirit into the temple:
And when the parents brought in the child Jesus,
To do for him after the custom of the law,
Then took he him up in his arms, and blessed God,
    and said,
Lord, now lettest thou thy servant depart in peace,
According to thy word:
For mine eyes have seen thy salvation,
Which thou hast prepared before the face of all
    people;
A light to lighten the Gentiles,
And the glory of thy people Israel.
And Joseph and his mother
Marvelled at those things which were spoken of
    him.
And Simeon blessed them, and said unto Mary his
    mother,
Behold, this child is set for the fall

And rising again of many in Israel;
And for a sign which shall be spoken against;
(Yea, a sword shall pierce through thy own soul
    also,)
That the thoughts of many hearts may be revealed.
And there was one Anna, a prophetess,
[And] . . . she was of a great age, . . .
And she was a widow of about fourscore and four
    years,
Which departed not from the temple,
But served God with fastings and prayers night and
    day.
And she coming in that instant
Gave thanks likewise unto the Lord,
And spake of him to all them
That looked for redemption in Jerusalem.
And when they had performed all things
According to the law of the Lord,
They returned into Galilee, to their own city
    Nazareth. . . .
Now when Jesus was born in Bethlehem of Judaea
In the days of Herod the king,
Behold, there came wise men from the east to
    Jerusalem,
Saying, Where is he that is born King of the Jews?
For we have seen his star in the east,
And are come to worship him.
When Herod the king had heard these things,
He was troubled, and all Jerusalem with him.
And when he had gathered all the chief priests and
    scribes
Of the people together,
He demanded of them where Christ should be
    born.
And they said unto him,
In Bethlehem of Judaea: for thus it is written by the
    prophet,
And thou Bethlehem, in the land of Juda,

Art not the least among the princes of Juda:
For out of thee shall come a Governor,
That shall rule my people Israel.
Then Herod, when he had privily called the wise men,
Inquired of them diligently what time the star
    appeared.
And he sent them to Bethlehem, and said,
Go and search diligently for the young child;
And when ye have found him, bring me word again,
That I may come and worship him also.
When they had heard the king, they departed;
And, lo, the star, which they saw in the east, went
    before them,
Till it came and stood over where the young child
    was.
When they saw the star, they rejoiced with exceed-
    ing great joy.
And when they were come into the house,
They saw the young child with Mary his mother,
And fell down, and worshipped him:
And when they had opened their treasures,
They presented unto him gifts;
Gold, and frankincense, and myrrh.
And being warned of God in a dream
That they should not return to Herod,
They departed into their own country another way.
(Luke 2:8–20; 3 Nephi 1:4–21; Luke 2:21–39;
    Matt. 2:1–12)

Part 4:
The Flight into Egypt
And when the [wise men] were departed,
Behold, the angel of the Lord appeareth to Joseph
    in a dream,
Saying, Arise, and take the young child and his
    mother,
And flee into Egypt,
And be thou there until I bring thee word:

For Herod will seek the young child to destroy him.
When he arose,
He took the young child and his mother by night,
And departed into Egypt:
And was there until the death of Herod:
That it might be fulfilled
Which was spoken of the Lord by the prophet, say-
    ing,
Out of Egypt have I called my son. . . .
But when Herod was dead,
Behold, an angel of the Lord appeareth
In a dream to Joseph in Egypt,
Saying, Arise, and take the young child and his
    mother,
And go into the land of Israel:
For they are dead which sought the young child's
    life.
And he arose, and took the young child and his
    mother,
And came into the land of Israel.
But, . . . being warned of God in a dream,
He turned aside into the parts of Galilee:
And he came and dwelt in a city called Nazareth:
That it might be fulfilled which was spoken by the
    prophets,
He shall be called a Nazarene. . . .
And the child grew, and waxed strong in spirit,
Filled with wisdom:
And the grace of God was upon him.
(Matthew 2:13–15, 19–23; Luke 2:40)

A God Is Born

Bruce R. McConkie

I HAVE CHOSEN AS MY SUBJECT, *The Birth of a God*. I shall attempt to present this holy happening in a hallowed and reverent way, knowing that few things of such a sacred nature have ever occurred in all the eternal ages of our endless lives.

A God is born—how glorious is the day; how wondrous are the works which the great Creator hath wrought among us!

A God is born—angels attend; divine proclamations go forth like rolling claps of heavenly thunder; and celestial choirs sing praises to his blessed name.

A God is born—and the word is carried to the edges of eternity, that all men on all the worlds of his creating may now know that there is One who can work out the infinite and eternal atonement; there is One who can now bring to pass immortality and eternal life for all the works which his hands have made.

Well might we ask: Where and under what circumstances was he born? And why would a God come to dwell among us men?

But first: Who is he? What is the source from whence he sprang, and who are the parents who gave him life? How can a tabernacle of clay be created for the great Creator?

We answer: He is the Firstborn of the Father, the noblest and greatest spirit being of all the endless host that bear the image of the divine Elohim. He is our Elder Brother, and like us needed to gain a mortal body, to die, and to rise again in glorious immortality—all to fill the full measure of his creation.

He is the Lord Jehovah who dwelt among us as the Lord Jesus. He is the Eternal One, the Great I AM, the One of whom the angel said to King Benjamin: "Behold, the time cometh, and is not far distant, that with power, the Lord Omnipotent who reigneth, who was, and is from all eternity to all eternity, shall come down from heaven among the children of men, and shall dwell in a tabernacle of clay. . . . And he shall be called Jesus Christ, the Son of God, the Father of heaven and earth, the Creator of all things from the beginning; and his mother shall be called Mary." (Mosiah 3:5–8.)

True it is that he, under the Father, is the Creator, Upholder, and Preserver of all things. He is the One of whom the Father said: "And worlds without number have I created; and I also created them for mine own purpose; and by the Son I created them, which is mine Only Begotten." (Moses 1:33.)

The Only Begotten, the Only Begotten in the flesh, the only person ever born of a mortal woman who had an immortal Father! The Immortal God was his Father, and the mortal Mary was his mother. And it was in consequence of this birth—a birth in which mortality and immortality joined hands—that he was able to perform his atoning mission and put into operation the great and eternal plan of redemption.

Worlds without number, how infinite and endless are his creations! He, under the Father, is the Creator of all things; and he, under the Father, is the Redeemer of all things. Even as he used the power of the Father to create them all, so he used that same power to redeem them all. As the Prophet Joseph Smith so beauteously and melodiously expressed it:

"And I heard a great voice bearing record from
heav'n,
He's the Saviour and Only Begotten of God;
By him, of him, and through him, the worlds
were all made,
Even all that careen in the heavens so broad.

"Whose inhabitants, too, from the first to the
last,
Are sav'd by the very same Saviour of ours;
And, of course, are begotten God's daughters
and sons
By the very same truths and the very same
powers."

(MORMON DOCTRINE, P. 66.)

Where then shall he be born? On which of all the worlds of his creating shall he dwell? Where shall he come to bow 'neath an infinite burden in a self-chosen Gethsemane? And where shall he find his Calvary where he can be crucified by sinful men?

For his own purposes the Eternal Father, who knoweth all things and doeth all things well, chose planet earth as the place for the birth, and for the ministry, and for the atoning sacrifice of the One who was his Beloved and Chosen from the beginning.

Why? Why this earth rather than any other? We are left to wonder. We know that among all the workmanship of the Father's hands there has not been so great wickedness as among the inhabitants of this particular earth. We know that Christ came among "the more wicked part of the world," and that there was "none other nation on earth that would crucify their God. For," as the scripture saith, "should the mighty miracles be wrought among other nations they would repent, and know that he be their God." (2 Ne. 10:3–5.)

Could it be that planet earth was chosen as the

place for the birth of a God because we on this earth are in greater need for direct and personal guidance than those who live on other earths? Could it be that a gracious Father arranged to tie the birth of his Son in with the history of Israel and with the house of David as a special favor to people here, to people who need to feel a closeness and a kinship to the Eternal One? Could it be that our knowledge of his life and ministry has come to us because we, above all peoples, need the enlightenment and encouragement found in the gospel accounts?

Whatever the reasons the decree went forth from the Father that his Beloved and Chosen One should find mortal habitation among us, among some of the lowest and weakest of his eternal children. And because he so decreed, we have great reason to rejoice. Our Lord's life here, in a setting familiar to us and under circumstances with which we can equate, gives us great encouragement. What he did here is an ever present beacon guiding us in the way to perfection.

The birth of a God—when should it be? It was programmed into the eternal scheme of things so as to take place in the meridian of time.

The meridian of time, the mid-point in time! It was to be four thousand years after the birth of the first man and, as we suppose, four thousand years before the great winding up scene when this earth shall become a celestial sphere.

The meridian of time, the high point in time! The high point, indeed—it was to be the one and only time in all eternity when a God would make flesh his tabernacle. It was to be the age of atonement, the age when the ransom would be paid, the age in which death would be swallowed up in victory. It was to be the age in which the crumbling dust in ten thousand tombs would cleave together and the saints of God would come forth from their graves in glorious immortality and be crowned with eternal life on the right hand of Him whose servants they had been.

The birth of a God—to whom would he be born? To the most blessed and favored one of all womankind; to the one prepared and foreordained for this signal honor from all eternity; to Mary of Nazareth of Galilee—she was chosen to be the mother of the Son of God.

And since God was to be the Father of his own Son, the Messianic word acclaimed: "Behold, a virgin shall conceive, and bear a son, and shall call his name Immanuel" (Isa. 7:14), *Immanuel,* meaning God with us!

Nephi bears this concordant testimony: "I beheld the city of Nazareth," he says, "and in the city of Nazareth I beheld a virgin, and she was exceedingly fair and white, . . . A virgin, most beautiful and fair above all other virgins." And from the lips of an angel he heard these words: "Behold, the virgin whom thou seest is the mother of the Son of God, after the manner of the flesh."

Then Nephi said: "And it came to pass that I beheld that she was carried away in the Spirit; and after she had been carried away in the Spirit for the space of a time the angel spake unto me, saying: Look! And I looked and beheld the virgin again, bearing a child in her arms. And the angel said unto me: Behold the Lamb of God, yea, even the Son of the Eternal Father!" (1 Ne. 11:13–21.)

What is more fitting than for the Holy One of Israel, whose mortal life was to be one without sin, what accords more perfectly with the whole nature of his life than that he should be born of a virgin, of the fairest and most gracious of all the virgins on earth. Indeed, how could it be otherwise for a Child whose Father was God?

And what is more fitting for the Promised Messiah, who is to be Lord and King over all the earth, what accords better with the concept that he shall rule and reign forever in the house of Israel, than to have him come into mortality as the Son of Israel's greatest king?

And so we read in the Messianic word: "For unto us a child is born, unto us a son is given." The Son of David shall come. "And the government shall be upon his shoulder." He shall reign gloriously over his saints forever. "And his name shall be called Wonderful, Counsellor, The mighty God"—note it, he is the great God—"The everlasting Father, The Prince of Peace." Christ is the Father, the Father of heaven and earth, the Father of all those who by faith are born again and become members of his holy family.

"Of the increase of his government and peace there shall be no end, upon the throne of David, and upon his kingdom, to order it, and to establish it with judgment and with justice from henceforth even for ever." (Isa. 9:6–7.) The ultimate and complete fulfillment of this is of course Millennial. And we know that in the not far distant day the Son of David shall come again. He shall come as the Second David to rule forever on the throne of his ancient ancestor.

Now, with these precious truths in our minds, let us see and hear what took place in the holy land as the hour approached for the birth of a God. Luke tells us:

"The angel Gabriel"—and he, be it remembered, stands second to Michael the archangel in the hierarchy of heaven—"The angel Gabriel was sent from God unto a city of Galilee, named Nazareth, To a virgin espoused to a man whose name was Joseph, of the house of David; and the virgin's name was Mary." Both Joseph and Mary were of the house of David; both were descendants of Israel's ancient king; both were of the royal lineage.

"And the angel came in unto her, and said, Hail, thou that art highly favoured, the Lord is with thee: blessed art thou among women." And how could any woman be more highly favored than to be chosen to be the mother of the Son of God after the manner of the flesh? What greater honor could come to any of the daughters of Eve than this? There was only one Christ; and there was only one Mary; and these two—the mother and the Son—were destined to play parts of infinite wonder and worth in the eternal drama of the ages. The One was the Son of God, and the other was the mother of that same holy being.

"And when she saw him, she was troubled at his saying, and cast in her mind what manner of salutation this should be. And the angel said unto her, Fear not, Mary: for thou hast found favour with God." The great God was her friend. What greater accolade of praise could be given to any mortal?

"And, behold, thou shalt conceive in thy womb, and bring forth a son, and shalt call his name JESUS. He shall be great, and shall be called the Son of the Highest: and the Lord God shall give unto him the throne of his father David: And he shall reign over the house of Jacob for ever; and of his kingdom there shall be no end." In him shall all the Messianic word be fulfilled.

As the Son of God, who is the Highest, and as the Son of Mary, who is of the house of David, it will be the right of the Lord Jesus to reign both on earth and in heaven. The Son of God, who also is God himself, shall be our everlasting Ruler. And he shall soon come as the Second David to reign personally upon the earth.

"Then said Mary unto the angel, How shall this be, seeing I know not a man? And the angel answered and said unto her, The Holy Ghost shall come upon thee, and the power of the Highest shall overshadow thee: therefore also that holy thing which shall be born of thee shall be called the Son of God." (Luke 1:26–35.)

Matthew is our witness that all things transpired as Gabriel promised. Our apostolic friend says: "Now the birth of Jesus Christ was on this wise: When as his mother Mary was espoused to Joseph, before they came together, she was found with child of the Holy Ghost."

According to the marriage discipline then prevailing among the Jews, Joseph a Jew and Mary a Jewess were espoused and considered to be husband and wife, although they could not properly live in the conjugal relationship until after a second marriage ceremony was performed, nor could Mary properly live with any other man. We can imagine Joseph's sorrows and feel the sadness of his tears when he learned that his beloved wife—for such she was considered to be—was with Child by Another.

As his sorrows weighed in upon him, "the angel of the Lord"—we suppose it was Gabriel—"appeared unto him in a dream, saying, Joseph, thou son of David, fear not to take unto thee Mary thy wife: for that which is conceived in her is of the Holy Ghost." That is to say, Mary had been overshadowed, as Luke recorded, and had conceived by the power of the Holy Ghost, and the Son of the Highest, who is God above all, was then in her womb.

And so the angelic promise came to Joseph: "And she shall bring forth a son, and thou shalt call his name JESUS: for he shall save his people from their sins." (Matt. 1:18–21.) Joseph took the angelic counsel and the Child Jesus was born of the blessed Virgin in due course.

The birth of a God—where shall it take place? If the Lord of the Universe is to take upon himself the form of a man, in what setting shall such a transcendent event unfold? Is there a place on earth worthy of such a birth? Or does the very universe itself contain a site of sufficient renown and eminence to be a fit place for the birth of its Eternal Creator? Can it take place anywhere but on Kolob itself?

Rome rules the world. Shall the Lord be born in Caesar's palace in the Eternal City? Herod is king in the land Jehovah promised to Abraham and his seed, of whom Christ is part. Is his palace an appropriate place for the birth of Israel's King? The Temple of Jehovah graces the Holy City. The walls around its courts are nearly a mile in length. The stones of its chief building are of majestic marble covered with solid gold. The great altar, the holy of holies (into which the high priest enters on the day of atonement to pronounce the ineffable Name and atone for the sins of the people) and the veil of the temple—all are there. Is this a proper place for the High Priest of our Profession to begin his mortal life?

What says the Messianic word? As to the place of his birth it says: "But thou, Bethlehem Ephratah, though thou be little among the thousands of Judah, yet out of thee shall he come forth unto me that is to be ruler in Israel; whose goings forth have been from of old, from everlasting." (Micah 5:2.) As to his dwelling place, it is to be in Nazareth of Galilee, "that it might be fulfilled which was spoken by the prophets, He shall be called a Nazarene." (Matt. 2:23.)

Let not Christ be born under the roof of Augustus where all the intrigue and sins of the world center. Let him stay far from the home of Herod who soon will slaughter the Innocents in Bethlehem as he thirsts for the blood of the new-born King. Let him not be in subjection to the ancient law administered in the Temple. Though it be his Father's house, those who administer its ordinances and regulate its affairs have made it a den of thieves. But let Christ be born and let him live as the Messianic word promises.

And so we find Joseph and Mary in Nazareth. The time for the birth of births is near, and Bethlehem is some eighty miles away by the closest route. Whether the married couple were even aware that "their" Son, as the world would assume him to be, must be born in Bethlehem we do not know. But at this point a divine providence began regulating the affairs of all concerned.

Caesar Augustus decreed "that all the world should be taxed," meaning that the citizens and subjects of his empire should be counted with each one paying a head tax. It was totally immaterial to him how and under what circumstances the counts were made. Herod who, under Caesar, was king of the Jews was an able and astute political leader. However much his reign reeked with evil and immorality and murder—he had ten wives and spent his life in debauchery and intrigue—however vile he was as a man, he had the political instinct to know that the Jews should be counted and taxed in the cities of their ancestors. Indeed, Herod himself was half Jew and half Idumean, and he is the one who ordered the journey that took Joseph and Mary—willingly or unwillingly—to Bethlehem, because Joseph "was of the house and lineage of David," and Bethlehem was the City of David.

The scriptures say only that Joseph and Mary went to Bethlehem. We know from other sources, however, how people travelled in that day, and we can picture with almost certainty the things they did. It is quite unlikely that they went through Samaria because of the animosities that existed between the two peoples. Probably their route led them through Perea, and certainly, having Mary's condition in mind, they would have spent a full week en route. To travel alone was unheard of; friends and relatives always banded together for their own protection and for the pleasant conversations that were a way of life in their religion-oriented society.

They used donkeys and oxen, sometimes camels, and they carried their own food and bedding. At night they camped at the everywhere present caravanserais. These established places of repose and sleep were all built to a common pattern. They consisted of a series of rooms of wood or stone, built in a square or rectangle, surrounding an open court, with the only doors opening onto the court. They were commonly built on a platform which was a foot or two higher than the courtyard. And the courtyard was the stable. It was there they tethered their animals. One would expect to find donkeys and oxen, sometimes camels, and occasionally sheep and goats in these enclosures.

It was to one of these caravanserais, in the environs of Bethlehem, that Joseph and Mary and their party came on the night appointed for the birth of a God. The travel of the day must have been restricted because of Mary's condition. In any event when they arrived all of the rooms were filled. These rooms in Hebrew are called *katalyma*, which word appears only twice in the New Testament. It has no English equivalent, the nearest meaning probably being hostel. In one New Testament instance the meaning is given as guestchamber. In the passage concerning our Lord's birth it is translated *inn*, which is corrected by the Prophet in the Inspired Version to read *inns* in the plural. Thus the statement, "There was no room for them in the inns," simply means that the rooms at the caravanserai were filled and they must of necessity sleep in the open air.

Joseph made the choice to sleep in the courtyard with the animals, in the stable if you will. And we cannot think other than that there was a divine providence in this. The great God, the Father of us all, intended that his Only Begotten Son should be born in the lowest of circumstances and subject to the most demeaning of surroundings.

There amid the lowing of cattle and the bleating of sheep; there where the calm of the night was filled with the sounds of braying asses and yelping dogs; there where the stench of urine and the stink of dung fouled the nostrils of delicate souls—there in a stable the Son of God was born. There the King of Heaven was wrapped in swaddling clothes and laid in a manger. That there were loving kinswomen who acted as midwives, we cannot doubt. And that a divine providence guided each step taken by all the participants is even more certain.

Each year at the Feast of the Passover, devout Jews ask: "Why is this night different from all others?" Well might we as Christians adopt their query and apply it to the birth of the Lord Jesus. Why was this night of nights different from all the others that ever have been or ever will be? Truly it was the night upon which a God was born. And his birth, demeaning and low and seemingly insignificant, was but a harbinger of his death. He was born in a stable and he died on a cross—all because his Father willed it so.

How well our friend Paul wrote: Christ "made himself of no reputation, and took upon him the form of a servant, and was made in the likeness of men: And being found in fashion as a man, he humbled himself, and became obedient unto death, even the death of the cross." (Philip. 2:7–8.)

Why was this night different from all others? Because on it One was born who was different from all others. A God was born. He came into this world inheriting from his Father the power of immortality and from his mother the power of mortality. His birth enabled him to work out the infinite and eternal atonement, than which there neither has been nor will be an event of such magnitude and import.

We testify that a God was born some two thousand years ago and that if we follow the course he charted for us and for all men, we will have peace and joy in this life and be inheritors of eternal life in the world to come.

In the name of Him who was born in Bethlehem, but whose goings forth have been from of old, from everlasting, who is the Lord Jesus Christ, Amen. ❁

For All Mankind

Mabel Jones Gabbott

Of Time

Into the midst of time, between the old
Law and the new, he came as was foretold.

Yet, all of time is his; his are the sun
And starshine. All the measured hours that run

Between are in his time . . . and so are we,
And they who were the very first to see

A sunset on the earth, or hear the birds
Carol his praises; they who heard his words,

And all who follow after to time's rim
Before and since the blessed Christmas morn
Are rich with time and life because of him.
For unto all mankind, the Son was born.

Of Place

That was an ancient year, a distant land
When Magi, richly dressed with gifts in hand,

Had traced the starlight unto Bethlehem,
Had seen the Holy Child, and worshipped him,

Yet all of earth is his, the restless dune,
The steadfast mountains, and the sea and moon,

The crowded city, trimmed and tinseled bright,
The country roadway drenched in lunar light.

Though stars are quiet now above the place
Where Christ was born, his light will always fill
With penetrating rays the ends of space,
As surely as it crowned Judea's hill.

On the Morning of Christ's Nativity

John Milton

I

This is the month, and this the happy morn,
Wherein the Son of Heaven's eternal King,
Of wedded Maid and Virgin Mother born,
Our great redemption from above did bring;
For so the holy sages once did sing,
    That he our deadly forfeit should release,
And with his Father work us a perpetual peace.

II

That glorious form, that light unsufferable,
And that far-beaming blaze of majesty,
Wherewith he wont at Heaven's high council-table
To sit the midst of Trinal Unity,
He laid aside; and here with us to be,
    Forsook the courts of everlasting day,
And chose with us a darksome house of mortal
        clay. . . .

V

But peaceful was the night
Wherein the Prince of Light
    His reign of peace upon the earth began:
The winds with wonder whist,
Smoothly the waters kissed,
    Whispering new joys to the mild ocëan,
Who now hath quite forgot to rave,
While birds of calm sit brooding on the charmed
        wave.

VI

The stars with deep amaze
Stand fixed in steadfast gaze,
    Bending one way their precious influence,
And will not take their flight
For all the morning light,
    Or Lucifer that often warned them thence;
But in their glimmering orbs did glow,
Until their Lord himself bespake, and bid them go.

Remembering Jesus
A Christmas Message to Children of the Church from the First Presidency

Harold B. Lee, N. Eldon Tanner, and Marion G. Romney

CHRISTMAS WILL SOON be here once again—Christmas, that joyous time of year when everyone thinks about giving and receiving gifts.

As your eyes sparkle with the excitement of this happy season and as you sing the lovely Christmas carols, may you remember the beautiful story of the Baby Jesus, who was born in a lowly manger in Bethlehem while shepherds watched their flocks by night on the plains of Judea. This was God's gift to the world.

When the angel Gabriel first visited young Mary in Nazareth, he told her she had been chosen to become the mother of the Son of God and that she should call his name Jesus, a special name meaning *Savior.*

Down through the ages, Jesus has been known by many other names that tell of His greatness and of His work. Among these names are Christ, Holy One, Redeemer, Immanuel, Son of God, Teacher, Messiah, Almighty, and, of course, Savior.

The first letters of these sacred titles spell the name of this season when we celebrate the wondrous birth of the Baby Jesus. As you think about gifts this Christmas, we hope you will think of the meaning of these names given to Jesus by those who knew and loved Him. Then you will be reminded of the blessings of this special holiday.

A few miles from Bethlehem where Jesus was born is the city of Jerusalem where He died for us. This too is part of the Christmas story.

Jesus gave not only His life but His gospel for each of us. His gift of the gospel was freely given to the world. But just as a gift is of little value if you put it on a shelf and never use it, the fulness of the gospel cannot bring the greatest happiness unless you understand its message of hope and gladly live its teachings.

You can make the gospel a wonderful part of your life by listening to your parents and obeying them, by giving thanks to our Heavenly Father for all of your blessings, and by showing your love for Him through caring for and sharing with others all through the year.

When you do this, then in your own small way you too are giving the greatest possible gift—the gift of yourself. And as you do, the sweet spirit of Christmas will glow and grow in your heart long after exciting new games and presents are lost or worn out.

No matter who you are or where you live, we give you at this Christmastime—and always—our blessing. Each one of you is special in our sight, and we know you are precious to our Heavenly Father and to His Beloved Son, whose birth on that first Christmas long ago was the greatest of all gifts. ❄

"The Birth of
Jesus Christ Was
on This Wise"

Gerald N. Lund

AND IN THE SIXTH MONTH the angel Gabriel was sent from God unto a city of Galilee, named Nazareth." (Luke 1:26.)

The rabbis of ancient Israel had a saying: "Judea is wheat, Galilee straw, and beyond Jordan, only chaff." The urbane and worldly wise Jerusalemites, privileged to dwell in the Holy City, looked down on all others with condescension; but they especially viewed the Galileans as crude, unlearned, and earthy peasants. For the most part the people of Galilee were men of the soil and of the sea. This kept them in touch with basic values; and in spite of the feelings of the Judeans, they were known for being hard-working and warm-hearted, and for showing unrestrained hospitality and uncompromising honesty.

As for Nazareth itself, like many other villages of Judea and Galilee, it sat amid steep, tree-covered hillsides so as not to utilize precious agricultural land. For a village now so famous to us, it seems to have been of singular insignificance then. It is not even mentioned in the Old Testament or in the extensive writings of the ancient historian Josephus. Nathanael expressed what must have been a common feeling even among the Galileans when he said, "Can there any good thing come out of Nazareth?" (John 1:46.) Evidently, the suggestion

that the Messiah had come from such a civic backwater was unthinkable.

But that is not to say that this home village of Mary and Joseph, and later the Master Himself, was a drab and dull setting. One writer describes it as follows: "You cannot see from Nazareth the surrounding country, for Nazareth lies in a basin; but the moment you climb to the edge of the basin . . . what a view you have. Esdraelon lies before you, with its twenty battlefields. . . . There is Naboth's vineyard and the place of Jehu's revenge upon Jezebel; there Shunem and the house of Elisha; the Carmel and the place of Elijah's sacrifice. To the east the valley of Jordan, . . . to the west the radiance of the Great Sea. . . . You can see thirty miles in three directions."

This was the setting in which our story begins.

Engagement of Joseph and Mary

"To a virgin espoused to a man whose name was Joseph, of the house of David." (Luke 1:27.)

As we are dropped into the midst of their lives, Joseph and Mary are "espoused." (Matt. 1:18.) Espousal among the Hebrews was significantly more binding than are our engagements today. The couple entered into it by written agreement and considered it the formal beginning of the marriage itself. While the couple might not actually live together for as much as a year after the betrothal— a time designed to allow the bride to prepare her dowry—the espousal was as legally binding as the formal marriage.

The scriptural text gives no hint of the age of either Mary or Joseph, but from existing sources we can make some educated guesses. We know that puberty began somewhat earlier in the Middle East than is common in Western countries today. Therefore, marriage at earlier ages than we are accustomed to was the general rule. Speaking of men, one rabbi described the stages of development as follows: At five he began study of Torah; at ten, study of the Mishnah (the oral laws); at fifteen, the study of Talmud (the extensive commentaries on the scriptures). *At eighteen,* he married; at twenty, he pursued a trade or business. For a girl, probably the most common age of marriage was fifteen or sixteen. Sometimes it was later, sometimes earlier, but it is likely that Mary was around sixteen and Joseph, her espoused husband, only two or three years older than that.

Nazareth was a small village. Joseph and Mary must have known each other well. How fascinating it would be to know the circumstances that brought them to the point of betrothal. Much is made of the fact that in those days families arranged marriages through the auspices of a matchmaker. No doubt that was true, but that does not mean that the individuals involved had no voice in the matter. We know from contemporary sources that, once the arrangements were made, the consent of the couple was required. The man had a direct say in the choice of his bride, and the woman could refuse the marital arrangements if not to her satisfaction. So what was it that drew these two together?

We know Mary must have been of unusual loveliness. Nephi saw her in vision six hundred years before her birth and described her as "exceedingly fair" and "most beautiful and fair." (1 Ne. 11:13, 15.) But did Joseph see only the outward beauty, or did he sense the same qualities that caused Gabriel to declare that this woman was "highly favoured" of the Lord? (Luke 1:28.) No wonder Joseph loved her! Imagine finding a woman of such remarkable grace and beauty in a small village in the mountains of the Galilee.

And what of Joseph? What was it about this man that caused Mary to give her consent to the marriage arrangements? Only a few scriptural verses tell us about Joseph. He was a carpenter, that we know. (See Matt. 13:55.) And because fathers commonly taught their sons their own trade, Joseph was likely reared in a carpenter's shop at his father's knees. His hands would have been rough and callused. He was a man of labor, a man who created things through his own craftsmanship.

Matthew also describes him as a "just man." (Matt. 1:19.) It is a simple phrase, yet it speaks volumes, for those same words are used to describe men such as Noah, Job, Nephi, and Jacob. Was it purely by accident that such a man was in Nazareth waiting to be Mary's partner in this most significant of dramas? Surely God the Father had seen in Joseph a man worthy to raise His Son and help prepare Him for His mortal ministry. While it would not be Joseph's privilege to actually father the "Firstborn," it would be his labor that would provide for His needs, his voice that would encourage His first steps, his hands that would guide the boy's fingers across the sacred scrolls of the Torah in those first Hebrew lessons. Joseph was also the one who would put a mallet and chisel and plane in those smaller hands so that one day this boy from Nazareth would also be known as "the carpenter." (Mark 6:3.) No wonder Mary loved him!

The Name Mary

"And the virgin's name was Mary." (Luke 1:27.)

One of the most common feminine names in the New Testament is Mary—*Miryam* (Miriam) in Hebrew. One Bible concordance identifies at least seven different Marys in the New Testament, so it is not surprising to find a virgin of that name in the village of Nazareth. But perhaps there is more to it than that. Among Book of Mormon prophets, even a hundred years before the birth of the Savior, the actual name of the woman who was to mother the Messiah was known: It was to be Mary. (See Mosiah 3:8; Alma 7:10.) If that was so among Book of Mormon prophets, is it not possible that the name was also known among Old Testament prophets as well, and therefore among the people of the Holy Land?

We know from existing records that the people at the time of Christ's birth generally believed that the birth of the long-awaited Messiah was imminent. What mother would not hope that her daughter might be the promised vessel for such an honor? Such maternal optimism might explain the frequency with which daughters were named Mary. But for whatever reason, Mary's mother fulfilled prophetic promises when she named her child, little dreaming that her daughter indeed would be the one to do so.

Gabriel's Salutation

"And the angel came in unto her, and said, Hail, thou that art highly favoured, the Lord is with thee: blessed art thou among women. And when she saw him, she was troubled at his saying, and cast in her mind what manner of salutation this should be. And the angel said unto her, Fear not, Mary: for thou hast found favour with God. And, behold, thou shalt conceive in thy womb, and bring forth a son, and shalt call his name JESUS." (Luke 1:28–31.)

It was early July in Galilee. The heat, even at night, can be stifling and oppressive. Luke indicates that Mary and Joseph were likely of poor families. If that be the case, the house of Mary's family would have been small, no more than one or two rooms curtained off for sleeping and privacy at night.

We are not told if it was day or night, or if she was alone in the house; surely she must have felt a sudden clutch of fear when she looked up and saw a personage standing there before her. All of us have had someone come up behind us or appear in a doorway unexpectedly and startle us. We give an involuntary cry of surprise and feel the quick burst of adrenaline that leaves the heart pounding, the palms sweaty, and the mouth dry. So it is not difficult to imagine the shock of having not just a man appear suddenly in your room, but a being of transcendent radiance and glory.

But the shock of Gabriel's sudden appearance could not have been any greater than the stunning impact of his words. First there was the "impossible" announcement that she was about to conceive. Her response is so spontaneous, so logical. It adds even further to the power and simplicity with which Luke tells us of this night. One can almost picture her blurting it out, in spite of the glory of the being standing before her: "How shall this be, seeing I know not a man?" (Luke 1:34.)

But that was only the first of the stunning pronouncements. The Messiah had been foretold for four millennia. Now to realize that the long centuries of waiting had come to an end, that the Messiah was about to be born, and that she—Mary of Nazareth—was to be the mother! Add to that the declaration that, for the first and only time in the history of the world, this was to be a virgin birth, and the revelation was even more staggering. This simple, pure woman from a little-known city in Galilee was to carry in her womb the divine offspring of the great Elohim Himself. Her son would be the Son of God!

Only when we consider the magnitude of those statements do we begin to appreciate how marvelous is Mary's answer. There were no questioning looks, no stammering demands of "Why me?" There were no murmurs of doubt. There was no disputation, no hesitation, no wondering. She simply said, in glorious and touching simplicity: "Behold the handmaid of the Lord; be it unto me according to thy word." (Luke 1:38.)

Mary's Pregnancy

"Now the birth of Jesus Christ was on this wise: When as his mother Mary was espoused to Joseph, before they came together, she was found with child of the Holy Ghost." (Matt. 1:18.)

At the command of Gabriel, Mary left Nazareth to visit her cousin Elizabeth, wife of Zacharias the priest, living in Judea. Elizabeth was six months pregnant with a miracle of her own, and Mary abode with her kinswoman about three months until the time came for Elizabeth to deliver.

Consider for a moment what coming back to Nazareth at that point must have meant for Mary. She suddenly, unexpectedly departed from her home for an extended stay far to the south. When she returned, the growing within the womb was pushing outward, expanding now to swell the mother's belly. It is not a secret that can be hidden for long.

This was not a society like our own where immorality is not only tolerated but often openly flaunted. Modesty and virtue were deeply ingrained into the fiber of the nation and were especially strong in the small towns and villages of Israel. Imagine the effect on that tiny village when Mary returned and the first of the village women began to notice the change in her.

Anyone who has ever lived in the tightly knit, closely bonded society of a small town or village can predict with some accuracy what happened next. At first there would have been only questioning looks

and quick shakings of the heads. Surely such could not be so. Not Mary. Perhaps she was just putting on a little weight. Then more and more voices would have questioned, not openly, of course, but in whispers, at the well each day as they came together for water, or while doing the laundry on the banks of a stream.

Was Mary allowed to tell others of her visit from Gabriel? Matthew's comment, "she was *found* with child," would imply not. (Italics added.) But even if she were allowed to tell, would such a "wildly fantastic" claim have quelled the rumors? A virgin birth? Mother of the Messiah? A child fathered by God Himself? Either she was mad or took them for absolute fools to imagine they would believe such a story. To the villagers, her departure from the village "with haste" took on new and ominous significance. (See Luke 1:39.) And poor Joseph. Victim of such "infidelity." What would he do now?

Joseph Takes Mary to Wife

"Then Joseph her husband, being a just man, and not willing to make her a publick example, was minded to put her away privily. But while he thought on these things, behold, the angel of the Lord appeared unto him in a dream, saying, Joseph, thou son of David, fear not to take unto thee Mary thy wife: for that which is conceived in her is of the Holy Ghost. . . . Then Joseph being raised from sleep did as the angel of the Lord had bidden him, and took unto him his wife." (Matt. 1:19–20, 24.)

Neither Luke nor Matthew gives us much detail, but we can read the pain and embarrassment between the lines. Here was a good man, faithful in every respect. What pain must have filled his soul to learn that his betrothed was with child! Surely not Mary, not his lovely and chaste Mary. We can only guess at the agony of spirit he must have experienced at the confirmation of her "unfaithfulness."

How many men would let the bitterness and anger of such betrayal fester and boil over into a blind desire for revenge that can cause people to strike out, seeking to hurt as deeply as they themselves are hurt? By Mosaic law, adultery was punishable by death. (See, for example, John 8:5; Lev. 20:10.) Joseph could have taken Mary to the elders of the village and demanded justice. But, despite the pain he must have felt, despite the personal humiliation, he would not put his beloved Mary through the shame and danger of a public trial. He would simply dissolve the marriage contract quietly.

But then again, in one blinding instant of revelation, all was explained and put right. In response to Gabriel's incredible announcement, Mary had simply said, "Behold the handmaid of the Lord." Now Joseph heard the same stunning pronouncement. We gain a glimpse of the greatness of the man from his response. Matthew says it in one phrase: "Then Joseph *being raised from sleep* . . . took unto him his wife." (Matt. 1:24; italics added.) The verse suggests that little time elapsed between the announcement and the marriage, perhaps even occurring entirely before dawn.

As with Mary, Joseph accepted without question the fantastic nature of the declaration. There was no vacillation. Surely he knew his fellow villagers well enough to know that a hasty marriage in the middle of the night would only fuel the rumors. All he would accomplish by such an action would be to bring the onus of doubt and shame upon himself. But the angel had spoken. His doubts were resolved. His Mary had been proven faithful. And so he arose from his bed and took her to be his wife.

The Town Called Bethlehem

"And it came to pass in those days, that there went out a decree from Caesar Augustus, that all the world should be taxed. . . . And all went to be taxed, every one into his own city. And Joseph also went up from Galilee, out of the city of Nazareth, into Judaea, unto the city of David, which is called Bethlehem; (because he was of the house and lineage of David:) to be taxed with Mary his espoused wife, being great with child." (Luke 2:1, 3–5.)

Bethlehem. The city of David. Ancient homeland of Israel's greatest king. In Hebrew it is called *Beth Lechem*. Literally, *Beth Lechem* means "The House of Bread." How perfect that He who was to take the throne of David and become Israel's ultimate king should come to earth in the city of His illustrious ancestor! How fitting that He who would be known as the "Bread of Life" should enter mortality in the tiny village called "The House of Bread." (See John 6:35.)

Though His birth is celebrated in December, latter-day revelation explains that it actually occurred in the spring. (See D&C 20:1.) The time would have been late March or early April when Joseph moved southward with Mary at his side, heavy with the living treasure in her womb. Spring is a time of glorious beauty in Israel. The "latter rains" water the parched soil, and in gratitude the earth responds with an explosion of grass and wildflowers. New life springs from the old with the wildest abundance. What better season to welcome him who would be called the "Prince of Life"? (See Acts 3:15.)

Search for Lodgings

"And so it was, that, while they were there, the days were accomplished that she should be delivered. And she brought forth her firstborn son, and wrapped him in swaddling clothes, and laid him in a manger; because there was no room for them in the inn." (Luke 2:6–7.)

No room in the inn. If, as we believe, it was April and not December, then it was very likely Passover season in Jerusalem. This could explain the reason Joseph took Mary on the rigorous, sixty-mile journey to Judea when she was in the final month of her pregnancy. The Roman "taxing" mentioned by Luke was more accurately a census or enrollment. Each family head had to register and give an accounting of their property so that taxes could be levied. But while there was considerable flexibility in timing allowed to meet this requirement, if it was Passover season, that would allow them to meet two responsibilities. The Mosaic Law required that every adult male bring his sacrifices before the Lord (i.e., to the temple) each year at Passover. (See Ex. 23:14–19.) So by choosing this time of year, Joseph could fulfill both requirements.

Today we can hardly conceive of the magnitude of this most important of all Jewish festivals. From all over the empire, Jews returned to their homeland at Passover. Though determining exactly how large Jerusalem was during this period is difficult, a fairly accurate guess would place the population between one and two hundred thousand. Josephus tells us that during Passover "innumerable multitudes came thither [to Jerusalem] out of the country." In another place, he was even more specific. Because the Paschal lamb had to be totally consumed by the family in the ritual meal, tradition stated that no fewer than ten and no more than twenty could gather for each lamb sacrificed. (See Ex. 12:10.) Josephus tells us that during one Passover of his time (about A.D. 70), 256,500 lambs were sacrificed. Even using the more conservative figure of ten, that still means the population of

Jerusalem at Passover had swollen by more than 1,000 percent to the staggering number of nearly three million people.

The throngs must have been incredible, the facilities throughout the city taxed beyond belief. And with Bethlehem only six miles south of Jerusalem, no wonder there was no room at the inn. Luke probably could have said with equal accuracy, "There was no room anywhere."

Often in the art and literature surrounding the Christmas story, the unknown, unnamed innkeeper of the scriptural account is viewed as selfish and uncaring, an insensitive oaf unmoved by the plight of a woman heavy with child. This may make for interesting art and literature, but it is not justified by the scriptural record. In the first place, the "inns" of the Middle East were not quaint and homey little buildings with thatched roofs and latticed windows from which warm lamplight beckoned the weary traveler. The inns of the Holy Land were typically large, fortress-like buildings, built around a spacious open square. Called *khans* or *caravanserai*, they provided stopping places for the caravans of the ancient world.

Just as modern hotels and motels must provide parking for automobiles, so did a *caravanserai* have to provide a place where the donkeys, camels, and other animals could be safely cared for. Inside the *khan*, which was usually of two-story construction, all the "rooms" faced the courtyard. They were typically arched, open antechambers facing out onto the square. Here the traveler could build a small fire or sleep within clear view of his animals and goods. "In these hostelries, bazaars and markets were held, animals killed and meat sold, also wine and cider; so that they were a much more public place of resort than might at first be imagined."

Even if there had been room at the inn, a

caravanserai was hardly the ideal place for a woman in labor. Perhaps the innkeeper, moved with compassion at Mary's plight and knowing of her need and desire for privacy, offered them his stable. Perhaps Joseph found the place on his own. The scriptures do not say. But one thing is very probable, and this contradicts another popular misconception. The birth likely did not take place in a wooden shed with pitched roof as is so commonly depicted in nativity scenes around the world.

In Bethlehem today stands the Church of the Nativity. Beneath the church is a large grotto or cave. In southern Judea, including the area around Bethlehem, limestone caves are common. Such caves provided natural shelter for the flocks and herds of ancient Israel. They were warm, safe from inclement weather, and could easily be blocked to keep the animals safe for the night. The tradition that this grotto was the stable of Luke's account is very old and accepted by many scholars. President Harold B. Lee, then of the Council of the Twelve, visited this grotto in 1958 and confirmed that in his mind it was "a hallowed spot, . . . a sacred place."

So there in the sheltered warmth of the cave, beneath the limestone hills of Bethlehem, He who was to become the Good Shepherd—not of the sheep that grazed the hills of Israel, but of the human flock—was born and cradled in a manger.

That seems almost beyond our comprehension. Here was Jesus—a member of the Godhead, the Firstborn of the Father, the Creator, Jehovah of the Old Testament—now leaving His divine and holy station; divesting Himself of all that glory and majesty and entering the body of a tiny infant; helpless, completely dependent on His mother and earthly father. That He should not come to the finest of earthly palaces and be swaddled in purple and showered with jewels but should come to a lowly stable is astonishing. Little wonder that the angel should say to Nephi, "Behold the condescension of God!" (1 Ne. 11:26.)

Announcement to the Shepherds

"And there were in the same country shepherds abiding in the field, keeping watch over their flock by night. And, lo, the angel of the Lord came upon them, and the glory of the Lord shone round about them: and they were sore afraid. And the angel said unto them, Fear not: for, behold, I bring you good tidings of great joy, which shall be to all people. For unto you is born this day in the city of David a Saviour, which is Christ the Lord. And this shall be a sign unto you; Ye shall find the babe wrapped in swaddling clothes, lying in a manger." (Luke 2:8–12.)

One of these verses is frequently misquoted: "Keeping watch over their *flocks* by night." But the verse does not say *flocks,* plural, but *flock,* singular. One scholar explained the significance: "There was near Bethlehem, on the road to Jerusalem, a tower known as *Migdal Eder,* or *the watchtower of the flock.* Here was the station where shepherds watched the flocks destined for sacrifice in the temple. . . . It was a settled conviction among the Jews that the Messiah was to be born in Bethlehem, and equally that he was to be revealed from Migdal Eder. The beautiful significance of the revelation of the infant Christ to shepherds watching the flocks destined for sacrifice needs no comment." The flock mentioned in the scripture, then, apparently was the one used for temple sacrifices, and the shepherds thus had responsibility for the most important flock in the region.

Sometimes in translation the power of the original language is considerably lessened. While the words, in English, of the angel to the shepherds are beautiful and significant, we miss much of the electrifying impact the original words must have had on those men of Judea. Let us just examine two or three of the phrases as we assume they were given in Aramaic to the shepherds that night.

"In the city of David." We have already seen that the Jews expected Bethlehem to be the birthplace of the Messiah. This in part stemmed directly from the prophet Micah, who centuries before had specified the place. (See Micah 5:2.)

"Is born a Savior." The word that meant "Savior" was *Yeshua.* In the Greek New Testament that name was transliterated into *Hee-ay-sous,* or, in English, "Jesus." When the angel announced to Joseph that Mary would bear a son, note what he said: "Thou shalt call his name Jesus [*Yeshua*]: for he shall *save* the people from their sins." (Matt. 1:21, italics added.)

"Which is Christ." Our English word *Christ* is derived directly from the Greek, *Christos.* It means "the anointed one." *Christos* was a direct translation of the Hebrew word, *Messhiach,* which meant exactly the same thing—the anointed one. *Messhiach* is of course transliterated into English as "Messiah."

"The Lord." The simple title, "Lord," is perhaps the most significant of all, yet we totally miss its importance in the translation. In the Old Testament the name of God was written with four Hebrew consonants: YHVH. Because they did not write vowels, there has been some debate as to its proper pronunciation. Modern scholars often write it as YAHVEH, but the King James translators wrote it as JEHOVAH.

The Jews of ancient times, however, viewed the name as being so sacred that it should not be pronounced out loud. Whenever they found it written, they would substitute the Hebrew word *Adonai,* meaning the Lord. The translators who produced the King James Version of the Old Testament honored that tradition of the Jews, and where they found the name YHVH, they wrote in (with very few exceptions) "the Lord." However, *adonai* can also be used as a title of respect for men, such as in the phrase, "My lord, the king." To distinguish between the two uses, the translators wrote *Lord* in small capital letters if it represented the name of deity, and regular upper and lower case letters if used normally. (See, for example, 2 Sam. 15:21, where both uses are found in the same verse.) The declaration of the angel to the shepherds obviously used *Lord* or *Adonai* in reference to deity; literally it could be translated *Jehovah.*

Now we begin to sense the impact of the angel's words upon these shepherds. In essence, here is his pronouncement: "Unto you is born this day in the city prophesied to be the birthplace of the Messiah, *Yeshua* [or Jesus], the Savior, who is the Anointed One (the Messiah), and who is also Jehovah, the God of your fathers."

"And they came with haste, and found Mary, and Joseph, and the babe lying in a manger. And when they had seen it, they made known abroad the saying which was told them concerning this child. And all they that heard it wondered at those things which were told them by the shepherds. But Mary kept all these things, and pondered them in her heart." (Luke 2:16–19.) ✳

You, Simeon,
Spirit-filled

Jay A. Parry

You, Simeon, Spirit-filled, went to the temple
The small voice whispered and you went,
And there you found our baby Lord
Newborn, helpless, a God in infant's flesh.

It was he who shared our human burden,
He who cleanses flesh from death,
He who washes soul from soil:
The baby Jesus
Who burns us clean with cooling light.

Now when Christmas says he's near,
And I recall that same small voice,
May I go newborn to his place
Helpless, an infant god in spirit,
But wrapped in holy swaddling clothes,
Trusting him to teach me life.

The Wonder
of the Story

Charles Irvin Junkin

O the wonder of the story
    Of the night so long ago,
In the glimmer of the starlight
    And the whiteness of the snow,
When the little Prince of Judah
    In His beauty came to birth,
While the angels sang His glory
    And His sweetness filled the earth!

O the wonder of the story,
    Of the gladness none can tell,
When the shepherds saw the rising
    Of the Star of Israel,
And a light from out the manger,
    Reaching far and waxing strong
Till it touched the darkened shadows
    And the world was wrapt in song!

O the wonder of the story,
    Of the tender joy supreme!
O the mystery of loving
    And the sweetness of the dream!
For the little head was pillowed
    On a Mother's loving breast,
And the Father's little children
    They shall find the perfect rest!

His Gift

Giles H. Florence, Jr.

above all
the gift
that came
this stillest night
of the year—
this gift
of king and priest,
this Word made flesh
for those with ears
to hear—
bears not the first birth
only
but the second,
on until the last.
His heirs know
the only way
back is onward
through air
then water
then fire.

The Mary-Song

Betty W. Madsen

I

Here is a cradle for my little Son,
　　Woven from summer-song upon the land.
When I first knew, I went where willow spun
　　Their shade, for they would understand
My need to sing this sudden wonder now.
　　And then I ran to meadows, warm with May,
And sang my song to them. A petalled bough
　　leaned, listening and white, across my way.
I sang my song all day, when I first knew,
　　And leaves and grass and flowers all were still.
I sang it when long shadow-fingers grew
　　Purple across the hollow and the hill.
No song had ever been so sweet to sing,
And all the earth lay quiet, listening.

II

The summer long I made a song of Him,
　　And sang it when I walked my path, apart.
Sometimes I hummed with grass or willow-limb,
　　But often kept it only in my heart.
Sometimes I told the wind or silver rain;
　　On sun-gold days I sang it to the sky.
The olive groves, the stands of yellow grain
　　All knew my song would be His lullabye.
And now a straw-thatched stable listens, too.
　　A little lamb comes searching at the door.
The manger whispers with the hay that grew;
　　A wind comes worshipping across the floor.
Songs of the grass and grain and willow-limb,
You are the cradle that I made for Him.

Thoughts on Christmas

Hugh B. Brown

Any man, I'm sure, who has a concept of the meaning of Christmas must stand amazed and humbled if he undertakes to speak of Christ and His transcendent mission. I'm thinking not only of the babe of Bethlehem, but of Jehovah, the Son of God, as He was in the beginning, as recorded in the Old Testament. He was present when the council was held in the heavens preparatory to the adoption of a plan for our salvation. The Bible tells us:

> *In the beginning was the Word, and the Word was with God, and the Word was God.*
> *The same was in the beginning with God.*
> *All things were made by him; and without him was not any thing made that was made.*
> *In him was life; and the life was the light of men. . . .*
> *And the Word was made flesh, and dwelt among us, (and we beheld his glory, the glory as of the only begotten of the Father,) full of grace and truth. (John 1:1–4; 14.)*

We think of Christ at Christmas time as the babe of Bethlehem, but we remember Him also as the boy on the shores of Galilee, and we remember those three transcendent years when He ministered among the poor of Judea. We think of His betrayal in Gethsemane, of Him hanging on the cross, and especially we think of His resurrection from the tomb with His glorified body.

As we celebrate Christmas time let us contemplate the majestic glory, the Godhood of Him whose birth we celebrate. He was the Jehovah of the Old Testament, the one who opposed Lucifer's plan to deprive men of freedom. He it was who spoke to prophets of old from Adam to Malachi. He strengthened and instructed Abraham; was with Moses in the wilderness and was the author of the ten commandments. He spoke through Isaiah, Jeremiah, Ezekiel and other prophets. He was in very fact one of the Godhead before He took a mortal body. This is an astounding thought that a God should become a mortal man born to a virgin of immaculate conception whose Father was God Himself. ❋

Keeping Christ in Christmas

Ezra Taft Benson

WITHOUT CHRIST THERE would be no Christmas, and without Christ there can be no fulness of joy.

In our premortal state we shouted for joy as the plan of salvation was unfolded to our view. (See Job 38:7.)

It was there our elder brother Jesus, the first-born of our Father's children in the spirit, volunteered to redeem us from our sins. He became our foreordained Savior, the Lamb "slain from the foundation of the world." (Moses 7:47.)

Thanks be to God the Son for the offering of Himself. And thanks be to God the Father that He sent Him. "For God so loved the world, that he gave his only begotten Son." (John 3:16.)

Jesus was a God in the preexistence. Our Father in Heaven gave Him a name above all others—the Christ. We have a volume of scripture whose major mission is to convince the world that Jesus is the Christ. It is the Book of Mormon. It is another testament of Jesus Christ and "the most correct of any book on earth." (Book of Mormon Introduction.)

In its pages we read "that there shall be no other name given nor any other way nor means whereby salvation can come unto the children of men, only in and through the name of Christ, the Lord Omnipotent." (Mosiah 3:17.)

As far as man is concerned, we must build "upon the rock of our Redeemer, who is Christ." (Hel. 5:12.)

The first and great commandment is to love Him and His Father.

Jesus Christ is "the Father of heaven and earth, the Creator of all things from the beginning." (Mosiah 3:8.)

"Wherefore," declared Jacob in the Book of Mormon, "if God being able to speak and the world was, and to speak and man was created, O then, why not able to command the earth, or the workmanship of his hands upon the face of it, according to his will and pleasure?" (Jacob 4:9.) God, the Creator, commands His creations even at this very moment.

Every prophet from the days of Adam knew of that first Christmas and testified of the divine ministry of the mortal Messiah. Moses prophesied concerning the coming of the Messiah. (See Mosiah 13:33.)

"We knew of Christ, and we had a hope of his glory many hundred years before his coming," reported Jacob in the Book of Mormon. (Jacob 4:4.)

In that same volume of scripture is recorded the manifestation of the Christ in His spirit body to the brother of Jared. "This body, which ye now behold," said the Lord, "is the body of my spirit; and man have I created after the body of my spirit; and even as I appear unto thee to be in the spirit will I appear unto my people in the flesh." (Ether 3:16.) And so He did.

He was the Only Begotten Son of our Heavenly Father in the flesh—the only child whose mortal body was begotten by our Heavenly Father. His mortal mother, Mary, was called a virgin, both before and after she gave birth. (See 1 Ne. 11:20.)

And so the premortal God, the God of the whole earth, the Jehovah of the Old Testament, the God of Abraham, Isaac, and Jacob, the Lawgiver, the God of Israel, the promised Messiah was born a babe in Bethlehem.

King Benjamin prophesied of Christ's advent and ministry in this manner:

"For behold, the time cometh, and is not far distant, that with power, the Lord Omnipotent who reigneth, who was, and is from all eternity to all eternity, shall come down from heaven among the children of men, and shall dwell in a tabernacle of clay, and shall go forth amongst men, working mighty miracles, such as healing the sick, raising the dead, causing the lame to walk, the blind to receive their sight, and the deaf to hear, and curing all manner of diseases.

"And he shall cast out devils, or the evil spirits which dwell in the hearts of the children of men.

"And lo, he shall suffer temptations, and pain of body, hunger, thirst, and fatigue, even more than man can suffer, except it be unto death; for behold, blood cometh from every pore, so great shall be his anguish for the wickedness and the abominations of his people.

"And he shall be called Jesus Christ, the Son of God, the Father of heaven and earth, the Creator of all things from the beginning; and his mother shall be called Mary." (Mosiah 3:5–8.)

The Lord testified, "I came into the world to do the will of my Father, because my Father sent me.

"And my Father sent me that I might be lifted up upon the cross." (3 Ne. 27:13–14.) And so He was.

In Gethsemane and on Calvary, He worked out the infinite and eternal atonement. It was the greatest single act of love in recorded history. Then followed His death and resurrection.

Thus He became our Redeemer—redeeming all of us from physical death, and redeeming those of us from spiritual death who will obey the laws and ordinances of the gospel.

His resurrection is well attested in the Bible. The Book of Mormon records the resurrected Lord's appearance on the American continent. To those people He said, "Behold, I am Jesus Christ, whom the prophets testified shall come into the world. . . .

"Arise and come forth unto me, that ye may thrust your hands into my side, and also that ye may feel the prints of the nails in my hands and in my feet, that ye may know that I am the God of Israel, and the God of the whole earth, and have been slain for the sins of the world." One by one, about 2,500 people "thrust their hands into his side, and did feel the prints of the nails in his hands and in his feet."

And they did "cry out with one accord, saying: Hosanna! Blessed be the name of the Most High God! And they did fall down at the feet of Jesus, and did worship him." (3 Ne. 11:10–17.)

Today in Christ's restored church, the Church of Jesus Christ of Latter-day Saints, He is revealing Himself and His will—from the first prophet of the Restoration, even Joseph Smith, to the present.

"And now," said the Prophet Joseph, "after the many testimonies which have been given of him, this is the testimony, last of all, which we give of him: That he lives!

"For we saw him, even on the right hand of God; and we heard the voice bearing record that he is the Only Begotten of the Father." (D&C 76:22–23.)

And now, my beloved brothers and sisters, what must we do this Christmas season—and always? Why, we must do the same as the Wise Men of old. They sought out the Christ and found Him. And so must we. Those who are wise still seek Him today.

"I would commend you," urged Moroni, "to seek this Jesus of whom the prophets and apostles have written." (Ether 12:41.) And God has provided the means—the holy scriptures, particularly the Book of Mormon—that all who seek may know that Jesus is the Christ.

In his lectures on faith, the Prophet Joseph Smith listed six divine attributes of God that men must understand in order to have faith in Him. (See *Lectures on Faith,* p. 35.) The Book of Mormon bears constant witness that Christ possesses all these attributes.

First, God is the Creator and upholder of all things. King Benjamin said, "He created all things"; "He has all wisdom, and all power." (Mosiah 4:9.)

Second, the excellency of the character of God, His mercy, long-suffering, and goodness. Alma testified that Christ is "full of grace, equity, and truth, full of patience, mercy, and long-suffering." (Alma 9:26.)

Third, God changes not. Moroni revealed that God is not "a changeable being; but he is unchangeable from all eternity to all eternity." (Moro. 8:18.)

Fourth, God cannot lie. The brother of Jared declared, "Thou art a God of truth, and canst not lie." (Ether 3:12.)

Fifth, God is no respecter of persons. Moroni testified that "God is not a partial God." (Moro. 8:18.)

Sixth, God is a God of love. Of this divine attribute Nephi wrote that the Lord "doeth not anything save it be for the benefit of the world; for he loveth the world, even that he layeth down his own life." (2 Ne. 26:24.)

The Book of Mormon was designed by Deity to bring men to Christ and to His church. Both we and our nonmember friends may know that the Book of Mormon is true by putting it to the divine test which Moroni proposed. (See Moro. 10:3–4.)

What a gift it would be to receive at Christmastime a greater knowledge of the Lord. What a gift it would be to share that knowledge with others.

To that end may I encourage you not only to read the biblical account of Christ's birth, but to read and share with a nonmember acquaintance the Book of Mormon account of Christmas Eve in America and Christ's personal manifestation following His resurrection.

Give them or lend them a copy of the Book of Mormon, even your own copy if necessary. It could bless them eternally.

In conclusion, in Book of Mormon language, we need "to believe in Christ and deny him not." (2 Ne. 25:28.) We need to trust in Christ and not in the arm of flesh. (See 2 Ne. 4:34.) We need to "come unto Christ, and be perfected in him." (Moro. 10:32.) We need to come "with a broken heart and a contrite spirit" (3 Ne. 12:19), hungering and thirsting after righteousness (see 3 Ne. 12:6). We need to come "feasting upon the word of Christ" (2 Ne. 31:20), as we receive it through His scriptures, His anointed, and His Holy Spirit.

In short, we need to follow "the example of the Son of the living God" (2 Ne. 31:16) and be the "manner of men" He is (see 3 Ne. 27:27).

With Moroni, I testify that "the eternal purposes of the Lord shall roll on, until all his promises shall be fulfilled." (Morm. 8:22.)

Not many years hence, Christ will come again. He will come in power and might as King of Kings and Lord of Lords. And ultimately every knee shall bow and every tongue confess that Jesus is the Christ.

But I testify *now* that Jesus is the Christ, that

Joseph Smith is His prophet, that the Book of
Mormon is the word of God, and that His church,
The Church of Jesus Christ of Latter-day Saints, is
true, and that Christ is at its helm.

I do so in the name of Him whose birth we
honor this Christmas season. ✳

Looking for a King

George MacDonald

They all were looking for a king
    To slay their foes, and lift them high;
Thou cam'st a little baby thing,
    That made a woman cry.

Mary and Her Son

Margery S. Stewart

You must have wondered
When he went away
How they would receive him . . .
Tall and gentle Son.
All his words were wheat
Within your fields,
But remembering Egypt
And the hidden flight,
You feared that stony
Acres stretched before
Him now and thorns.
In firelanes at dusk
You heard the laws
Fall, as if fresh minted,
From his tongue. His
Parables were beautiful
To you, yet I believe
You sensed the coming sword. . . .
All this before his shadow
Quit your door,
Your warm loaf napkined
In his lonely hand.
For you
The spinning, candlemaking,
Fleece. . . .
Oh, heavy, heavy wheel
Oh, wheel of wood
Turning toward the doorway
Where he stood.

A Christmas Carol

Gilbert K. Chesterton

The Christ-child lay on Mary's lap,
  His hair was like a light.
(O weary, weary were the world,
  But here is all aright.)

The Christ-child lay on Mary's breast,
  His hair was like a star.
(O stern and cunning are the kings,
  But here the true hearts are.)

The Christ-child lay on Mary's heart,
  His hair was like a fire.
(O weary, weary is the world,
  But here the world's desire.)

The Christ-child stood at Mary's knee,
  His hair was like a crown,
And all the flowers looked up at Him
  And all the stars looked down.

As Joseph Was A-Walking

Old English Carol

As Joseph was a-walking
  He heard an angel sing,
"This night shall be the birth-time
  Of Christ, the Heavenly King.

He neither shall be born
  In house nor in hall,
Nor in a place of paradise,
  But in an ox's stall.

He shall not be clothèd
  In purple nor in pall;
But in the fair white linen,
  That usen babies all.

He neither shall be rockéd
  In silver nor in gold,
But in a wooden manger
  That resteth on the mold."

As Joseph was a-walking
  There did an angel sing,
And Mary's child at midnight
  Was born to be our King.

Then be ye glad, good people,
  This night of all the year,
And light ye up your candles,
  For His star it shineth clear.

CHAPTER TWO

Faith & Testimony

The Wondrous Gift

Spencer W. Kimball

CHRISTMAS TIME IS A GLORIOUS TIME of happy friendliness and unselfish sacrifice; a time of increased hospitality, devotion, and love; a time of the subduing of selfish impulses; a time of renewing friendships, cementing loosening ties, and the swelling of the heart. It transcends the individual, the family, the community, the nation; it approaches the universal, crosses borders, and touches many nations of the earth. Our caroling voices sing the sweet songs of Christmas reminiscent somewhat of the host of heavenly angelic voices in the long ago, praising God and saying: "Glory to God in the highest, and on earth peace, good will toward men."

We set up the evergreen tree with its gleaming, brightly colored lights; we hang wreaths and bells; and we light candles—all to remind us of that wondrous gift, the coming of our Lord into the world of mortality.

We send Christmas cards to numerous friends and relatives, pulling back into happy memories the loved ones who have moved out of our immediate association. Like the wise men who opened their treasury and presented to Jesus gifts of gold and frankincense and myrrh, we present to our loved ones things to eat and wear and enjoy.

Though we make an effort to follow the pattern of gift giving, sometimes our program becomes an exchange—gift given for gift expected. Never did the Savior give in expectation. I know of no case in his life in which there was an exchange. He was always the giver, seldom the recipient. Never did he give shoes, hose, or a vehicle; never did he give perfume, a shirt, or a fur wrap. His gifts were of such a nature that the recipient could hardly exchange or return the value. His gifts were rare ones: eyes to the blind, ears to the deaf, and legs to the lame; cleanliness to the unclean, wholeness to the infirm, and breath to the lifeless. His gifts were opportunity to the downtrodden, freedom to the oppressed, light in the darkness, forgiveness to the repentant, hope to the despairing. His friends gave him shelter, food, and love. He gave them of himself, his love, his service, his life. The wise men brought him gold and frankincense. He gave them and all their fellow mortals resurrection, salvation, and eternal life. We should strive to give as he gave. To give of oneself is a holy gift.

I often think of an experience in giving that occurred a number of years ago. In one of the stakes of Zion lives a family who gave to me a crisp fifty dollar bill, saying, "Today is the Lord's birthday. We always give gifts to our family members on their birthdays. We should like to give a gift to the Savior. Will you place this money where it will please the Redeemer the most?"

Two days later Sister Kimball and I were on our way to Europe for a six-month tour of all the missions. As we made hasty and extensive preparations, we kept thinking about the birthday gift entrusted to us, and then the thought came to us that perhaps in Europe we would find the most appreciative recipient.

For months we toured the missions, held meetings with the missionaries and Saints, and met many sweet folk. There were numerous opportunities to present the gift, for the majority of the Saints there could use extra funds. But we waited. Toward the end of the mission tour we met a sweet little woman in Germany. She was a widow—or was she? She had been alone with her family of children for ten years. Whether her husband was deceased or not, she did not know. A victim of war, he had disappeared, and no word had ever come from him. The little children, who were small when he was taken away, were now nearly grown, and the son was a full-time missionary among his people.

It was nearing the time of the temple dedication at Bern, Switzerland. I said to this sweet woman, "Are you going to the temple dedication?" I saw the disappointment in her eyes as she said how she would like to go but how impossible it was for her because of lack of finances. I quietly checked with the mission president as to her worthiness and the appropriateness of her going to the temple, and then I gave him half the gift, which he assured me would pay the bus transportation to Bern and return.

A few weeks later we were in southern France. We had driven from Geneva, Switzerland, south to the Riviera. The long circuitous route had taken most of the day. The crowds of fun-lovers along the beaches delayed us so that for some twenty or thirty miles we moved slowly, bumper to bumper, to reach our destination. When we arrived, we were one hour late for our meeting. It was a hot night. The building was filled to capacity. An elderly woman sat at the piano, entertaining this large crowd until our arrival. For one hour she had played. I was so embarrassed for our delay, and so grateful to her for what she had done to hold the group and entertain them, that I inquired concerning her. Her husband, a professor, had died, and the sweet little widow was making a meager living through her musical talents. She was a fairly recent convert. The mission president and the elders assured me that she was worthy, and so I left with the president the other half of the gift for her.

We completed our tours of the ten missions and finally arrived in Bern for the dedication service of the Swiss Temple. The prophet of the Lord was present, as were three of the apostles. After the glorious dedication meetings were over, the regular temple services were conducted in the various languages. As I assisted the French Saints in their session, I was conscious of the sweet little musician, and she literally beamed as she was enjoying the Savior's birthday gift. It had paid her transportation to the temple. Her eyes shone with a new luster; her step was lighter; she radiated joy and peace as she came through the temple with new light, new hope. And I whispered to myself, thank the Lord for good folk who remember the Redeemer on his birthday.

I was present again when the three German-speaking missions had their sessions in the temple. These faithful Saints were assembling for their first time in a holy temple of the Lord. Some of them had been in the Church for many years, and this was their first opportunity to be in a temple. And as these German Saints congregated, I saw a lovely mother rush over to a group of missionaries, single out her handsome missionary son, and embrace him. Their eyes were glistening as they were reunited after many months of separation. To meet in the temple of God, what a joy to them both! I whispered to the Prophet their story of devotion and sacrifice and uncertainties. He was touched by their tender affection. How they wished the lost father could be restored and that they all could be sealed this day! The light in this mother's eyes was like that of one of the other German sisters, who shook my hand warmly and with deep emotion said to me, "Now I can face anything. Now that I have been through the Lord's temple, have made my covenants with my Heavenly Father, and have had my own temple work done, I can meet any situation—hunger, cold, uncertainties. Even war with all its terrors will have less fear. Now I can take anything."

The light that shone in the eyes of these women reflected love and joy and the peace that are truly part of Christmas. In this season we need to listen carefully to the words of a glorious Christmas hymn that proclaims: "How silently, how silently, the wondrous gift is given! So God imparts to human hearts the blessings of his heaven." Our Savior who was the Babe in Bethlehem has given us the recipe for inner peace, for a soul that glows with joy, for a heart that loves life even though it may be strewn with trials.

When I think of Christmas and what it means to me, I think of the question I have often been asked: "How can I find meaning in the celebration of Christmas?" In attempting to answer this question, I seem always to revert to the same formula.

First, we must get to know Jesus Christ—really know him. To do this, it is appropriate that we celebrate his birth, but also our thoughts must turn to his life.

Next, we must learn everything we can about him.

Then, as an exercise, we can select the twelve greatest men in all history according to our own appraisal. Next to each name we will put the outstanding characteristic of that man that made him great in our sight. If we could wrap up all these twelve outstanding attributes that made these twelve men stand out as great personalities, we would find that Jesus of Nazareth had every characteristic, but in a perfected degree. I challenge any person to add even one little thing to Jesus to make him better. We can't make him more just, more righteous, more honest, more loving, or more kind.

Jesus stands on the horizon of human experience as the only one who cannot be improved.

In my own knowledge and acquaintance and experience, I have come to know men to a degree. Now, if we could take all of the qualities of all twelve men and weld them together, our created man would still be inferior to Jesus the Christ, whom we know and love and worship.

He whose birthday we celebrate is the Son of God, the Eternal Father. In him is all majesty and power. No life is comparable to his. He stands alone on the pinnacle of all that is holy and good and righteous and exemplary. My heart is filled with joy to know that he marked for us the plan, the way of life, whereby if we are faithful we may someday see him and express our gratitude personally for his perfect life and his sacrifice for us.

Listen again to the words of this wonderful hymn that celebrates the birth of him whom we worship and follow.

How silently, how silently, the wondrous gift is
*   given!*
So God imparts to human hearts the blessings of
*   his heaven.*
No ear may hear his coming; but in this world
*   of sin,*
Where meek souls will receive him, still
The dear Christ enters in.

It is my prayer that each of us will recognize that the most wondrous gift of all is the selfless gift given to us by our Savior. We can do nothing more to show our love for him than to give of ourselves in a silent, quiet, loving way. This, the gift of self, is the highest gift of all. ❋

Let Every Heart Keep

Phillips Brooks

Then let every heart keep its Christmas within,
Christ's pity for sorrow, Christ's hatred for sin,
Christ's care for the weakest,
    Christ's courage for right,
Christ's dread for darkness,
    Christ's love of the light,
Everywhere, everywhere,
Christmas tonight!

That Holy Star

William Cullen Bryant

O Father, may that holy Star
    Grow every year more bright,
And send its glorious beam afar
    To fill the world with light.

O Holy Child

Phillips Brooks

O holy Child of Bethlehem!
    Descend to us, we pray;
Cast out our sin, and enter in,
    Be born in us today.

Time for Hope

Joann Jensen McGrath

Hanging on the wall of my living room is a wooden clock. It is not an elaborate timepiece but a rather simple one, fashioned from an odd-shaped piece of wood. It has Roman numerals and delicate gold hands, and it is without a crystal or covering. This clock has dutifully tried to keep our family on schedule for the last dozen years. At Christmastime, however, the clock serves as more than a timepiece. Its perpetual, steady ticking summons to mind recollections of important lessons learned at Christmas thirteen years ago.

It was December 1978. My husband and I had just moved into a new home with our infant daughter. As the holidays approached, I was eagerly anticipating the Christmas celebrations, and I busied myself with the usual preparations.

The gaiety of the holiday season was marred, however, by my brother's failing health. Alan was four and a half years older than I and had never been blessed with good health. Because of his lifelong health problems, he'd never married and was living with Mom and Dad. During that autumn, his condition had deteriorated, and Alan had spent a couple of months in and out of the hospital. We were encouraged by a spurt of energy he enjoyed early in December. He felt well enough to shop for gifts, attend his Sunday meetings, and go to a ward Christmas party. He had enough energy to visit the barber and have his shaggy hair trimmed, much to the delight of my mother.

Then, the week before Christmas, Alan had to be rehospitalized. The doctors summoned us to his bedside on December 20 and warned of his imminent death. I arrived at the hospital ahead of the other family members and entered his room alone. A small stream of sunlight shone between the curtains and danced across the darkened room. I straightened his bed covers and pulled a chair next to the bed.

Taking his fragile hand in mine, I held it close. The atmosphere was solemn, and even the skipping sunbeams could not chase away death's shadow. I spoke to him. I wasn't sure if Alan could hear or understand, but I was determined to speak to him anyway. As I whispered of my love, I prayed in my heart that somehow our spirits would be able to communicate. When a faint smile drew across his lips and he gently squeezed my hand, I thanked God for an answer to my prayer. I stroked his blond hair and softly kissed his forehead, savoring the moment, somehow knowing that it was our last.

Alan died in the early morning hours of December 21. The next day was filled with funeral and burial plans. We scheduled his funeral for December 23. As other families gathered for their holiday parties, our family gathered to bury my brother.

At the funeral, our family greeted friends and relatives, seeking solace in one another's presence. I was standing next to my younger sister when someone commented that it was such a tragic time of year for a death. I took great comfort in my sister's reply: "No, this is a beautiful time of year, reminding us that without our Savior's birth, we would have no hope of ever seeing or being with Alan again."

Christmas morning was bittersweet as our family gathered at my parents' home. We nestled about the Christmas tree and exchanged gifts. We cried and laughed as we unwrapped our presents. Soon there were only a few gifts under the tree. My sister crawled beneath the tree boughs to read the tags. She whispered, "They're from Alan."

Weeks earlier, Alan must have selected and wrapped our gifts, placing them beneath the tree to wait for Christmas morning. The room was hushed, and I glanced around through tear-filled eyes. My sister placed a large, oddly shaped present in my lap. Tears splashed on the brightly colored wrapping paper as I slowly opened the gift. My heart was overflowing as I gazed down at the beautiful wooden clock. It seemed to be Alan's way of reminding me that although his stay on earth was over, I still had time—time to love, time to serve, and time to learn. Yet the clock was also a beautiful reminder that our existence isn't just for time, it is for eternity. The clock reminds me that I can be with Alan again someday. ❈

In Temptation

Weiss Wenig

THE GLOOM OF A DISMAL winter's night had already begun to settle down in the streets of a large city in the German Empire, when there emerged from a pawn-shop a man of perhaps thirty-five years of age. He shivered with the cold, being without an overcoat, and wearing merely a light jacket in the pockets of which he sought warmth for his hands. His clothing though neither torn nor patched, was worn threadbare in nearly every part. His countenance, though showing evidences of care and want was nevertheless attractive, and beamed with intelligence. It was very evident that this man had seen better days.

It was just before Christmas. The stores and show windows teemed with attractive presents. Art and science vied with each other in offering their best productions to the brilliant display. Within the mirrored windows gas or electric jets sparkled, and multiplied the glittering array many times to arouse the wonder of youth and the covetousness of age.

Gerhard Kostlin forgot both darkness and cold in his observation of the show-windows. Now it was toys, next instructive picture books, and again presents for females which fastened his longing eye, for he had wife and children at home whom he in spirit placed among those happy ones to whom such gifts were sent on every recurring Christmas. Of himself and his wants there arose no thought.

Suddenly he found himself before the large window of an immense bank. He was unable to suppress a sigh as he saw the crisp bank notes of all countries, the glittering yellow piles of gold pieces arranged in baskets or heaps upon the tables. For one handful of that shining metal he could obtain all that which in the various stores he had so much desired for his wife and children; a single one of those notes would have driven want from his door for many days to come!

While Kostlin gazed on the bank notes and gold pieces there passed restlessly up and down the walk behind him a tall man clad in a coat of the most costly fur. Several times he was on the point of entering the bank, but as often did he alter his mind. Undetermined he now placed himself by the side of Kostlin in front of the window, and from the side he closely scrutinized the poor man for a brief time. Finally he seemed to reach a satisfactory conclusion, and addressing the object of his inspection said, "Sir, will you have the kindness to do me a favor?"

Kostlin looked up. "If it is in my power, willingly," he answered.

The stranger motioned him away from the window, and they went a few steps to one side. Then he said, as he produced a small packet and carefully wrapped it in a newspaper, "Will you be so kind as to give this to the banker Barrot?"

"You mean the president of the bank?"

"Yes."

"Why do you not deliver it yourself?" inquired Kostlin to whom the request appeared somewhat strange.

"For reasons," answered the stranger, "which I cannot here explain."

"Well, I will then do as you request," replied Kostlin.

"I thank you," said the gentleman bowing low as he placed the packet in Kostlin's hand. "But pray," he added, "give it only to the banker himself;

I know that he is within. And this you will please accept for your trouble."

Kostlin felt the pressure of a silver piece in his hand, and blushingly handed it back, for it was the first time in his life that he had ever been "tipped" for his service.

"I shall feel sorry if you refuse the trifle," said the stranger. "Perhaps you have children at home for whom you can purchase therewith a little something for Christmas to please them."

Kostlin had just pawned two wedding rings— the last articles he possessed on which money could be had. His wife at home hoped the broker would be willing to loan at least eight marks thereon, but no amount of pleading increased the amount offered beyond five marks. This piece of silver made exactly the amount expected by his wife. Was it therefore proper pride to absolutely refuse the proffered gift? No, certainly not! He therefore slipped the money into his pocket, blushingly thanked the giver and passed into the brilliantly lighted banking room. This consisted of a succession of small compartments whose doors were open.

Kostlin now for the first time realized that he had accepted no easy but rather a very difficult task. He was asked as to his wish, and when he expressed a desire to speak to the head of the firm his poor clothing and personal appearance were scrutinized closely. The clerks shrugged their shoulders and offered excuses—the banker did not wish to see beggars, and was at any rate very busy at present.

"I am no beggar," remonstrated Kostlin; "I have a commission from another to deliver something to the banker himself, and will not detain him more than a minute."

The firm and fearless tones in which these words were uttered did not fail in effect. Kostlin was directed to the last door. It was no pleasant thing to walk past the long rows of desks occupied by clerks, many of whom cast questionable glances at his worn clothes as he passed along towards the "sanctuary," where only the heaviest customers had access. Many a scornful titter reached Kostlin's ear as he moved along the aisle. The scoffers did not know that the object of their mirth once occupied with honor a desk in one of the leading banking businesses of the city, and had only lost it by the falsehood of a companion.

Finally Kostlin stood at the entrance of a princely furnished room, where the banker sat at a table hastily overlooking some letters and dispatches. The poor man waited until the banker looked up, when he bowed and said: "I am commissioned, sir, to give this into your hand only," and then passed the packet to the somewhat aged and haughty man.

The bank was located on a corner with two large windows facing the street in the room where the banker sat. Through one of these openings Kostlin saw the tall form of the stranger, who seemed to be anxious to know that his errand was faithfully executed. As soon as the packet passed into the hand of the banker the watcher vanished.

Kostlin was about to withdraw, when the banker checked him with the question, "Who sent you?"

"I do not know," was the reply.

"You do not know who sent you?" questioned the banker, deigning now for the first time to look straight at the messenger. "How am I to understand that?"

"A strange gentleman addressed me as I stood by your window outside," replied Kostlin. "He asked me to do him the kindness to hand this packet to you personally. More than this I do not know."

The rich man looked suspiciously at the clothing of his visitor, viewed the packet from all sides, and then tossed it back to Kostlin, as though he feared its contents to be dynamite, with the icy remark, "That may be as you say; I do not know you, and it is one of my business principles not to accept anonymous packages. You will please take it with you."

Then turning to his work without taking further notice of his visitor, there was nothing left for Kostlin to do but withdraw. As the latter reached the street he sought the stranger in vain—he was to be found in neither street. Good or bad, therefore, he could do nothing but take the packet home with him. As he traversed the long distance to his home he considered what was best to be done about the matter, and finally decided to submit the case to his wife, who had frequently given him wise counsel.

It was already late when he arrived at the house, of which he occupied the attic. Involuntarily he went on tiptoe as he passed the door on the third landing, for in that room lay a young woman near death's door with the typhoid fever. He ascended the stairs very quietly and entered his poorly furnished single room, wherein two beds in addition to several other necessary articles of furniture were to be found. The light of the dimly burning lamp revealed a woman of perhaps thirty years of age, who, notwithstanding her pale, careworn face, might still be called beautiful, engaged in the labor of repairing children's clothes.

Kostlin gave his wife a warm kiss and then walked lightly to one of the beds, where were sweetly slumbering three lovely boys in age between four and nine years. After looking at them tenderly for a few moments he turned to the poorly heated stove, where he sought to warm himself.

"Have you not heard, Mary, how the sick lady below feels?" he inquired.

"The doctors think she will scarcely live through the night," answered Mary. "Her mother has already arrived, the servant told me."

"Sad, very sad," exclaimed Kostlin, full of sympathy. Then he drew from his pocket the pawn receipt, in which was wrapped the money, and laid them on the table before his wife.

"Only five marks!" cried Mary astonished.

"My goodness! That disarranges all my plans. All our supplies are exhausted: potatoes, flour, petroleum and everything else. We are burning the last coal in the stove."

"Thank heaven that I suppressed my pride," said Kostlin, again feeling in his pocket. "For a slight service which I rendered a gentleman as I was homeward bound I received three marks. The Lord sent me the stranger, I believe."

At the request of his wife he related minutely the circumstances connected with the request of the stranger and his interview with the banker. With close attention she listened to his narration. Her inquisitiveness was aroused to know the contents of the packet, which she weighed carefully in her hand, and viewed from all sides.

"What will you do with it," she finally asked.

"I have thought that perhaps it would be best to leave it at the police station and have it advertised as lost property."

"Would it not be best for us to first open it?" inquired Mary, "perhaps the contents will give some information as to the owner, and you can then be able to restore it to him."

"You always suggest the best plan," replied Kostlin, and to open it they began.

Mary took off the paper and had scarcely removed the last wrapper of white paper when she gave expression to a faint scream. Kostlin himself was almost overcome by the sight which met his gaze. It was a packet of bank notes, each one of which was a thousand mark bill.

In the utmost astonishment the couple stared at the display. Then Mary began to spread the notes around on the table. There were thirty bills. Thirty thousand marks in real money now within that poor dwelling which daily witnessed scenes of poverty and distress of the most heart-rending character!

To Kostlin in his poor circumstances this amount seemed an immense fortune. The stranger, who had given him the packet believed it to be in the possession of the banker, for he had seen it passed to his hands, and the banker, without any suspicion as to its contents, had thrown it back to its bearer. Thus was the money cast into a channel where it would be retained with scarcely a probability that it would ever be discovered by either the sender or the one who should have received it. That was the thought of the husband and wife as they viewed the money, he with pale countenance, she with burning cheeks, the blood having mounted quickly to her hitherto whitened face.

She first broke the silence. With her eyes cast down she murmured, "You just now said that God sent the stranger to you."

He understood her meaning: she did not refer to the three mark piece; but to the thirty thousand marks.

"Yes, God sent him to me," he answered with a mournful, upward glance, "of this I am now con vinced more than ever. God sent him to me that I might be tried, and that we may learn the true import of the petition, 'Lead us not into temptation,' which we make a part of our daily prayer."

"Oh, it is cruel to send us only a temptation when we daily pray for help," moaned the poor woman in agony. "Had you by evil deeds merited the misfortune that has daily followed us, then would I have seen the wisdom of our trials. But this is not the case, and therefore such trials as we endure, such misfortunes in the smallest affairs, such cares for daily living have no tendency to elevate but rather to degrade mankind. There is no justice. All is luck or misfortune, and a lucky accident has cast the lot in our favor. Do not be a fool, Gerhard, and speak of temptation, but view this as a stroke of luck. You have only to retain this money and our wants can be supplied."

"Unfortunately, Mary, I have long since noticed that our suffering has shattered your faith in God and man," said Gerhard sadly. "But do you really believe that blessing would attend us were we to retain this money?"

Mary laughed bitterly. "How many tears and drops of life's blood cling to the money of those who have amassed wealth by usury, or by the oppressions of the poor, and yet I have not discovered that a curse rests upon such accumulations. On the contrary, these persons enjoy life—live in palaces, ride in carriages, are held high in the esteem and respect of their fellows, and such would view with contempt anyone who would even suggest that they should be ashamed of possessing riches thus accumulated. These thirty thousand marks you can call your own, and have the satisfaction of knowing that they have not been obtained by the oppression of your fellow-men."

"Mary," replied her husband, "I would not yield the consciousness of being an honest man for one hundred times the amount."

"Ah, Gerhard, with the consciousness of integrity one cannot today entice a dog from behind the stove," answered Mary coldly. "What have you succeeded in bringing us to with all your honor?

Only to a beggar's condition. Look back at your past life. You are a man of brilliant business talent; you write and speak three languages; you neither drink nor gamble, but are devoted to your labor and your family. You had a good position, and your employer was inclined to make you a partner, when a covetous and unprincipled relative came between you and your prospective fortune, and deprived you of everything which you had hoped in a business way to obtain. This was your reward for ten years of faithful and diligent service. You succeeded in obtaining another situation, where after years of faithful toil you again attained a position of trust and honor; but this house failed. In vain do you now apply for work, the supply by far exceeds the demand; your recommends for ability and honor are valueless to you now. The people to whom you apply for employment are suspicious because of your long enforced idleness; they shrink from contact with your well-worn clothing which every day becomes more threadbare; on your unexampled misfortune they do not believe, but think there must be some hidden disqualification in your character. Indeed, one loses immediately the good opinion of his fellows when luck deserts him. You accept of any kind of employment of which you are capable, but this uncertain and poorly paid employment, together with the pittance which my sewing brings, is not even sufficient to provide our daily necessities. From one dwelling to another poverty has driven us, and each place has been worse than the one just vacated, until now we are confined to this small, miserable, filthy room. Soon this will also be too good for us, for I really do not know how we will pay the rent on New Year's day. We will then be put into the street in mid-winter. And then? O, Gerhard, will you not think of your poor children? Neither man nor God has pity on us, so do you be merciful! There lies the relief, there is no other, keep it!"

Mary sank with sobs at the feet of her husband, pointing to the treasures which lay spread upon the table before him. Gerhard was deeply moved. Almost overpoweringly was the temptation pressed home to him. Not in the love of gold did his weakness lie, but in the pleadings of his poor wife, her touching picture by which she had drawn before his eyes the hopelessness of his sad circumstances.

"Mary," he said, at length as he gently raised his wife from the floor, "there is something more valuable than money or land, and that is a clear conscience, and there is something worse than poverty and want, and that is sickness and death. The first we have been able till the present to retain, from the latter God has thus far preserved us, for which kindness we cannot give Him sufficient thanks. Think of the poor, sick woman below. How often have we envied that young couple! They have all the gold they desire, the husband occupies an independent position, and his wife by her dowry added to his wealth. And yet with all my poverty I would not exchange with him, for that which is dearest of all to him now quivers between life and death. Look, Mary," continued the weeping man as he took the lamp and drew Mary to the humble cot, where the three children slept in peaceful embrace, "look at that picture; see how peacefully they slumber, how regular and quiet their breathing. Our children are healthy and we may, as their happy and blessed parents, look down at them—"

At this moment a piercing cry ascended the stairs and almost chilled the marrow of Gerhard and his wife. It came from the sick woman who in the delirium of fever began now to rave as one who is crazy. Perhaps for a half an hour did this continue, when all became still. Only for a moment, however, when the weeping tones of those below indicated that another precious spirit had passed to the great beyond.

On Gerhard's shoulder had Mary listened with terror to the acts of the tragedy which was occurring beneath them, nor did she move until the last stifled tones of the bereaved were heard.

"Gerhard, you spoke the truth," she whispered in the midst of her terror, "poverty is not the severest trial placed on mortals. Take that away so that I cannot see it again, and do with it as you think best."

• • •

"Papa, will you not soon send me to the school again where I went before? It was so nice there, and I could learn so fast, much more than I could learn in the other school where there are so many bad boys." This was the question asked by the nine-year-old Arthur as the family were eating their breakfast of dry bread and coffee the morning following the events narrated above.

"In my class are bad boys, too," complained Carl, who was two years younger, "and because I am the smallest they thrash me on the way home, though I don't do anything to them."

"You will give me the pretty ship with white sails, won't you papa," now broke in five-year-old Fritz.

"Which ship is that?" inquired Arthur.

"The one he saw in the toy store on the corner," said Carl. "The box of building blocks I would like better, which will make castles and houses with towers. Whoever receives that for Christmas can laugh. The Christmas tree is also nice, just like the one we had two years ago."

"How many times must I sleep yet before Santa Claus will come with the pretty ship?" asked Fritz.

"He won't come to us this time, Fritz," whispered Arthur, leaning toward his brother, "because we are poor. Santa Claus only visits rich people. We were rich once, were we not, mamma?"

A tear trickled down Mary's cheek as she listened to the talk of the innocents. She cast an almost reproachful look at her husband, and he closely buttoned his coat in the pocket of which he carried the thirty bank notes which he was about to convey to the banker Barrot. Just as he turned to go he extended his hand to Mary.

"I think," said Mary softly, "the rich man will scarcely allow so noble an act as yours to go unrewarded, perhaps he will by some kind act drive the wolf from our door for a short time to come. And should it so happen, Gerhard, that you enter into conversation with him, do not be bashful, but explain fully to him our circumstances. Perhaps he can find for you a humble situation in his large establishment."

"I will see what can be done," replied Gerhard, "but do not allow yourself to build too many hopes on this chance. The hearts of business men are not always easily moved. Good-bye for a short time."

"Good-bye, God bless you!" heartily responded Mary.

As Gerhard again found himself in front of the large bank he experienced no happy presentiment of success in his desire to be provided with work. Now he has crossed the threshold, but there is nothing to prevent his withdrawal again. He hesitated as he felt the valuable packet in his breast pocket, but only for a moment did this last and terrible struggle last and then he walked with firm step and entered the room of Millionaire Barrot. The latter was just engaged in reading a letter which the early post had brought, and was so deeply interested that he did not notice the entry of his visitor. He was even reading it a second time which with him was unusual. It read as follows:

"Mr. Barrot, Banker:

"You will still have sad recollections of the undersigned. Fifteen years ago I occupied a situation in your establishment. I betrayed the confidence which you reposed in me, and was guilty of embezzlement. Threatened with discovery I fled to America. There in a hard struggle for my daily bread and amid indescribable suffering and want, I atoned in a measure for my sin. Later, fortune favored me and the horn of plenty was emptied into my lap. I am thus enabled, while on a visit to my fatherland, to return the misappropriated sum, together with the accrued interest, amounting in all to thirty thousand marks. I at first determined to return this personally. For a long time yesterday evening I stood before your place of business endeavoring to acquire the moral courage to again face you, but the feeling of shame restrained me, and I must confess that the sin of my younger days neither the changes of fortune nor the lapse of years have succeeded in erasing from my memory. For this reason I entrusted my commission to a poor stranger, and the money has already been passed to your hands. Please accept this sum as an assurance of my repentance, and do not condemn with too great severity the foolish act of a thoughtless youth who now pleads humbly for your forgiveness.

"JULIUS LUDERS."

A slight shuffling caused the banker to look up.

"Ah," he exclaimed, astonished at the sight of his visitor, "I surely am not mistaken. You were here last evening."

"Yes, sir," answered Kostlin, "I come again with the packet which you refused last evening. As I was unable to find the stranger who gave it to me, I took it home and opened it, and after I had acquainted myself with its contents I became convinced that you would not again reject it. Be kind enough, Mr. Barrot, to count the money; there should be thirty thousand marks."

With these words he handed the packet to the banker, who cast a searching glance at Kostlin, then counted the money and threw it carelessly and coldly on his desk.

"It is right," he nodded with a second searching look at the bringer, "I thank you."

Gerhard was released. After this curt dismissal by the cold business man it would have appeared like beggary to have asked for work, or to have mentioned his circumstances. He could not have uttered a word even had his wife and children starved on the spot. He politely bowed and withdrew quietly from the grand room of the financier.

Can one be astonished at the bitter murmurings of the troubled wife as the husband returned without a word of comfort or joy to his dismal home? Why was it that in the midst of their deep trials a ray of sunshine broke through the clouds only to be withdrawn leaving the surrounding gloom the more intense! Scarcely can she be blamed for reviewing with still greater bitterness their tribulations which their integrity and industry had failed to remove. Even the terrible reminder of the uncertainty of all things mortal, occasioned by the death of the woman below on the previous night, now lost its effect for Mary. As Gerhard called her attention to the heavy tread of the men who had come to convey to its last resting place the body of the deceased, she only exclaimed in answer, "I wish I were in her place."

• • •

Banker Barrot was not the man, however much his appearance might otherwise indicate, to allow such an honorable act as Gerhard's to pass without consideration. He was fully aware that this poor man might have safely retained the means entrusted to his care without the slightest fear of discovery. Such an example of integrity amid what was, doubtless, the severest temptation, was seldom if ever seen, and the shrewd banker did not for one moment intend that such a valuable jewel should be lost to him. This was his thought as he received the notes from Kostlin's hand, and it was not without being inwardly moved that he saw the noble fellow modestly and politely withdraw without the slightest kindly recognition from him of his noble act.

Immediately thereafter, however, he gave an employee the commission to follow and learn the residence of his visitor, and in the course of the afternoon the banker made a personal visit to Gerhard Kostlin's home, and you may be sure the latter was no little surprised at the rich man's entrance. The remarkable poverty which was here exhibited, only increased the esteem of the banker for the strength of character which the occupants exhibited. He heard in detail the series of circumstances which had reduced Kostlin to his present circumstances, and reviewed with pleasant smile the recommendations of his former employers which Mary had hastily and tremblingly laid before him.

"It happens just right, Mr. Kostlin," said the banker, "that you are acquainted with office business. Your recommends testify to your capabilities. The most valuable recommend to me, however, you have yourself presented in your act of this morning. For some time there has been a vacancy in the office of first assistant cashier of my bank, a position of such importance and requiring such strict integrity that I have not been able to fill it since the elevation of its former occupant. Now, if you will accept this position it will benefit us both, and you may consider yourself employed from this moment at an annual salary of eight thousand marks."

Gerhard scarcely knew what had happened. His only answer was a flow of grateful tears. The banker seized and warmly pressed the hand of Gerhard which he extended in grateful acknowledgment to his benefactor.

Arising to go the banker said pleasantly, "Well, it is then understood and accepted? You will, of course, begin your duties by paying to yourself a sum of money with which to surround yourself more comfortably, and to prepare a pleasant and happy Christmas for your family. Now, I hope to see you soon again, Mr. Kostlin. Good-day!"

After politely bowing himself out, Gerhard accompanied him to the street. When the latter returned to the room his wife threw herself joyfully into his arms.

"You are right," she exclaimed in a choking voice. "Honor is best of all. About us there is thrown a kindly Providence, however dark our pathway may sometimes appear. Never again will I lose confidence in God and man." ❈

Pilgrimage to Christmas

Dorothy J. Roberts

Peace is warmth and sound of pigeons, pining,
And silhouette of camels weaving by. . . .
I have fanned old ashes into ember
And overhead a star grows in the sky.

By rose or thorn the pilgrim paths return
And I will take the first, as once before,
Content to walk the dimly cloistered land
And lay no sole to sink beyond the shore.

For once, while he walked calmly, sea's horizon,
As Peter, sinking, I implored *his* name,
Reaching for help of parable and promise;
I could not walk the water till *he* came.

Upon that path I paced meridian.
The bitter thorn was doubt, a weapon then,
Yet as the nailed act of destruction, doubt
But crucified *him* into life again.

Now I have welded weapon into plowshare,
That, grain *he* savored on a Sabbath meal
Nourish the flesh of speech; I have known famine
More vast than earthly appetite can feel.

Treading the path of rose, of faith, of wonder,
I find *his* healing hand held out to save,
His robe, trailing the crested mount forever,
His sandaled signature upon the wave.

The Little Match Girl

Hans Christian Andersen

It WAS BITTERLY COLD, snow was falling and darkness was gathering, for it was the last evening of the old year—it was New Year's Eve.

In the cold and gloom a poor little girl walked, bareheaded and barefoot, through the streets. She had been wearing slippers, it is true, when she left home, but what good were they? They had been her mother's, so you can imagine how big they were. The little girl had lost them as she ran across the street to escape from two carriages that were being driven terribly fast. One slipper could not be found, and a boy had run off with the other, saying that would come in very handy as a cradle some day when he had children of his own.

So the little girl walked about the streets on her naked feet, which were red and blue with the cold. In her old apron she carried a great many matches, and she had a packet of them in her hand as well. Nobody had bought any from her, and no one had given her a single penny all day. She crept along, shivering and hungry, the picture of misery, poor little thing!

The snowflakes fell on her long golden hair which curled so prettily about her neck, but she did not think of her appearance now. Lights were shining in every window, and there was a glorious smell of roast goose in the street, for this was New Year's Eve, and she could not think of anything else.

She huddled down in a heap in a corner formed by two houses, one of which projected further out into the street than the other, but though she tucked her little legs up under her she felt colder and colder. She did not dare go home, for she had sold no matches and earned not a single penny. Her father would be sure to beat her, and besides it was so cold at home, for they had nothing but the roof above them and the wind whistled through that, even though the largest cracks were stuffed with straw and rags. Her thin hands were almost numb with cold. If only she dared pull just one small match from the packet, strike it on the wall and warm her fingers!

She pulled one out—scr-r-ratch!—how it spluttered and burnt! It had a warm, bright flame like a tiny candle when she held her hand over it—but what a strange light! It seemed to the little girl as if she were sitting in front of a great iron stove with polished brass knobs and brass ornaments. The fire burnt so beautifully and gave out such a lovely warmth. Oh, how wonderful that was! The child had already stretched her feet to warm them, too, when—out went the flame, the stove vanished and there she sat with the burnt match in her hand.

She struck another—it burnt clearly and, where the light fell upon the wall, the bricks became transparent, like gauze. She could see right into the room, where a shining white cloth was spread on the table. It was covered with beautiful china and in the centre of it stood a roast goose, stuffed with prunes and apples, steaming deliciously. And what was even more wonderful was that the goose hopped down from the dish, waddled across the floor with carving knife and fork in its back, waddled straight up to the poor child! Then—out went the match, and nothing could be seen but the thick, cold wall.

She struck another match, and suddenly she was sitting under the most beautiful Christmas tree. It was much larger and much lovelier than the one she had seen last year through the glass doors of the rich merchant's house. A thousand candles lit up the green branches, and gaily coloured balls like those in the shop windows looked down upon her. The little girl reached forward with both hands— then, out went the match. The many candles on the Christmas tree rose higher and higher through the air, and she saw that they had now turned into bright stars. One of them fell, streaking the sky with light.

"Now someone is dying," said the little girl, for her old grandmother, the only one who had ever been good to her but who was now dead, had said, "Whenever a star falls, a soul goes up to God."

She struck another match on the wall. Once more there was light, and in the glow stood her old grandmother, oh, so bright and shining, and looking so gentle, kind and loving. "Granny!" cried the little girl. "Oh, take me with you! I know you will disappear when the match is burnt out; you will vanish like the warm stove, the lovely roast goose and the great glorious Christmas tree!"

Then she quickly struck all the rest of the matches she had in the packet, for she did so want to keep her grandmother with her.

The matches flared up with such a blaze that it was brighter than broad daylight, and her old grandmother had never seemed so beautiful before, so stately before. She took the little girl in her arms and flew with her high up, oh, so high, towards glory and joy! Now they knew neither cold nor hunger nor fear, for they were both with God.

But in the cold dawn, in the corner formed by the two houses, sat the little girl with rosy cheeks and smiling lips, dead—frozen to death on the last evening of the old year. The dawn of the new year rose on the huddled figure of the girl. She was still holding the matches, and half a packet had been burnt.

"She was evidently trying to warm herself," people said. But no one knew what beautiful visions she had seen and in what a blaze of glory she had entered with her dear old grandmother into the heavenly joy and gladness of a new year. ❋

Winter Quarters

Berta Huish Christensen

"Such winter we have never known before,"
She said, "Such darkness, Stephen,
And you know
How much my heart is torn.
I bore
The child that morning
Seven years ago
Back home among the hills of Tennessee.
I should be strong to brave
This bitter hour,
But it is Christmas day,
And memory stabs the will
Past resolution's power.
(Our Linda smiled last night
But did not speak.)
Stephen, I ask,
What flame or inner lamp
Kindles your quiet peace
Although your cheek
Seems whiter than the snow
That shrouds the camp?
Tell me, I beg,
Where is the start that gleams
Beyond the heart's ache
And ashes of dreams?"
Then Stephen touched her slightly greying hair
And squared his shoulders,
Never bowed in fear.
"Hunger we both have known,
But now we share
A newer grief . . . nor is the trail's end near.
But Wise Men once were guided

By a star;
No less, my love, are we
This Christmas night.
It flashes truth eternally,
Although our tears may briefly
Dim its light.
Beyond the cedared mountains
And the plain,
The lamp of faith
We must forever keep,
Though part of us remain
Upon that hill
Where silence guards her sleep.
Then shall we know the star of peace—
Then see
Its light beyond
This dark Gethsemane.

Yuletide in a Younger World

Thomas Hardy

We believed in highdays then,
And could glimpse at night
On Christmas Eve
Imminent oncomings of radiant revel—
Doings of delight:—
Now we have no such sight.

We had eyes for phantoms then,
And at bridge or stile
   On Christmas Eve
Clear beheld those countless ones who had crossed it
   Cross again in file:—
Such has ceased longwhile!

We liked divination then,
And, as they homeward wound
   On Christmas Eve
We could read men's dreams within them spinning
   Even as wheels spin round:—
Now we are blinker-bound.

We heard still small voices then,
And, in the dim serene
   On Christmas Eve,
Caught the far-times tones of fire-filled prophets
   Long on earth unseen . . .
—Can such ever have been?

Three Levels of Christmas

William B. Smart

CHRISTMAS IS A BEAUTIFUL TIME of the year. We love the excitement, the giving spirit, the special awareness of and appreciation for family and friends, the feelings of love and brotherhood that bless our gatherings at Christmastime.

In all of the joyousness, it is well to reflect that Christmas comes at three levels.

Let's call the first the Santa Claus level. It's the level of Christmas trees and holly, of whispered secrets and colorful packages, of candlelight and rich food and warm open houses. It's carolers in the shopping malls, excited children, and weary but loving parents. It's a lovely time of special warmth and caring and giving. It's the level at which we eat too much and spend too much and do too much—and enjoy every minute of it. We love the Santa Claus level of Christmas.

But there's a higher, more beautiful level. Let's call it the Silent Night level. It's the level of all our glorious Christmas carols, of that beloved, familiar story: "Now in those days there went out a decree from Caesar Augustus. . . . " It's the level of the crowded inn and the silent, holy moment in a dark stable when the Son of Man came to earth. It's shepherds on steep, bare hills near Bethlehem, angels with their glad tidings, a new star in the East, wise men traveling far in search of the Holy One. How beautiful and meaningful it is; how infinitely poorer we would be without this sacred second level of Christmas.

The trouble is, these two levels don't last. They can't.

Twelve days of Christmas, at the first level, is about all most of us can stand. It's too intense, too extravagant. The tree dries out and the needles fall. The candles burn down. The beautiful wrappings go out with the trash, the carolers are up on the ski slopes, the toys break, and the biggest day in the stores in the entire year is exchange day, December 26. The feast is over and the dieting begins. But the lonely and the hungry are with us still, perhaps lonelier and hungrier than before.

Lovely and joyous as the first level of Christmas is, there will come a day, very soon, when Mother will put away the decorations and vacuum the living room and think, "Thank goodness that's over for another year."

Even the second level, the level of the Baby Jesus, can't last. How many times this season can you sing "Silent Night"? The angels and the star and the shepherd, even the silent, sacred mystery of that holy night itself, can't long satisfy humanity's basic need. The man who keeps Christ in the manger will, in the end, be disappointed and empty.

No, for Christmas to last all year long, for it to grow in beauty and meaning and purpose, for it to have the power to change lives, we must celebrate it at the third level, that of the *adult* Christ. It is at this level—not as an infant—that our Savior brings His gifts of lasting joy, lasting peace, lasting hope. It was the adult Christ who reached out and touched the untouchable, who loved the unlovable, who so loved us all that even in His agony on the cross He prayed forgiveness for His enemies.

This is the Christ, creator of worlds without number, who wept, Enoch tells us, because so many of us lack affection and hate each other—and then who willingly gave His life for *all* of us, including those for whom He wept. This is the Christ, the adult Christ, who gave us the perfect example, and asked us to follow Him.

Accepting that invitation is the way—the only way—to celebrate Christmas all year and all life long. ❋

CHAPTER THREE

Shepherds & Wise Men

The Three Kings

Henry Wadsworth Longfellow

Three Kings came riding from far away,
   Melchior and Gaspar and Baltasar;
Three Wise Men out of the East were they,
And they travelled by night and they slept by day,
   For their guide was a beautiful, wonderful star.

The star was so beautiful, large, and clear,
   That all the other stars of the sky
Became a white mist in the atmosphere,
And by this they knew that the coming was near
   Of the Prince foretold in the prophecy.

Three caskets they bore on their saddlebows,
   Three caskets of gold with golden keys;
Their robes were of crimson silk with rows
Of bells and pomegranates and furbelows,
   Their turbans like blossoming almond-trees.

And so the Three Kings rode into the West,
   Through the dusk of night, over hill and dell,
And sometimes they nodded with beard on breast,
And sometimes talked, as they paused to rest,
   With the people they met at some wayside well.

"Of the child that is born," said Baltasar,
   "Good people, I pray you, tell us the news;
For we in the East have seen his star,
And have ridden fast, and have ridden far,
   To find and worship the King of the Jews."

And the people answered, "You ask in vain;
   We know of no king but Herod the Great!"
They thought the Wise Men were men insane,

As they spurred their horses across the plain,
   Like riders in haste, and who cannot wait.

And when they came to Jerusalem,
   Herod, the Great, who had heard this thing,
Sent for the Wise Men and questioned them;
And said, "Go down unto Bethlehem,
   And bring me tidings of this new king."

So they rode away; and the star stood still,
   The only one in the gray of morn;
Yes, it stopped,—it stood still of its own free will,
Right over Bethlehem on the hill,
   The city of David, where Christ was born.

And the Three Kings rode through the gate and the
     guard,
   Through the silent street, till their horses turned
And neighed as they entered the great inn yard;
But the windows were closed, and the doors were
     barred,
   And only a light in the stable burned.

And cradled there in the scented hay,
   In the air made sweet by the breath of kine,
The little child in the manger lay,
The child, that would be king one day
   Of a kingdom not human but divine.

His mother Mary of Nazareth
   Sat watching beside his place of rest,
Watching the even flow of his breath,
For the joy of life and the terror of death
   Were mingled together in her breast.

They laid their offerings at his feet:
   The gold was their tribute to a King,
The frankincense, with its odor sweet,
Was for the Priest, the Paraclete,
   The myrrh for the body's burying.

And the mother wondered and bowed her head,
    And sat as still as a statue of stone;
Her heart was troubled yet comforted,
Remembering what the Angel had said
    Of an endless reign and of David's throne.

Then the Kings rode out of the city gate,
    With a clatter of hoofs in proud array;
But they went not back to Herod the Great,
For they knew his malice and feared his hate,
    And returned to their homes by another way.

The Miracle

Claire S. Boyer

Into each man's life comes the miracle—
    The wonder of manger and star;
But 'tis only the wise men see the light,
    And the shepherds who watch afar;

And only the wise men follow its gleam
    Through a desert of dusty days,
And the purple murk of appalling nights,
    And the terror of Herod-ways;

And only the shepherds hear the song
    Of "Glory to God on High;"
For their hearts are rich with humility,
    And tuned to the heavenly cry.

Yet His star is hung for all to see,
    And each has the right to bring
The gift of his soul in the palm of his hand
    To the manger that cradles the King.

For to all of the people of East and West
    Come the tidings of joy each year,
But few are the shepherds and wise men
    With the faith to see and to hear.

Into each man's life comes the miracle—
    The joy of the Christ Child's birth—
But human love alone can bring
    A second Peace to the earth.

Good Tidings of Great Joy

David O. McKay

And there were in the same country shepherds abiding in the field, keeping watch over their flock by night.

"And, lo, the angel of the Lord came upon them, and the glory of the Lord shone round about them: and they were sore afraid.

"And the angel said unto them, Fear not: for, behold, I bring you good tidings of great joy, which shall be to all people.

"For unto you is born this day in the city of David a Saviour, which is Christ the Lord.

"And this shall be a sign unto you; Ye shall find the babe wrapped in swaddling clothes, lying in a manger.

"And suddenly there was with the angel a multitude of the heavenly host praising God, and saying,

"Glory to God in the highest, and on earth peace, good will toward men." (Luke 2:8–14.)

That is the sweetest story ever told; and though it may be repeated time after time, it never fails to move and satisfy, for there is inherent in it much of the meaning of life.

The scene is Bethlehem, a city in Palestine in point of historic interest second only to Jerusalem.

In Micah, the fifth chapter, Bethlehem, the city of David, is mentioned by that prophet as the birthplace of the Messiah. I wonder if the shepherds to whom this revelation of Christ's birth was given had not that prophecy in mind as they kept watch over their flocks by night. A revelation of God does not come to man unless he prepares himself for it and lives worthy of it. Evil influences will thrust themselves upon men, but God will be sought. Evil is always crowding and tempting and promising. God asks us to put forth effort and seek. "Seek, and ye shall find; knock, and it shall be opened" (Matt. 7:7), but we must seek, we must knock, and I think these humble shepherds were treasuring in their hearts the hope, as all Judea was treasuring it, that the Messiah would soon come. Those humble men had opened to them the vision of God.

"And it came to pass, as the angels were gone away from them into heaven, the shepherds said one to another, Let us now go even unto Bethlehem, and see this thing which is come to pass, which the Lord hath made known unto us." (Luke 2:15.)

The shepherds did not say, "I wonder if this be true." They did not say, "Let us go and see if this thing be true"; they said, "Let us go and see this thing which is come to pass which the Lord hath made known unto us"—an assurance that God had revealed his Son, that the angels had given to the world the message that he who should be King of kings and Lord of lords had come as a mere babe in the humblest part of that little Judean town.

What would you give—you who may not have that assurance—to have in your hearts that same confidence that Christ is born, that Christ lives, that God had heralded his birth by angels in heaven? All doubt would be banished, all worry concerning our purpose here in life would cease. That is what such a testimony means. If we could only say: "Let us go now and see this thing which has come to pass, which the Lord hath made known to us." The revelation that Jesus Christ, the Savior of the world, is a divine personal Being, is a wonderful thing. Is it not the most sublime in all the world? With it comes the assurance that Christmas has a divine significance.

It is the spirit of Christmas that counts; it is the feeling that we are his brethren, and that we want to live to come back into his presence, so that we can go, as the shepherds went, right into the very presence of the King of kings, the Lord of lords.

Let us have the spirit of Christmas with the assurance that the shepherds had as they heard the message of the angels, and with that spirit go to him. Therein is life. Unless we can find God and Christ and know them, we shall not have eternal life, for "this is life eternal, [to] know thee, the only true God, and Jesus Christ, whom thou has sent." (See John 17:3.) ❈

How Simple

Angelus Silesius

How simple we must grow!
How simple they who came!
The shepherds looked at God
Long before any man.
He sees God nevermore
Not there, nor here on earth
Who does not long within
To be a shepherd first.

Dividers of the Stars

Vesta P. Crawford

" . . . When Jesus was born in Bethlehem of Judea in the days of Herod the king, behold there came wise men from the east . . . "

From out the orient hills in haste they come
To seek a nameless Prince whose star shall rise
From out the shadowed kingdoms of the earth
To shine forever in the eastern skies.

The Magi move by ancient prophecy
Against the columns of a lesser law,
And know of chariots in the aisles of time
More brief than those the Medes and Persians saw.

    (Swift their shadows pass,
    Swift as a blade on seeded grass. . . .)

Perhaps where sceptered Nineveh is dust,
The thrones departed and the temples gone,
They cross the channeled rivers of the plain
And mark the walls of shattered Babylon.

    (Oh, hurried travelers on the path of stone,
    Seek the tall gate, seek the hill town.)

Dividers of the stars and keepers of the spheres,
Moving through shadows in a cone of light,
They come unto the high Judean hills
With haste, across the broken fields of night. . . .

• • •

(Oh, men of earth,
Listen to the words again—
As wise men heard them long ago,
"Good will—good will to men.")

When the Wise Man Appeared

William Ashley Anderson

....

It WAS A BITTERLY COLD NIGHT, vast and empty. Over Hallett's Hill a brilliant star danced like tinsel on the tip of a Christmas tree. The still air was as resonant as the inside of an iron bell; but within our snug farmhouse in the Pocono Mountains of Pennsylvania it was mellow with the warmth of our cherry-red stoves.

The dinner things had been cleared away, and I relaxed when Bruce came downstairs—an apparition in a long white nightgown with a purple cloak of tintexed cotton over his shoulders. In one hand he held a tall crown of yellow pasteboard and tinsel. From the other swung an ornate censer. On his feet were thin flapping sandals.

"What in the world are you supposed to be?" I asked.

My wife looked at the boy critically, but with concern and tenderness.

"He's one of the Wise Men of the East!" she explained with some indignation.

The look she gave me was an urgent reminder that I had promised to get him to the schoolhouse in town in time for the Christmas pageant. I shuddered at the thought of the cold and went out into the night, pulling on a heavy coat.

The battery in the old car had gone dead, but by one of those freaks of mechanical whimsy, the engine caught at the first turn of the crank. That was a trick of the devil, for the engine died before we got out to the main road. My heart sank. I glanced at Bruce, with the crown and censer clasped in his arms, staring down the endless lane that disappeared in the lonely hills. Hallett's place was more than a mile and a half away, and the nearest turn of Route 90, with the thin chance of a lift, was more than two miles away.

Well, I thought, it's not tragically important. Bruce still said nothing, but his eyes were staring now at the big star twinkling just over the ragged edge of the mountain. Then an uneasy feeling stirred in me, because I knew the boy was praying. He had made his promise, too, and he was praying that nothing would keep him from being one of the Three Wise Men on this magic Christmas Eve.

I strained and heaved at the crank, but it was useless. I thought it over. When I looked up, Bruce was scuttling down the lane, one hand holding his skirts, the other swinging the censer, the high golden crown perched cockeyed on his head. I hesitated between laughing at him and yelling for him to stop. Then I began once more to crank.

Finally the engine coughed throatily. I scrambled into the car. Just about where the road enters town I overtook Bruce.

"You shouldn't have gone off that way," I growled. "It's too cold."

"I made a fire in the censer," he said. "I kept warm enough. I took a bearing on the star, made a short cut across Basoine's farm, and came out right by the new cottage." He shivered.

"But look at your feet! You might have frozen them!"

"It wasn't so bad."

We arrived at the school on time. I stood in back and watched. When I saw Bruce appear, walking stiff-legged on cut and chilblained feet, kneeling by the crèche declaiming his lines, I regretted my laughter at the dinner table. Then an uneasy awe rose up within me. Something stronger than a promise, I knew, had brought him through the bitter night to this sacred pageant.

Going home, Bruce showed me where the shortcut came out. "That's where the Thompsons live," he said, and added, "Harry Thompson died there."

As we passed the Basoine farm there were lights burning. I thought this was strange. Since George Basoine had gone off to war, the old grandmother, who had lost her youngest son in the first war, had sort of shriveled up, and a gloom lay over the house; but as I slowed down I could see Lou Basoine through the kitchen window, smoking his pipe and talking with his wife and mother.

That was about all there was to the evening. But on Christmas Day a friendly farmer's wife came by with gifts of mincemeat, made from venison, and a jug of sassafras cider. She went into the kitchen where my wife was supervising the Christmas feast. I drifted toward the kitchen, too, when I heard laughter there, since I have a weakness for the gossip of the countryside.

"You must hear this!" said my wife. The farmer's wife looked at me with a glittering but wary eye.

"You hain't a-goin' to believe it either," she said. "Just the same I'm tellin' you, folks up here in the hills see things and they do believe!"

"What have you been seeing?"

"It was old Mrs. Basoine. Last night when she was a-feelin' low she thought she heard something back of the barn and she looked out. Now I'll say this for the old lady—she's got good vision. There warn't no moonlight, but if you recollect it was a bright, starry night. And there she saw, plain as day, one of the Wise Men of the Bible come a-walkin' along the hill with a gold crown on his head, a-swingin' one of them pots with smoke in them—"

My wife and I looked at each other, but before I could say anything our visitor hurried on:

"Now don't you start a-laughin'. There's other testimony! Them Thompsons. You know the ones whose oldest boy died? Well, the children heard him first—a singin' 'Come, All Ye Faithful' plain as day. They went runnin' to the window, and they seen the Wise Man a-walkin' in the starlight across the lane, gold crown and robes, and fire pot and all!"

The farmer's wife looked defiantly at me. "Old folks and children see things that maybe we can't. All I can say is this: Basoines and Thompsons don't even know each other. But old lady Basoine was heartsick and lonely for her lost boy, and the Thompsons was heartsick and lonely because this was the first Christmas without Harry, and you dassent say they wasn't a-prayin' too! Maybe you don't believe that amounts to anythin'—but I'm tellin' you it was a comfort to them to see and believe!"

In the quiet of the kitchen the eyes of the two women searched my face—for disbelief, perhaps, since I'm not a very religious person. But whatever they expected, they were surprised at what they got.

I hadn't seen a vision that Christmas Eve, but what I had seen was to me far more impressive than any apparition: a flesh-and-blood small boy with a promise to keep, following over a trackless countryside the star which centuries ago led the Wise Men to Bethlehem. And it was not for me to deny the courage and the faith I saw in my son's eyes that night.

And so I said, with a sincerity which must have startled those two good women as much as it obviously pleased them:

"Yes, I believe that God is very close to us at Christmas." ❈

The Shepherds and the Magi

Young Men's Mutual Improvement Association Manual, 1897–98

I**T WILL BE OBSERVED THAT** the testimonies concerning the birth of the Messiah are from two extremes, the lowly shepherds in the Judean field, and the learned magi from the far east. We cannot think this is the result of mere chance, but that in it may be discerned the purpose and wisdom of God.

All Israel was looking forward to the coming of the Messiah, and in the birth of Jesus at Bethlehem, the hope of Israel—though unknown to Israel—is fulfilled. Messiah, of whom the prophet spake, is born. But there must be those who can testify of that truth, and hence to the shepherds who watched their flocks by night an angel was sent to say: "Fear not, behold I bring you good tidings of great joy, which shall be to all people; for unto you is born this day, in the city of David, a Saviour, which is Christ, the Lord." And for a sign of the truth of the message, they were to find the child wrapped in swaddling clothes, lying in a manger in Bethlehem. And they went with haste and found Mary and Joseph, and the babe lying in a manger; and when they had seen it, they made known abroad the saying which was told them concerning this child. God had raised up to Himself witnesses among the people to testify that Messiah was born, that the hope of Israel was fulfilled.

But there were classes of people among the Jews whom these lowly shepherd witnesses could not reach, and had they been able to reach them, the story of the angel's visit, and the concourse of angels singing the magnificent song of "Peace on earth, good will to men" would doubtless have been accounted an idle tale of superstitious folk, deceived by their own over-wrought imaginations or idle dreams. Hence God raised up another class of witnesses—the "wise men from the east"—witnesses that could enter the royal palace of proud King Herod and boldly ask: "Where is he that is born king of the Jews? for we have seen his star in the east, and are come to worship him"; a testimony that startled Herod and troubled all Jerusalem.

So that indeed God raised up witnesses for Himself to meet all classes and conditions of men— the testimony of angels for the poor and the lowly; the testimony of wise men for the haughty king and proud priests of Judea. So that of the things concerning the birth of Messiah, no less than of the things of His death and resurrection from the dead, His disciples could say, "these things were not done in a corner." ❊

A Hymn on the Nativity of My Saviour

Ben Jonson

I sing the birth was born tonight,
The author both of life and light;
 The angels so did sound it.
And like the ravished shepherds said,
Who saw the light and were afraid,
 Yet searched, and true they found it.

We Three Kings of Orient Are

John Henry Hopkins, Jr.

Kings: We three kings of Orient are,
   Bearing gifts we traverse afar,
   Field and fountain, moor and mountain,
   Following yonder star.
    Refrain:
   O star of wonder, star of night,
   Star with royal beauty bright,
   Westward leading, still proceeding,
   Guide us to the perfect light.

Melchior: Born a babe on Bethlehem's plain
   Gold I bring to crown Him again;
   King forever, ceasing never
   Over us all to reign.
    Refrain:

Caspar: Frankincense to offer have I;
   Incense owns a Deity nigh,
   Prayer and praising all men raising,
   Worship Him, God on high.
    Refrain:

Balthasar: Myrrh is mine; its bitter perfume
   Breathes a life of gathering gloom;
   Sorrowing, sighing, bleeding, dying,
   Sealed in the stone-cold tomb.
    Refrain:

All: Glorious now behold Him arise,
   King and God and Sacrifice;
   Heaven sings "Hallelujah!"
   "Hallelujah!" earth replies.
    Refrain:

From a Far Country

Vesta P. Crawford

"Now when Jesus was born in Bethlehem of Judea in the days of Herod the king, behold there came wise men from the east . . . Saying, Where is he that is born King of the Jews? for we have seen his star in the east, and are come to worship him."

Why should they seek another lamp in diamond
      galaxies,
Whose fathers knew the planets back a thousand
      years;
Who saw Orion and the belts of Pleiades,
The flame of Vega, the meteors and the spheres?

   (So wondered old Chaldea—
   So questioned Babylon. . . .)

And were there not unnumbered roads
In Median lands among the satrapies
Where questing caravans might go?
Why leave the palace and the ivory gate
For paths as desolate as these?

   (Thus they asked in Nineveh
   And on the Euphrates. . . .)

    • • •

Thin-lined as a silver thread the road runs back
Through long meridians to Bethlehem,
And in the jeweled watches of the night
We trace the Magian path and walk with them.

For we have known the orbit of a broken world,
And we have seen the fire and the stone,
Have searched the fields of space of signs. . . .

As Magi on the Persian roofs who once had
      watched alone.

And we who sought for wisdom long latent to our
      sight
Have found the answer and the prophecy
Revealed upon the scripture of the night!

The Song of a Shepherd-boy at Bethlehem

Josephine Preston Peabody

Sleep, Thou little Child of Mary:
    Rest Thee now.
Though these hands be rough from shearing
    And the plough,
Yet they shall not ever fail Thee,
When the waiting nations hail Thee,
Bringing palms unto their King.
    Now—I sing.

Sleep, Thou little Child of Mary,
    Hope divine.
If Thou wilt but smile upon me,
    I will twine
Blossoms for Thy garlanding.
Thou'rt so little to be King,
    God's Desire!
    Not a brier
Shall be left to grieve Thy brow;
    Rest Thee now.

Sleep, Thou little Child of Mary.
    Some fair day
Wilt Thou, as Thou wert a brother,
    Come away
Over hills and over hollow?
All the lambs will up and follow,
Follow but for love of Thee.
    Lov'st Thou me?

Sleep, Thou little Child of Mary;
    Rest Thee now.
I that watch am come from sheep-stead
    And from plough.
Thou wilt [surely remember] me
When Thou'rt lifted, royally,
Very high for all to see:
    Smilest Thou?

The Holy Night

Elizabeth Barrett Browning

We sate among the stalls at Bethlehem;
The dumb kine from their fodder turning them,
   Softened their hornèd faces
   To almost human gazes
   Toward the newly Born:
The simple shepherds from the star-lit brooks
   Brought visionary looks,
As yet in their astonied hearing rung
   The strange sweet angel-tongue:
The magi of the East, in sandals worn,
   Knelt reverent, sweeping round,
   With long pale beards, their gifts upon the ground,
   The incense, myrrh, and gold
These baby hands were impotent to hold:
So let all earthlies and celestials wait
   Upon thy royal state.
   Sleep, sleep, my kingly One!

CHAPTER FOUR

Love &
Sharing

Food for Santa

Anna Marie Scow,
as told to Jack M. Lyon

A FEW YEARS AGO, we wondered if we were even going to have a Christmas. We were struggling financially and hardly had enough money to buy food, let alone buy presents. Our cupboards were actually bare. When our bishop announced the ward Christmas party in sacrament meeting, our children were really excited. They especially looked forward to visiting with Santa, who would be there to give them some candy. We thought that candy might be the only present they would receive. Then the bishop said the party would also be a chance to help the poor. Each child who wanted to talk to Santa would first have to donate a can of food. Our hearts sank—with our seven children, we couldn't afford a can of food for each one.

At first we thought we would just stay home and not go to the party. But as the days passed, I prayed about what to do. I felt that I should act in faith and things would work out. Acting on my impression, I went to the grocery store to see what food items I might buy, although I really didn't know what I would be able to afford. On one aisle was a display of Chinese noodles, and they were on sale: eight packages for a dollar. And I had a dollar! I bought seven packages, which our children took to the party and happily added to the large pile of food near Santa's chair. This may not seem like much, but in our position even that was a sacrifice.

After the party, we went home. We were preparing for bed when someone pulled into our driveway. It was the bishop—and he was bringing all that food to us. In the following days, we thanked the Lord over and over for his love and goodness to us during that Christmas season. ❋

Most Gentle Love

Anonymous

Though He be Lord of all,
The Christ Child is but very small.
Kneel then, and at His cradle lay,
Most gentle love this Christmas Day.

Christmas Is for Sharing

Richard Warner, as told to
Emma Lou Warner Thayne

I KNEW THAT HOMER HAD WANTED canyon boots for as long as I could remember. He was eleven and I ten, and we had spent many nights under the blue quilts at the cabin talking about how great it would be to have some real boots—boots that would climb through thorny bushes, that would ward off rattlesnakes, that would nudge the ribs of the pony; we had planned the kind of leather they should be and what kind of decoration they should have.

But we both knew it was just talk. The depression had been hard on Father's business, and even shoes for school were usually half-soled hand-me-downs.

Christmas that year had promised as always to be exciting, though mainly because of the handmade things we'd worked on in school for our parents. We never had money to spend on each other, but we had caught early in our lives a sort of contagion from our mother. She loved to give, and her anticipation of the joy that a just-right gift would bring to someone infected our whole household. We were swept up in breathless waiting to see how others would like what we had to give. Secrecy ruled—open, exaggerated secrecy, as we made and hid our gifts. The only one whose hiding place we never discovered was my Grandmother's. Her gifts seemed to materialize by magic on Christmas morning and were always more expensive than they should have been.

That Christmas I was glowing because Mother had been so happy with the parchment lamp shade I'd made in the fourth grade, and Father had raved over the clay jewelry case I had molded and baked for him. Gill and Emma Lou had been pleased with the figures I'd whittled out of clothespins, and Homer had liked the Scout pin I'd bargained for with my flint. Then Grandma started to pass out her presents.

Mine was heavy and square. I'd been in the hospital that year and then on crutches, and I'd wondered how it would be to have an Erector set to build with. Grandma had a knack at reading boys' minds, and I was sure that's what it was. But it wasn't. It was a pair of boots, brown tangy-smelling leather boots.

I looked quickly to Homer's package. His was a sweater. He'd needed one all fall. I wanted to cover my box before he saw what it was. I didn't want the boots; they should have been his. He came toward me, asking to see, and I started to say, "I'm sorry, bruv."

But he was grinning. And he shouted, "Hey, everybody—look what Richard's got." He swooped the boots out of the box, fondled them like treasure, and then sat on the floor at my feet to take off my half-soled shoes and put on the brand new boots.

I don't remember how the boots felt, nor even how they looked. But Christmas rang in my soul because my brother was glad for me. ❋

The Gift

Elaine Reiser Alder

I᷈T'S TIME TO GO NOW, MOM," he called through the
front door. "Better get some gloves on, 'cause it's
getting kind of cold out here."

The midwinter grey and the street lights defied
the time. It was just five o'clock, and my son, the pint-
sized newspaper carrier, had been folding and putting
rubber bands on his ninety papers ever since he came
home from school. Now he packed them sardine-tight
into a double bag; the single bag was for me.

He called from the porch again, "Let's get
going before it's dark."

For Christmas we gave "gifts of self" that year.
When I asked eleven-year-old Nate what would be
most special for me to give him, he didn't hesitate.
"Come with me on my paper route, will you?" His
impish grin forewarned that it would be memorable.

Ironically, I scheduled the day to give my gift
without knowing it would follow the season's
biggest snowstorm. So, with dinner simmering in
the oven and our bodies bundled against the cold,
we headed down the street. Twenty inches of snow
lay on the ground, a slight breeze wisping its surface
into feather-like drifts.

It was two blocks to the first door, then a
ramble through the student trailer court, breaking
trails in the fresh snow.

Drifting snowflakes added a holiday atmosphere to the dusk, while little Christmas lights in
trailer windows told us that mini-families on shoe-
string incomes lived inside. Their gift-giving, like
their monthly newspaper bill, would be carefully
budgeted, and their Christmas trees and window
decorations signaled traditions handed on to a new
generation.

My bag was heavy, though my seventy-five-
pound guide bore the double burden. His year's
experience as a carrier had taught him all the tricks,
including how to tote a bag with papers balanced
front and back. He suggested that I deliver on one
side of the road as he called out the numbers to me.
He would do the opposite side.

The first few trailers were fun. There is a simple
satisfaction to a paper route—service, orderliness,
completion.

"See that trailer?" my sidekick asked as he
pointed toward the small, metal home. "They had a
baby this week."

"How do you know?"

"Well, when I collected from them I could tell
she was going to. Then they printed it in the window with shoe polish," he reported.

As an afterthought, "It was a girl."

A few steps more and he remarked, "I don't
like to collect from the people in this trailer."

"Why?" I puzzled.

"Oh, . . . they don't seem to have very much
money."

"What makes you think that?"

"They always get it out of a fruit bottle.
Sometimes it's all in pennies and dimes."

We walked along in silence for a few moments.

"I just wish I didn't have to collect from
people who don't have much money. It kind of
makes me feel sad." I was moved by his sensitivity.

As the snow fell thicker and the bags became
lighter, the calves of my legs felt tight and my boots
irritated the skin. The novelty was beginning to
wear off, the trailer court looked much bigger.

But I had to admit that the snow was post-card
pretty and the company charming.

"These people are really neat," he began as he placed a paper on one porch.

"How come?"

"Whenever I collect from them they give me a cupcake or a cookie. They always make me feel like I'm important," he added self-consciously.

We trudged along without a word for many minutes. But my mind was anything but blank: *He gets three cents per paper per night for this . . . No wonder he hates to get up at six on Sunday mornings . . . If only his customers knew what a sacrifice this is . . . Is it really worth all this effort every day?*

My musings were interrupted when Nate asked, "Mom, what is frankincense and myrrh?"

Surprised, I tried to answer.

"What does that have to do with a paper route?" I teased.

"Nothing. But we were talking about it in Primary. They're sure different-sounding words, aren't they?"

So we talked about frankincense and myrrh. That was good for a few more trailers.

"Do you know who lives there?" He pointed to a trailer.

"No," I replied. To me these were all just numbers on an emergency list tacked to the bulletin board at home.

"The USU quarterback. I'll bet he makes All-American next year, he's so good. He used to be one of my customers, but then he stopped. I don't know why. I sure wish he still was."

He grinned. "I told all my friends at school that I was his paper boy. They thought that was pretty cool."

I was dragging along, but he ran ahead to a cluster of out-of-the-way trailers.

"Just a minute, Mom," he called. "I've got to put these in the milk boxes. These customers don't

like their papers left on the porch." *Now what? They even expect extra service.* A little further on, he showed me a trailer where "Dad's secretary lives" and another where "she saves the rubber bands for me." Two trailers beyond he said, "These people gave me a Christmas card and a plate of cookies last week."

Around the corner he showed me where "one of Dad's students lives. He asked me if we were related when he wrote my name on the check."

Our conversation continued as I visualized the customers he was describing.

"The people in number 40 gave me a tip for Christmas. I didn't expect it, but it sure made me happy," he admitted.

"The next ones here just got married," Nate said. "In the temple, too. Pretty neat, huh?"

"How do you know it was in the temple?"

"Oh, they have a picture on their TV set. They're standing out in front of the temple."

"He's a student body officer besides. I'd like to be just like him."

He stopped at the next trailer. "Something sad happened to this family," he said as he walked toward the door.

"What was that?"

"Do you remember when I told you about the little baby that died? This is where that family lives."

"Yes, and I remember cutting out the obituary from the paper. Did you take it to them?"

"I did. But it was sort of hard to know what to say to them. He was the only baby they had."

We neared the end of the route; but he had one more hero to tell me about.

"Did I tell you that I've got a golf champion on my route? He won the tournament."

"Look in that living room window. See all those trophies? He's just in college, but he'll probably be a pro."

"What's he like?"

"He's nice. His wife is always telling me she appreciates it when I get the paper right by the door. They've got a cute little girl, too. They aren't hard to talk to, even though he's important."

By now we were ready to leave the trailer court. It was nice having a lighter bag on my shoulder, and I was sure he felt better with his bag nearly empty, too.

"Well, that's the trailer court. I'll show you an easy way over to the dorms." Tromping through an adjoining field, we looked like two white ragamuffins.

"Let's make tracks through here," Nate called as he moved ahead of me. "There's nothing in the snow. I'll go first. I love to do this between the trailers on a snowy day," he informed me.

"How may customers do you have in the dorms?" I asked.

"Just fifteen. They're a cinch." I was ready for a cinch at this point.

We trudged, single file; I aimed for his footprints. Then he turned around toward me.

"It's more fun to deliver in the new snow than anything."

"What?" I wasn't sure I had heard him correctly.

"Oh, you know. Making tracks and watching the snow fall by the street lights. It's kind of warm and soft and quiet."

I felt silly for feeling the cold instead of appreciating the setting.

Seven dorms were ahead of us now, each one with four stories. "How can you tell these dorms apart, anyway?" I questioned.

"It's just like a checkerboard, Mom." He described the apartment numbers and the letters for the buildings. I listened, suddenly glad that little boys, instead of their mothers, have paper routes.

One by one he delivered his last few papers. At the "B" dorm he instructed, "Wait down here in the lobby, mom. I'll run this paper to the fourth floor."

At the next, "I have to leave this paper on the vent and then ring their bell."

In Dorm "E" he called back, "This one's just on the first floor. I'll do it fast."

Two buildings later: "I have to put this one on the head resident's desk. My customer picks it up there."

At the last dorm he had been entrusted with the combination to a lock box, and each day he tucked the paper inside and locked the box back up.

In a moment of awe, I began to genuinely appreciate this little boy with his computer memory. *I hope he never gets sick, I thought. There's no way we'd be able to substitute for him and come out even on the papers.*

"Well, we're done," he said as he delivered the last paper. "Wasn't too bad, was it?" he asked, sensing my amazement that we hadn't run short or quit along the way.

We were just two blocks from home now. The sky was dark, light snow still falling.

"Pretty neat customers, aren't they?"

"Sure are," I agreed.

"And you give nice Christmas presents, Mom," he confided. "It's more fun when there's someone to talk to."

But the gifts were manifold that day. My gift was time and company; his was a message that years of mothering had not been wasted. His teachers had given him simple faith; his customers gave him trust in humanity and confidence in himself.

"Next Christmas will you give me two days, Mom?

"Why not?" I squeezed his gloved hand extra tight, warming inside with pride, even renewal.

Sometimes the best gifts aren't wrapped in paper and bows. And sometimes the giver gains the most. ❋

The Visit of the King

Bertha Irvine

MANY YEARS AGO, IN ENGLAND, monasteries were a familiar sight, and the monks belonging to them were well-known, for they numbered at times into the thousands, having entered into those institutions for the purpose of leading lives of contemplation and self-denial, and of service to their fellowmen.

At the beginning, the monastic life was not one to be envied by those who loved comfort and pleasure, for such things were to be done away with when they entered these religious orders, and the strictest self-denial had to be practiced. Coarse clothing was worn next to the body; long fasts were required, and food was partaken of sparingly at all times. They endured cold and hunger, with the full belief that the punishment of the flesh brought about spiritual growth. They believed, too, that the extreme tortures which they inflicted upon themselves could only give them the slightest idea of the sufferings endured by their great Master, whom they thought to serve in this way.

Although this was the desire in the beginning of these orders, and many lived out such lives of self-sacrifice, nevertheless, history shows that later on the selfish feelings of the natural man gained the ascendency, and it was then only a question of time until the monasteries and their inmates were looked upon as a menace to the country morally rather than an uplift to it spiritually.

The changed condition was brought about chiefly through the great wealth that was bestowed by charitably inclined people upon these monasteries. This included large grants of land and the means with which to build fine abbeys as homes for the monks and to furnish them with all the comforts that the age afforded, and that would make life pleasant.

It was then that the monks gradually gave way to their selfish desires, and the true ideal of their monastic life was forgotten in revelry and even sin, spending the means placed in their hands as a sacred trust for their own gratification.

This of course did not come about all at once. While some so far forgot the life which was expected of them as religious leaders of the people, at the same time there might be found others filled with zeal and willing to deny themselves in order to live lives which they believed to be acceptable in the sight of the Lord, and wherein they might serve their fellows who needed comfort and aid.

However, corruption gradually increased until the time came when the monastery was no longer worthy of the name of religious order, and in time the government of the country itself had to take a hand in their banishment, and now only the ruins remain of the once magnificent abbeys that occupied so important a place in the religious history of England.

Our story takes us back to the time when they were in a flourishing condition.

Had we then traveled through a certain county of Northern England, we might, in our journey, have seen two monasteries situated within sight of each other, one at the foot and one on the side of a high hill.

The one in the valley was in a richly wooded country, well sheltered, while the other was in an exposed situation, without the friendly shelter of trees, and where the soil had been washed away and vegetation of any kind was scarce.

The one was situated so high that the wind forever whistled in chill blasts around it, while the other was so sheltered that an unkind wind rarely reached it.

As we have said, one might be seen from the other, and often in the still evenings the chanting of the monks at their service could be plainly heard from one to the other.

The monastery in the valley had the appearance of luxury which wealth supplies, while the one on the hillside was bleak and bare, with no adornment. And these outward conditions were but an index to what might be seen inside—the one extravagant with the comforts which the age afforded, and the other extremely plain.

The monks of the two monasteries were also easily distinguished. Though all were arrayed in the somber black robe of their order, still the difference was quite marked in the texture and make of the garment—the one long and flowing, gathered with silken cords, while the other was scant and coarse, and girded with the same material.

On the countenances of the valley monks were the marks of self-seeking and pride, while on those of their hillside brethren were plainly stamped self-denial, gentleness and a noble purpose.

Where there was either sorrow or suffering in the regions far and near, where the dying were, and the plague-stricken, there could invariably be seen the latter, while at the feasts and ceremonies both of church and state one might always have seen the former.

The valley monastery was presided over by a haughty, selfish abbot named Hugo, while its sister institution had at its head the good Francis, whose purpose throughout his four score years had been to serve his Master with most unselfish zeal. He had gathered those around him to the number of many hundreds whom he led as a gentle shepherd, and whose happiness it was to be like their beloved abbot. And as like clings to like, Hugo had gathered around him those of his own kind—the selfish and proud, the lazy and the self-righteous.

The time of our story is in late December, the Christmas season near at hand.

The news had come to both monasteries that the good king of the land, beloved of all his subjects, was traveling in that county, and would visit the monasteries either on Christmas eve or day, for he was known to be of pious mind, and the monks and their labors had his especial interest as he traveled throughout the land.

Abbot Hugo and his companions felt proud to think that they had so much to offer so royal a guest. They believed he would linger in their stately abbey when he reached there, for they did not look upon the hillside monastery as worthy of even a short visit from one so rich and mighty. In their pride they scorned their humbler brethren, and made light of their endeavors to do good.

Therefore great preparations were made. Cooks were kept busy preparing food for the feasts. The best wine was sought out and brought forward. The woodmen were ordered to bring in a large supply of fuel, so that blazing fires might be everywhere to keep out the wintry weather.

"A king must have the best," agreed all the monks. And they considered that best which they themselves revelled in most, and for which they thought best to spend their time and means.

On the hill side the visit was also looked forward to with joy, for they had heard of the good deeds of the king, and their hearts were loyal towards him, and while they expected him, yet they trembled to think of so great a visitor within their humble home.

They could make no great preparations, for there was but a scanty supply of either food or drink in their storehouse, and but little money in their treasury, for the constant demand of those in need at this season kept it low.

There was one thing however they did excel in, and that was their singing. The clear, high air, their temperate living, and their pure lives all contributed to make the music of their choirs more divine than earthly.

Many and many a time had Abbot Hugo and his monks paused to listen to the strains of sweetest harmony that came floating to them upon the stillness of the night, and were jealous, too, for they themselves could not make music; try as they would, it was harsh and coarse. Often, too, had travelers, in passing in the vicinity of the hillside monastery, gazed upward with the expectation of seeing a heavenly chorus singing and praising the Lord.

It was well known that the king was a lover of music, and therefore the hope of the poorer monks was in their singing. They spent more time now every day in their practice, for they wished to do better than they had ever done, if it should happen that the king should visit them.

Christmas eve came.

"Surely the king will be here today," was the word passed in both monasteries, and there was more or less excitement noticeable, for a visit from a king was no small event, and the present monarch had thus far not visited either of them.

The snow lay so deep as to almost bury the monastery in the valley, but with huge fires, plenty of clothing, and with wine to warm and cheer the inner man, Hugo and his monks were far from suffering in the keen air, and taking them altogether, they certainly presented a jolly, comfortable com-

pany as they gathered on Christmas eve to hold services.

They went through the form, but the thoughts of each one were more upon the expected visit, with its feasts and enjoyments, than upon the singing and prayers. They knew that if the king came at all that day he must now be near at hand.

While they were thus engaged a loud knocking was heard at the outer door, and they exclaimed in one voice, "The king."

The Abbot himself hurried to the entrance, and in his grandest manner threw wide open the door with words of welcome on his lips, when, to his surprise and disgust, he beheld, instead of the commanding figure of their king, the bowed form and gray hair of an aged minstrel, cloaked and hooded, and leaning upon his staff, with a harp upon his back.

"Can you afford shelter and warmth for the night?" said a trembling voice.

"The storm has made traveling hard, and it is bitter cold. I have lost my way, and I fear I am far from home."

The Abbot's face, already red from a late wine feast, now grew redder with disappointed anger, and the monks crowding near him reflected his countenance. Scowls were seen on every side.

"What mean you to come at this hour and disturb our holy service," cried the Abbot. "Begone, the monastery on the hill is for such as you. We are expecting the king, and cannot have our stately halls disgraced with the presence of a beggar."

"Could I not make music at your feasts?" inquired the old man.

"No, indeed," they all cried.

"Then I will go to the hillside home, and will trouble you no more."

So saying he turned away and was soon lost in the darkness.

The door was closed. The Abbot and the monks returned to their interrupted service, while the minstel made his way through the deep snow, over slippery paths, toward the one light he could see far above him.

As he drew nearer to the monastery he heard soft, sweet strains of music coming, it seeing to him, from above. He paused, and distinctly to his ears came the words, "Glory to God in the highest, and on earth peace, good-will to men."

He looked up, but could see nothing, though he expected no less than an angelic vision. His mind was carried far away from the wintry scene around him to the Judean hills, where in fancy he saw the gentle shepherds and the heavenly choir that sang to them so long ago, and his own soul glowed within him until he was sure he felt the warmth of that beautiful night when the message had come to those humble men that a Savior was born into the world.

The cold and weariness had been forgotten and he had journeyed up the slippery paths with haste, and now found himself very near to the light that had been his guide. He hastened on.

Reaching the door of the monastery, he now realized that the strains of music came from within its walls, and in astonishment he again paused and wondered, while his spirit was moved within him. Could they be human voices that had stirred his heart? At least they must, he felt, be aided by the heavenly choirs.

He knocked at the door, and the knock resounded through the bare passages and empty rooms, echoing and re-echoing.

Soon the door was slowly opened by a very old man, holding a torch high above his head, and say-ing in a gentle voice, as a greeting oft repeated, for it was apparent that he could see but little, "Welcome, stranger or friend, enter."

The minstrel stepped in and was invited to be seated.

He now noticed that there was no interruption in the beautiful singing, though he felt certain that his knock had resounded through every part of the building.

After waiting but a moment he heard footsteps. A door opened, and the venerable Abbot came forward with outstretched hands to greet him.

The minstrel said in his trembling voice: "I wish shelter for the night. The wind is keen and I am far from home."

"Welcome, friend," said the Abbot. "This house is ever open to the lost and the needy. Come with me."

Together they walked down the dimly lighted passage, coming nearer and nearer to the sound of the music, and the Abbot was passing on, when the old man said:

"Let me pause here, so that I may hear those beautiful strains. They led me up the mountain; they made my heart glow until I felt the bitter cold no more. At first I thought it was the heavenly choir singing of the Savior's birth."

"Would you not like to go where they are?" asked the Abbot.

The minstrel expressed his great desire to do so, and the Abbot then opened a door and ushered the stranger into a vast unadorned chapel, where the monks were assembled singing.

They saw the visitor and paused an instant. The Abbot said, "Brethren, a stranger has come to our door for shelter. Your singing led the way for him. He is a minstrel, and we bid him welcome. He wishes again to hear your songs of praise."

Every head bowed assent. Then the beautiful harmony again filled the chapel, the very walls seemed to resound with the music of their voices.

The stranger sat with bowed head beside the Abbot until the singing was ended.

After this the Abbot called a few of his brethren to him, and they conferred together in low tones.

"The stranger has first claim," spoke the Abbot. "Will it not be well to give him the room we have prepared for the king?"

"What if the king should come?" said one.

"Then he must fare as this needy stranger would have done had he not come first. This poor minstrel is in greater need of the little warmth and comfort we have to give than the king will be when he comes."

They all assented to this.

Then the Abbot led the minstrel to the best chamber the abbey afforded, where a fire of logs gave an air of comfort. And they spread a table with their plain fare and bade him eat, with a hearty welcome. The minstrel gave thanks and ate.

Many of the monks had gathered around, and some desired the stranger to sing and play. He requested them to be seated.

Then he told them of his long journey and that he was now weary, but if they desired it, before going to rest, he would sing to them of that which fitted the season so well.

He played a short prelude upon his harp, and in a sweet, low voice he sang the story of the birth of Christ in the lowly manger, of the shepherds on the Judean hills, of the angelic visitation, and of their finding the divine child in the Bethlehem stable; of the wise men led by the star and of their gifts and adoration. It was all sung in beautiful,

quaint language, and his audience was charmed, listening with reverent attention to every word.

After this they bade each other good night, and very soon quiet reigned throughout the monastery. Peace was upon their slumbers.

The monks of the valley monastery grew impatient waiting for their royal guest, and at length sat down to the banquet which had been prepared, nor did they arise therefrom until far into the night, when all had partaken too freely both of food and drink. After a few unseemly brawls each retired to his cell to slumber heavily, but not in peace.

• • •

Christmas morning was bright and clear. On the hillside the air was extremely keen. Very early the monks were astir. They thought the king might even now be at the valley monastery, and surely they would receive a visit today. They hoped he would come, but could not feel sure, for kings had visited the richer monastery before without troubling to come to them, and especially in the winter season.

However, they had many things else to think about and plan for. There were errands of mercy to go, many sick to cheer, the poor to feed with extra care because of the day, and they had their own services of praise to attend. So while they were filled with expectancy they did not waste their time in idle looking for what might not happen.

The sun shining so brightly into his room awoke the minstrel. He started from his couch, but not the bowed old man of the night before. He was tall and straight, with wavy black hair, and in rich attire, which the heavy cloak and hood of the night before had altogether concealed. No one seeing him now could fail to recognize the king.

The recollections of the evening before were clear upon his mind. He could hear the low chants in the distance, and as the monks passed to and fro in procession their musical voices were heard keeping time to their steps.

The king made his way, without disguise, to the chapel, where the monks had not as yet assembled, and there he awaited their coming.

Soon the measured tread of their footsteps drew near, the door was opened, and Abbot Francis led the procession. They came with bowed heads, chanting solemnly, and took their places. Then they raised their heads and saw their royal visitor as with one eye.

"The king," was the united exclamation, as they bowed in reverence.

"It is the king," their guest responded. "What you thought to do unto a poor wandering minstrel you did unto me."

He earnestly requested that they go through their usual service of praise. They did so in humility, and never before had praise sounded so rich to his ears as it did from the lips of those who were acting out what they believed in their hearts to be the true Christian life.

The king remained at the hillside monastery throughout that day and many that followed, quietly resting under the peaceful influence, and rejoicing in the lives of the inmates as well as in their tuneful voices. He closely watched their system of caring for the needy and was satisfied with their devotion to duty. His heart was filled with thankfulness to know that in his kingdom there were so many true servants of the Master. On leaving them he bestowed a kingly gift, in full confidence that they would know how to use it well.

It was not long after his visit that Abbot Hugo received word from the king that the abbey occupied by himself and his monks was theirs no longer; that it was to become a hospital to be in the charge of the hillside monks, and that Hugo and his companions were to be disbanded, to return to their former avocations until they might learn humility and the love of fellowman, so necessary in those who claim to be engaged in the work of the Master. ✻

A Christmas Hymn

Christina Georgina Rossetti

Love came down at Christmas,
Love all lovely, Love Divine;
Love was born at Christmas,
Star and Angels gave the sign.

. . .

Love shall be our token,
Love be yours and love be mine,
Love to God and all men,
Love for plea and gift and sign.

I Think You Have
a Fire at Your Store

LaRue H. Soelberg

THIS CHRISTMAS HAD BEGUN like any other. The laughter of our happily excited children was evidence that Santa had indeed been able to decipher the hastily scrawled notes mailed weeks before.

As was our custom, LeRoy and I would wait until the children had sufficient time to inspect, test, compare, and segregate their new treasures before we would open our gifts.

The similarity of this Christmas to any other ended here.

The loud knock on the front door demanded immediate answer.

"Come quick!" There was urgency in our friend's voice. "I think you have a fire at your store!"

Fears flooded my mind as I ran through the vacant lot to the store, a small grocery business, which was not yet half paid for.

There were no flames rising from the building, but the windows were solid black.

A fireman came running up and put his hand against the window.

"No heat." He seemed relieved. "There's no fire now—let's open it up."

Our hopes were raised. Perhaps we had not lost everything!

He turned the key and pushed open the door. The dense, choking smoke that had filled every minute space of the small building drifted out into the street.

My heart sank. It was like looking at the inside of a coal-black furnace. Not a crack, not a corner, not one can stacked beneath another had escaped the ugly black filth!

LeRoy, with the help of some of the firemen, removed the motor that had burned itself out. We stood gazing in disbelief at the result.

True, the store had not burned, but was it salvageable? Perhaps the building and equipment could be cleaned, but what about the thousands of bottles, cans, and cartons? Even if they could be saved, how could we possibly survive the closing of business for even a few days?

"Only one thing to do." The fireman's voice was surprisingly cheerful. "Let's see if we can clean it up."

We were reluctant to accept his offer of help. After all, wasn't this Christmas, a day to be spent with family and loved ones?

"Come on," he joked. "My son will be glad to have me out of the house so that he can play with his electric train. Get me a bucket and some soap.

No sooner would we equip one volunteer with cleaning items than another would appear at the door, demanding, as one neighbor put it, "a chance to participate in this joyful holiday project."

Each person who came to the door uttered an astonished "Oh, no!" and then, "Where do you want me to start?"

By 11 A.M. there were over forty people: friends, neighbors, firemen, patrons, and new acquaintances, scrubbing away at the terrible black goo. Still they kept coming! We were overwhelmed!

The men had taken over the cleaning of the ceiling, the most stubborn and difficult task of all. The women were working in twos, taking items off the shelves, cleaning what they could, and boxing the rest.

One young lad who was recuperating from a broken leg made trips to the cafe to get hamburgers and potato chips to feed the workers. Another brought turkey and rolls which, I'm certain, were to have been the biggest part of his family's Christmas dinner.

An energetic teenager must have run twenty miles emptying buckets and refilling them with clean hot water.

A service station operator brought hundreds of old cleaning rags.

An electrician worked on a motor replacement and soon had the refrigerator case operating again.

This was no ordinary cleaning job. Every inch had to be scrubbed, scoured, washed, and rinsed. Sometimes this procedure had to be repeated seven times before the white of the walls and ceiling would show through, yet everyone was laughing and joking as though they were having a good time.

"Actually, I only dropped by to supervise," came a comment from behind the bread rack.

"I bet this cures you of following fire trucks," a fireman chided his wife.

We all laughed when an attractive blonde woman, who was perched on top of the vegetable case and now bore a striking resemblance to a chimney sweep, burst out with a chorus of "Chim Chim Cheree."

It was shortly after 2 A.M. when we locked the front door. Everyone had gone. As they finished their jobs, they just slipped out—not waiting for a word of thanks or a smile of appreciation.

We walked home hand in hand. Tears flowed freely down my cheeks. Not the tears of frustration and despair that had threatened earlier, but tears of love and gratitude. Business would open as usual tomorrow—because fifty-four kind people had the true spirit of Christmas in their hearts.

Our children had left the tree lights burning, and our presents lay unopened in a neat pile on the floor. They would wait until morning. Whatever those gaily wrapped packages contained would be dwarfed, indeed, by the great gift of friendship given to us that Christmas Day. ❈

Gifts for the Poor

Shirley G. Finlinson

SISTER MELBOURNE WAS MEAN and grouchy. There was no other way to describe her. Just the other day I heard her telling the bishop that children took too much time in testimony meeting. She even said that most of us didn't understand what we were saying; we just wanted attention. I walked out of the chapel feeling very angry.

My anger didn't last, however. It was December, and Christmas was in the air. Excitement filled me right up to the top of my head. I had to smile and laugh, or I think I would have burst. We began singing "Jingle Bells" as we rode home from church, just to let some of the excitement out.

After dinner, Mom and Dad called us into the family room. We all knew what we were going to discuss. Every year for as long as I could remember, we had chosen a family in our ward who needed some extra help at Christmastime, and we had secretly taken gifts and food to their house. It was one of our family's favorite traditions.

When we were all together, Dad said, "It's time we decide which family to help this year. Do any of you children have a suggestion?"

Some years it had been really easy to decide because of a particular family's needs, but this year we couldn't think of anyone. When none of us said anything, Dad looked at Mom. "Maybe Mom has a suggestion. Sometimes she notices things the rest of us miss."

Mom smiled. "As a matter of fact, I do know of someone who needs our help. Before, we have always chosen a family with children, but this year I think we should help Sister Melbourne."

I couldn't believe what I was hearing! "But, Mom," I protested, "she's not poor or sick, and she's really grouchy. She doesn't even like kids. I think we should choose someone else."

"I agree with April," said my older sister, Beth. "She really is grouchy. It wouldn't be any fun doing something for her. She might even kick our gifts off her porch. Besides, she seems to have plenty of money. She dresses in nice clothes."

I looked at Beth gratefully. It was comforting to have someone older agree with me. Peter spoke up. "She's always telling me to shush, even when I'm quiet."

Lynn and Josh didn't say anything. They were too small to know who Sister Melbourne was.

"I know that Sister Melbourne has enough money to take care of herself," Mom said. "And I know that she isn't very pleasant to be around. But that's exactly why I think she needs our help."

I wasn't convinced, but I listened as Mom continued: "Sister Melbourne has had an unhappy life. She was divorced before she moved here. She has three children who are married. They have children of their own but never come to see her or let her get to know her grandchildren. Perhaps she has done something to make them want to stay away. I don't know about that, but I do know that she is very lonely and unhappy. I think she needs someone to let her know that she is loved. You see, April, you weren't quite right when you said that she wasn't poor."

"You mean she's poor in love?" I asked.

"Yes, and sometimes it's much more painful to be poor in love than it is to be poor in money."

We were all quiet for a few minutes. Then Dad said, "Let's take a vote. How many of you would like Sister Melbourne to be our special family this year?"

Slowly Beth's hand went up. Lynn and Josh raised theirs. Then Peter raised his. Looking around at everyone, I reluctantly raised mine.

Mom said that instead of buying all our gifts for Sister Melbourne from the store, we should make most of them. All the next week we cut out snowflakes, strung popcorn and cranberries, pasted together red and green chains from paper strips, and made cookies and candy. We bought apples and oranges to go with all the things we had made.

It was Dad's job to get a box just the right size for our gifts and to decorate it. We carefully arranged everything inside the box and put on the lid. Dad added a huge red and green plaid bow on the top.

We gathered around the dining room table to have a prayer and make our final plans before we delivered the box. In the prayer, Dad asked Heavenly Father to please soften Sister Melbourne's heart and help her to receive our gift in the spirit of love with which we were giving it. I was comforted by those words, because I remembered what Beth had said about Sister Melbourne kicking our gift off the porch, and I had visions of cookies, candy, paper snowflakes, apples, oranges, strings of popcorn and cranberries, and red and green chains strewn all over the ground.

We all put on our coats and piled into the car. Since the box was pretty big, we decided Dad would carry it to the porch. After he returned to the car, it would be my job to ring the doorbell and run back to them before Sister Melbourne opened her door.

I could feel my heart pounding with excitement as Dad parked far down the street from her house. "April and I will walk to Sister Melbourne's

house," he said. "The rest of you must be very quiet so that you don't attract attention." He lifted the box out of the car and motioned for me to follow him.

"Dad," I said, "I'm afraid Sister Melbourne will catch me and get mad."

"She'll never catch you!" He grinned at me. "You're the fastest runner in our family. But if you're really worried, I'll wait for you behind those bushes over there on the far side of her yard. When she's inside again, we'll go back to the car together."

"I'd like that," I said, smiling gratefully up at him.

Dad carefully set the box on the porch. I waited until he was hidden behind the bushes, and then I ran up the steps, rang the doorbell, and flew down the steps and across the yard to the bushes, where I crouched down next to Dad. "Good work," Dad whispered, putting his arm around me.

The door opened, sending a ray of light out across the snow. Sister Melbourne didn't see the box at first, but as she was about to close the door, she saw it and stopped. She just stood there for a second. Then she bent down and read her name on the top. She lifted the lid, and once again she was very still. Finally she picked the box up and looked around the yard. She was smiling, but there were tears running down her cheeks. "Thank you," she called out. "Thank you, whoever you are."

Dad and I were both quiet for a few moments after she went inside and closed the door. I whispered, "I think she really liked our presents, don't you?"

"Yes, I think she really did."

The next Sunday as we were driving home from Church, we looked at everyone's Christmas decorations and we began singing "Jingle Bells" again. When we passed Sister Melbourne's house, I saw our snowflakes in her big front window, and the popcorn and cranberry strings and red and green chains on a Christmas tree that hadn't been there the week before. "I think Sister Melbourne's getting richer," I said.

Mom stopped singing long enough to give me a hug. "So are we." ❄

Trouble at the Inn

Dina Donohue

FOR YEARS NOW whenever Christmas pageants are talked about in a certain little town in the Midwest, someone is sure to mention the name of Wallace Purling. Wally's performance in one annual production of the nativity play has slipped into the realm of legend. But the old-timers who were in the audience that night never tire of recalling exactly what happened.

Wally was nine that year and in the second grade, though he should have been in the fourth. Most people in town knew that he had difficulty in keeping up. He was big and clumsy, slow in movement and mind. Still, Wally was well-liked by the other children in his class, all of whom were smaller than he, though the boys had trouble hiding their irritation when Wally would ask to play ball with them or any game, for that matter, in which winning was important.

Most often they'd find a way to keep him out, but Wally would hang around anyway—not sulking, just hoping. He was always a helpful boy, a willing and smiling one, and the natural protector, paradoxically, of the underdog. If the older boys chased the younger ones away, it would always be Wally who'd say, "Can't they stay? They're no bother."

Wally fancied the idea of being a shepherd with a flute in the Christmas pageant that year, but the play's director, Miss Lambard, assigned him to a more important role. After all, she reasoned, the innkeeper did not have too many lines, and Wally's size would make his refusal of lodging to Joseph more forceful.

So it happened that the usual large, partisan audience gathered for the town's yearly extravaganza of crooks and crèches, of beards, crowns, halos, and a whole stageful of squeaky voices. No one on stage or off was more caught up in the magic of the night than Wallace Purling. They said later that he stood in the wings and watched the performance with such fascination that from time to time Miss Lambard had to make sure he did not wander onstage before his cue.

Then came the time when Joseph appeared, slowly, tenderly guiding Mary to the door of the inn. Joseph knocked hard on the wooden door set into the painted backdrop. Wally the innkeeper was there, waiting.

"What do you want?" Wally said, swinging the door open with a brusque gesture.

"We seek lodging."

"Seek it elsewhere." Wally looked straight ahead but spoke vigorously. "The inn is filled."

"Sir, we have asked everywhere in vain. We have traveled far and are very weary."

"There is no room in this inn for you." Wally looked properly stern.

"Please, good innkeeper, this is my wife, Mary. She is heavy with child and needs a place to rest. Surely you must have some small corner for her. She is so tired."

Now for the first time, the innkeeper relaxed his stiff stance and looked down at Mary. With that, there was a long pause, long enough to make the audience a bit tense with embarrassment.

"No! Begone!" the prompter whispered from the wings.

"No!" Wally repeated automatically. "Begone!"

Joseph sadly placed his arm around Mary, and Mary laid her head upon her husband's shoulder, and the two of them started to move away. The innkeeper did not return inside the inn, however. Wally stood there in the doorway watching the forlorn couple. His mouth was open, his brow creased with concern, his eyes filling unmistakably with tears.

And suddenly this Christmas pageant became different from all others.

"Don't go, Joseph," Wally called out. "Bring Mary back." And Wallace Purling's face grew into a bright smile. "You can have *my* room."

Some people in town thought that the pageant had been ruined. Yet there were others—many, many others—who considered it the most Christmas of all Christmas pageants they had ever seen. ❋

Loving Father, Help Us

Robert Louis Stevenson

Loving Father, help us remember the birth of Jesus, that we may share in the song of the angels, the gladness of the shepherds, and the worship of the wise men.

Close the door of hate and open the door of love all over the world.

Let kindness come with every gift and good desires with every greeting.

Deliver us from evil by the blessing which Christ brings, and teach us to be merry with clear hearts.

May the Christmas morning make us happy to be Thy children, and the Christmas evening bring us to our beds with grateful thoughts, forgiving and forgiven, for Jesus' sake. Amen! ❋

CHAPTER FIVE

Blessing Others

Are You Ready for Christmas?

Harold B. Lee

THE YEARS HAVE BEEN FULL and plentiful since I was called as president of the old Pioneer Stake nearly 40 years ago. It was a large stake by today's standards, a stake of nearly 7,500 members living in 11 wards. It was in the southwest part of Salt Lake City; the people there were feeling the economic depression, and times were hard.

One Christmas (I believe it was the first one during my presidency), our small daughters quickly opened their Christmas morning gifts and soon dashed over to show their little friends the new dolls and other gifts. Shortly they returned home, both in tears.

"What in the world is the matter?" we asked.

Sobbing, they said: "Our friends did not have any Christmas. Santa Claus did not come to their home."

All too late we remembered that just across the street was a family whose father was not a member of the Church, although the children were, and the mother passively so; he had been out of work, and we had forgotten. Our Christmas was spoiled.

We sent for those children and tried to divide what we had in an attempt to make up for our lack of thoughtfulness, but it was too late. Christmas dinner that day did not taste very good to me. I was unhappy. I realized that upon my shoulders rested the welfare of the people of the stake.

We made a survey and were startled to discover that 4,800 of our membership were either wholly or partially dependent—the heads of families did not have steady employment.

There were no government make-work projects in those days. We had only ourselves to look to. Church finances were declining. We were told that we couldn't expect much help from the general funds of the Church. Thus, it was in this same condition that we approached another Christmas season.

We knew that we had about one thousand children under ten years of age for whom, without someone to help them, there would be no Christmas.

We started to prepare. We found a second floor over an old store on Pierpont Street. We gathered toys, some of which were broken, and for a month or two before Christmas, fathers and mothers were there. Some arrived early or stayed late to make something special for their own little ones.

That was the spirit of Christmas giving—one only had to step inside the door of that workshop to see and feel it. Our goal was to see that none of the children would be without a Christmas.

There was to be Christmas dinner in all the homes of the 4,800 who, without help, wouldn't have Christmas dinner. Nuts, candy, oranges, a roast, and all that went with it would be their Christmas menu.

It so happened that I was then one of the city commissioners. On the day before Christmas that year we had had a heavy snowstorm, and I had been out all night with the crews getting the streets cleared, knowing that I would be blamed if any of my men fell down on the job. I had then gone home to change my clothes to go to the office.

As I started back to town, I saw a little boy on the roadside, hitchhiking. He stood in the biting cold, with no coat, no gloves, no overshoes. I stopped, and he climbed into the car beside me.

"Son," I asked, "are you ready for Christmas?"

"Oh, golly, mister, we aren't going to have any Christmas at our home. Daddy died three months ago and left Mamma and me and a little brother and sister."

Three children, each under ten!

"Where are you going, son?"

"I am going up to a free picture show."

I turned up the heat in my car and said, "Now, give me your name and address."

Further conversation revealed that they were not members of the Church.

"Somebody will come to your home; you won't be forgotten. Now, you have a good time today—it's Christmas Eve."

That night I asked each bishop to go with his delivery men and see that each family was cared for, and to report back to me.

While waiting for the last bishop to report, I painfully remembered something. In my haste to see that all my duties at work and my responsibilities in the Church were taken care of, I had forgotten the boy in my car and the promise that I had made.

When the last bishop reported, I asked, "Bishop, have you enough left to visit one more family?"

"Yes, we have," he replied.

I told him the story and gave him the address.

A little later he called to say that that family too had received some well-filled baskets. Christmas Eve was over at last, and I went to bed.

As I awoke that Christmas morning, I said in my heart, "God grant that I will never let another year pass, but that I, as a leader, will truly know my people. I will know their needs. I will be conscious of the ones who need my leadership most."

My carelessness had meant suffering the first year because I did not know my people. But now I had resolved never again to overlook the needs of those around me. ❄

For Them

Eleanor Farjeon

Before you bid, for Christmas' sake,
   Your guests to sit at meat,
Oh please to save a little cake
   For them that have no treat.

Before you go down party-dressed
   In silver gown or gold,
Oh please to send a little vest
   To them that still go cold.

Before you give your girl and boy
   Gay gifts to be undone,
Oh please to spare a little toy
   To them that will have none.

Before you gather round the tree
   To dance the day about,
Oh please to give a little glee
   To them that go without.

Three Christmas Gifts

Mildred Goff

THE WISE MEN BROUGHT THREE GIFTS: gold, frank-incense, and myrrh.

This Christmas, try adding three gifts to your list. Yes, I know your Christmas gift list is already overly long, that you have neither time nor money for extra gifts. But these will cost you little in time, and less in money, and they will capture for you the true Christmas spirit so often lost in the rush and flurry of the season.

First gift: to a stranger. This might be a note to the bus company, mentioning that bus driver who is unfailingly pleasant and courteous, even under the most trying conditions. Send a Christmas card to the waitress who is so cheerful and quick to serve you. Write a letter to the author whose book, story, or poem you have enjoyed recently. Drop a note to the department store whose windows entice you, with a word of praise for the work of the window dresser. You can think of many more. Choose at least one.

Second gift: to someone you find it hard to like, or to someone you feel does not like you very much. It might be your cross old great-aunt, or a sharp-tongued cousin; perhaps it is a business asso-ciate who annoys you, or an irritable neighbor. Send a small, inexpensive, but thoughtful gift to one in this group. It might be no more than a clipping or an article about some hobby for the neighbor; a magazine you know she would enjoy for the cranky relative. Remember, it is easy to give to those we love, but God's love includes the whole world.

Third gift: to someone in trouble. Think of those enduring a cheerless old age, who would be so grateful for an unexpected caller. There are many in hospitals who have no one to visit them, to read to them, to talk to them. And consider those in prisons; yes, we are told we should visit them, too. An hour spent with one of these lonely and half-forgotten persons will do much for them, and more for you.

This Christmas, give these three gifts. You will be repaid a thousand-fold. ✻

The Joy of Giving

John Greenleaf Whittier

Somehow, not only for Christmas
    But all the long year through
The joy that you give to others
    Is the joy that comes back to you.
And the more you spend in blessing
    The poor and lonely and sad,
The more of your heart's possessing
    Returns to make you glad.

On the Night of the Nativity

Anonymous

WHOSOEVER ON THE NIGHT of the nativity of the young Lord Jesus in great snows shall fare forth bearing a succulent bone for the lost and lamenting hound, a wisp of hay for the shivering horse, a cloak of warm raiment for the stranded wayfarer, a flagon of red wine for him whose marrow withers, a garland of bright berries for one who has worn chains, gay arias of lute and harp for all huddled birds who thought that song was dead, and divers lush sweetmeats for such babes' faces as peer from lonely windows—

To him shall be proffered and returned gifts of such an astonishment as will rival the hues of a peacock and the harmonies of heaven, so that though he live to the great age when man goes stooping, yet shall he walk upright and remembering, as one whose heart shines like a great star within his breast. ❈

Harry's Carol

Lisa Dahlgren

I HAD MY MOTHER TO THANK that I was cooking breakfast for 120 elderly people on Christmas morning. Instead of Santa waking us, the phone rang with a call for help from the nursing home where I worked part-time. No one, the head nurse explained, had shown up for work, and they were desperate. Could I possibly come down for a few hours. My mom said we all would!

Morning is everyone's least favorite time except for Mom, who managed to be extra coherent with Christmas spirit as she announced the news. "Get up! They need us down at the home. We'll have our Christmas later. First, we have to go cook lots of eggs."

"What about the presents?" Todd and Christine, my younger brother and sister, wailed.

"We've waited *all night*," Christine pleaded.

"It'll be here when we get home. Now get the lead out. Mom and Dad are serious about this," I said without much sympathy.

Somehow we managed to pile in the car, and we drove the two miles in silence. The nurse met us at the door looking disheveled and frantic. "Oh, thank goodness," she said. Not wasting any more time with gratitude, she pushed us towards the kitchen in unison. The only cook to show up that morning, Gladys, was rushing from stove to steam table, scooping out scrambled eggs and shouting orders to Frank, the janitor.

"Get moving on that O.J., will you," Gladys said. She hadn't noticed her bleary-eyed crew yet.

"They'll be down in 45 minutes, and I can't find the bread, let alone the toaster."

"Uhmmm, maybe we could be of help," offered my dad, a bit reluctantly.

"We're Diane's family," Mom introduced us, steering Todd and Chris over to the newly found toaster. "I think the children can make toast. Oh, by the way, I'm Irene, and this is my husband, Bill," she pointed to Dad. "You know Diane, and the toast makers are Christine and Todd."

"Hi," muttered Chris and Todd together. They were thinking about opening presents, not about buttering toast.

Gladys stood in the middle of the kitchen supporting her latest batch of eggs. After a moment's hesitation, she sized us all up and decided we'd do. Gladys shoved the bowl in Dad's stomach. "Here, you look like an egg man to me. You can take over scrambling."

Dad caught the bowl and his breath. "Sure, I can do that," he gasped.

"And you, Diane," Gladys turned me toward the hot cereal. "Oatmeal duty."

We all set to work and before we knew it the breakfast rush was on, over, and breakfast dishes were just beginning.

"Mom, can't we go home *yet*?" Christine whimpered, emphasizing *yet*. "It's almost eight and every child in America, probably the entire world, has opened their gifts except us. Doesn't that bother you even a little?"

Mom didn't mince words. "No, not even a little, Chris," she answered watching Dad and Todd squirt each other with the high powered hoses. "I know it isn't easy to be here on Christmas, honey, but could we really be anywhere else?" When neither Chris nor I responded, Mom started humming a cheery carol. "Let's sing a song," she encouraged.

I honestly wasn't in the mood. Helping others was supposed to make a person feel good, but I was right there with Chris, wanting to be opening gifts and away from the smell of eggs and nursing home.

Mom continued without us, singing her favorite, "I Heard the Bells on Christmas Day." At first she sang softly, but by the second verse she picked up the volume. Chris and I gave in, joining Mom, and sliding dishes down the metal chute on beat.

"Let's sing 'Rudolph,'" Todd shouted. "Rudolph, the Red-Nosed Reindeer" it was, Dad leading the family along in a loud baritone. This might have ended our musical contribution on that unusual Christmas morning, if it hadn't been for Brother Greenwall.

I turned to pick up one of the last dish stacks, and there he stood, listening at the kitchen serving window. Brother Greenwall had lived in our neighborhood and attended church with us until his wife passed away.

"Hi, Brother Greenwall," I said. His lonely eyes stared back, not recognizing me.

My dad smiled over his shoulder and walked to the window. "Harry, how are you? It's Bill. Did you hear us singing away in here?" Dad chuckled, "Hope we didn't disturb you."

Harry Greenwall smiled back at Dad. I wasn't sure if he remembered him or not, but something had been triggered. "Just a minute," he muttered, hurrying off to the TV lounge.

Dad watched him go. "I wonder what he's up to," he said as Harry returned with two or three friends and their chairs. Before we figured out what Harry had in mind, he'd pushed open the door and

seated them by the stove, then hobbled back to the TV room.

Eyebrows raised, Mom checked out the three seated in the kitchen. "Well, Bill, do you think we're supposed to keep singing?" When no one volunteered an opinion she added, "I think Harry wants a performance."

"Oh, Mom, do we have to?" Todd groaned, blasting his dishes with an extra hard squirt.

Dad put his arm around Todd, "You've heard of singing for your supper haven't you?"

"Yeah, but . . . "

"Well, you get to sing for your presents."

Chris and I laughed. "Come on and give me a hand helping Brother Greenwall with his friends," said Dad.

By now Harry had returned, cramming in seven more concertgoers. Eight more joined the group, bringing the crowd to about twenty. Fully staffed, the kitchen never held more than eight people.

Harry stared at us without recognition, interested only in the music. Mom and Dad exchanged their you'd-better-do-something look, and Dad picked up the cue. "Well, folks, Harry thought you'd all like a little Christmas music."

We sang, starting with family favorites like "Jingle Bells," "Silent Night," and "Oh, Come, All Ye Faithful." Actually, "Oh, Come, All Ye Faithful" is Dad's favorite. Mom says his eyes twinkle when he sings that song. I looked over at Dad to catch that twinkle, and its shine filled me with warmth. My voice cracked, and I stopped singing, bowing my head to hide the tears.

Looking down at the floor, I felt love for each of those people listening to my family sing. I tried to join in the music, but the same feeling came again, repeating the impression. This time I knew the Savior wanted them to know of his love. Doubting myself, I hesitated a moment and was overwhelmed for the third time with the same desire to comfort them.

My family finished the last few measures of music, and I began without thinking, "I just want to tell you I know Jesus lives. He is concerned for you and loves you. I didn't really want to come here today, but I'm glad we did. Most of all, I hope you can feel the Savior's love for you like I have. He really wants you to know this."

Dad put his arm around me. "I couldn't give any of you a better gift at Christmas than the knowledge that Jesus lives, as Diane has said."

The kitchen was silent for a minute, the spirit of Christ in our hearts. "Let's sing a carol together," Mom suggested. "What one would you like, Harry?"

Considering all the carols available and Harry's love for Christmas music, we should have been surprised when his choice wasn't a traditional Christmas song.

"I Know That My Redeemer Lives," he said.

Everyone sang his "carol," filling the kitchen with the words, "He lives, my kind, wise heav'nly Friend. He lives and loves me to the end."

That day became a treasure and started a family tradition of Christmas Day service we enjoy. And, out of all the carols we sing at Christmastime, Harry's carol is our favorite and the finest way to get a twinkle in any of our eyes.

By the way, my dad says we still sound the best in kitchens. ❋

On Another Street

Berta Huish Christensen

No, my child,
These are not for us—
Not the fruit, nor the bread,
Nor the round raisin cookies—
Not for us to eat.
We will take them to a woman who lives
In another place, on another street.

No, my son,
There are no children there,
None at all. Why?
Because they grew up tall, and moved away.
She will come softly to the door—
This woman who lives in another place—
She will come smiling, and with Christmas words,
But there will be a look of all-alone
And many years—upon her face.

CHAPTER SIX

Giving & Receiving

Charity Christmas

Alma J. Yates

As soon as Brother Malone announced that the priests quorum was going to give a Christmas to a needy family for our December service project, I knew our family was in trouble. Since Danny's operation and Luke's mission call eight months earlier, things were tight around our place. I don't know what the official poverty level was for a family of nine, but I knew we were miles below it, and I was convinced that we were prime targets for all the ward service projects and Christmas charity drives.

"Hey, Jason," I said, cornering my younger brother that night before we climbed into bed, "we're in trouble. I think we're on the list."

Jason just looked at me and retorted innocently, "I haven't done anything. Honest!"

"How many weeks till Christmas?" I asked solemnly.

He shrugged and pulled the quilts back from his bed, fluffed up his pillow and remarked indifferently, "I don't know, but I've got a test in English tomorrow and I need some sleep or I'll . . ."

"Would you believe three?"

"Hey, I'll believe anything. Just let me get to sleep," he said, yawning and pushing his feet under the covers and snuggling up in a ball. "Besides, I'm not counting on anything for Christmas this year. Mom and Dad are broke."

I turned the covers down on my bed, flipped off the light, and dropped heavily onto the mattress. "Well, when your teachers quorum chooses our family for their December service project, don't say I didn't warn you."

The light flipped back on. Jason was sitting on the edge of his bed. "What'd you say?"

"Have you seen the storeroom lately?"

"Yeah, Mom sent me for a bottle of fruit tonight."

"Was the door locked?" Jason shook his head. "It should have been. It always is this time of year. That's where Mom and Dad hide the loot, but there's no loot this year."

Jason shrugged. "We'll survive."

"You don't get the point," I growled. "We're charity material. Charity as in service project, needy family."

"Come on, Brett," he grinned nervously. "Mom fixes a few beans now and then, and we have lots of whole wheat bread, but that doesn't make us candidates for welfare. Dad's got a job. We're not out on the street or anything."

I flipped the light off again. "Wait till Christmas and find out the hard way," I warned.

Five minutes later the lights came back on. "That's just great!" he muttered. "All we need is 50 care packages on our front step Christmas Eve." He groaned, shaking his head morosely. "How embarrassing!"

"The trouble is there's not much we can do," I complained. "How can you stop a charity project?"

"Let's just tell them we don't want anything."

"Tell who? It could come from anybody. It's not like we can send letters to everyone in the ward declining their good will."

"Let's move," Jason growled.

"Where?"

He shrugged. "Could we hide?"

"For a month?"

Glumly we sat on our beds and brooded as we pondered the inevitable. "I know," Jason suggested after a moment of silence. "We'll beat them to the punch."

"Huh?"

"We'll pull off our own charity job, on somebody else." He grinned, enthusiasm brightening his eyes. "If we're helping another family—anybody— nobody will bother us. Everybody will think we've got enough to throw away."

"Maybe," I whispered, considering the plan's plausibility. "It just might work. But who? Who's in worse shape than we are?"

"What about the Bradleys? She's a widow, three kids. You home teach there. You'd know what they could use."

I smiled, but the smile was temporary. "We're forgetting one thing. We're broke. How do we help if we don't have anything to help with?"

Jason sighed. "I forgot about that," he mumbled.

It was true. We had no money, no job, and we struggled with a pride that prevented us from going down on main street with a bell and pot to solicit contributions.

"I know," Jason volunteered, the excitement obvious. "We can collect pop cans and sell them. Twenty cents a pound."

"In the middle of winter? Nobody drinks pop in the winter, and I'm not about to rummage through garbage cans just to pinch a few pennies."

"How about newspapers. Morgan's Shopping Center gives 30 dollars a ton for them. Everybody's got newspapers, winter or summer."

"Can we make enough money collecting newspapers?" I asked.

He shrugged.

"Could you go around begging for newspapers?" I asked skeptically.

Jason cleared his throat. "Maybe. As long as we don't go to people we know."

"When do we start then?"

Jason chewed on his thumb. "Couple of weeks from now."

"You're stalling."

"I've got some tests coming up and a paper to write and . . ."

"I wonder what your teachers quorum will get you for Christmas."

He glared at me. "Maybe we better start tomorrow afternoon."

So with dubious motives we embarked on our questionable Christmas crusade. The next day after school we dragged ourselves over to Fruit Heights. We were sure no one there knew us, so we figured we could commence our campaign without fear of being recognized.

The trace of an icy mist hung in the afternoon air, bit through our coats and sweaters, and numbed our cheeks and noses. Pulling our collars up around our ears and digging our hands deep into our pockets, we approached our first house with an emotional mixture of trepidation, loathing, and melancholy endurance. I took a deep breath, gingerly pushed the door bell, and stepped back, shivering from cold and abject embarrassment.

Hearing someone approach, Jason turned to me and whispered nervously, "Maybe you'd better do the talking. I don't know anything about this."

"And what do I know?" I hissed back. "We're in this together, you know."

"Yeah, but you're the oldest," he added, stepping behind me just as the door opened and an older man greeted us with a curt nod and a withering scowl.

For a moment I just stood and stared, unable to call to mind the door approach Jason and I had rehearsed. Finally the man demanded gruffly, "Well?"

"Do you have some paper?" I blurted out.

"Paper?"

I gulped. "Newspaper."

"Oh, yeah," he said, waving us away and turning to go. "The Collins boy brings it. I don't need another paper. I hardly read the one I take now."

"No," I called out in desperation, "we don't sell papers. We're collecting old papers. To sell."

"What?" the man asked.

"We're trying to help a family for Christmas," I explained. "The papers are for them."

"It's a widow's family," Jason volunteered from behind me. "It's not really for us. The money from the papers, I mean."

The man rubbed his chin with the back of his hand and looked us up and down. "I've got a few papers, I guess."

"Could you save them? We're not picking them up today. We'll be back in two weeks. On a Saturday."

"It's for the widow and her kids," Jason called out again. "And we're not her kids either. We're just trying to help her out. We're not . . ."

I poked Jason to shut him up. "We'll be back in two weeks then," I repeated, my cheeks flushed purple.

By the time we made it out into the street again, I had to unbutton my coat because I was sweating so much. "I don't know how many more of those I can do," I muttered. "That wiped me out."

"That wasn't bad at all," Jason grinned, pleased with himself.

"You didn't say anything either," I returned. "At least anything sensible. But the next door's yours."

"Mine?" he protested.

"And leave out the part about us not being the widow's kids. Just act natural or they really will think we're the widow's kids."

Our whole operation that afternoon lay between abject drudgery and acute torture, but we persisted. Our commitment did waver at times, but each time one of us faltered in our resolve to continue, the other would comment matter-of-factly, "It's this or care packages Christmas Eve." With that humiliating possibility looming before us, we beat down our pride and trudged on to the next house.

It was getting dark when we knocked at the last house on the block. We had already promised ourselves that if we could endure till then, we would call it quits for the night.

An older woman, Mrs. Bailey, hobbled to the door, leaning heavily on a cane. She peered skeptically over the rims of her glasses and pressed her thin, pale lips together.

"Hello, ma'am," I greeted her, a pinched smile frozen to my blue lips. "We're collecting old newspapers," I announced. "For a needy family." Mrs. Bailey didn't respond, and I began to wonder if she could even hear me. "We're going to sell the papers and help this family with Christmas," I all but shouted, just in case she was slightly deaf. "Do you have any old newspapers lying around?"

"Well, my husband has collected a few," Mrs. Bailey said in a shaky voice.

"Would he like to donate them to the cause?" Jason asked.

"Well, he planned to read them."

"Do you think he could read them by a week from Saturday? That's when we'll pick them up."

"Oh, I doubt it," she answered bluntly.

It wasn't exactly a turn down, but neither was

it an offer. In nervous perplexity we stood shifting our weight from one foot to the other. "Well, thanks just the same," I said, turning to go.

"What'd you say they're for?" she spoke up suddenly.

"We're helping a widow and her kids."

Mrs. Bailey cocked her head to one side and tapped her cane on the front step. After a moment of contemplation, she shuffled into her house and returned with a sweater thrown about her frail shoulders. She motioned for us to follow her. We inched along behind her as she limped her way to the driveway. She led us to her garage and stopped. Banging on the door with her cane, she commanded, "You'll have to open it."

Jason and I jumped for the door and pushed it up. It squeaked and creaked and finally crashed into place overhead. We squinted into the black interior but could see nothing.

"There's a light on the back wall," she remarked. "One of you will have to turn it on."

Jason volunteered me by giving me a shove. Reluctantly, I ventured into the darkness.

"Straight back," Mrs. Bailey directed. "You can't miss it."

Before I had taken four steps, my feet smashed into a lawn mower. I teetered forward and tried to regain my balance, but in stepping over the mower, my feet became tangled in a garden hose and I crashed to the floor, knocking over cans, boxes, rakes, and hoes.

"Watch your step," Mrs. Bailey cautioned from behind me.

"It's on the back wall," Jason encouraged from the safety of the driveway.

Muttering, I extricated myself from the tangle of tools, wire, and hose and continued my perilous journey to the back wall, this time with my hands outstretched, groping the blackness for other obstacles. After banging my shins on cans and boxes and scraping my head on a bucket hanging from the ceiling, I finally reached the back wall and flipped on the switch.

A pale yellow light cast a thousand shadows throughout the garage, and it was hard to determine just how effective the light was. The garage was stacked almost to the ceiling with a lifetime collection of odds and ends—tools, pots, old furniture, tires, and boxes. I was amazed that I had even managed to reach the light switch without maiming myself permanently or losing my life.

"There they are," Jason sang out, pointing to two boxes right inside the garage door. "We didn't even need the light for these," he laughed.

"Now you tell me," I growled under my breath.

"Oh, that's only part of them," Mrs. Bailey whined. "The others are in the corner under the tarp."

In the shadows, I hadn't noticed the dark mound in the far corner. I waded through some ragged lawn furniture, stumbled over two saw horses, and finally fell against the enormous mystery hidden under an old army tarp, gray with years of dust.

Grabbing one corner of the tarp, I jerked it back. A suffocating cloud of dust choked and blinded me. I sputtered, gasping for breath, and rubbed the dirt from my eyes, tripping over a croquet mallet and sitting down hard in a rusty, battered wheelbarrow filled with flower pots. My nostrils were filled with the musty smell of dirt and dried and decaying flowers, and there was a gritty film between my lips and teeth.

Jason whistled. "Would you look at that," I heard him say in amazement.

Flailing the air with my arms to beat the dust away, I cracked my eyes and stared in disbelief at the huge mountain of newspapers before me. "How long's he been saving them?" I gasped.

"I lost track after 20 years," Mrs. Bailey replied simply. "Some people collect stamps. Some collect coins. My husband collected newspapers. He didn't have time to read them, so he stacked them in here to read later. He insisted that the time would come when he'd be able to sit down and enjoy them. Nothing I could say ever changed his mind. And he wouldn't let me get rid of them until he read them. So here they are. And he still hasn't read them."

"Is he going to care if we take them?" I wondered out loud.

"Oh, it's hard to say with him."

"We could leave some of the newer ones in case he wants to read them," Jason offered.

Mrs. Bailey waved his remark aside with her hand and shook her head. "He won't read them. Any of them. Not now. He died three years ago. They're yours if you'll haul them off."

It was just a wild guess, but we estimated that there was at least a ton of newspapers in Mrs. Bailey's garage. All ours! As we hurried home that night, a new enthusiasm was born. What had begun as a sheepish attempt to conceal our own poverty suddenly became a personal quest.

"You know," Jason said, "I think we can really do it. Mrs. Bailey's papers alone are enough to give the Bradleys a little Christmas. But we can get more, lots more. All we've got to do is keep knocking on doors."

"And maybe tomorrow we better split up," I suggested. "We can cover more ground."

Two weeks later everyone in Fruit Heights had been contacted. We had even swallowed our pride and asked people in our own neighborhood to donate papers.

The Saturday before Christmas we were getting ready to collect our newspapers in Dad's ancient, temperamental truck. The truck was a battered antique, but it was all we had to make our Christmas drive. It had traveled its share of miles and was now content to live its remaining moments rusting in front of our house. On a good day, which was rare, and if it was treated just right, it might consent to run. Unfortunately, that particular Saturday didn't seem to appeal to the truck. When I turned the key and pushed the starter, it coughed and emitted a blue puff of smoke from the exhaust, but it refused to start. I tried again and again, but each time the cough became weaker and the smoke from the exhaust more faint.

We fumed and fussed. We pleaded with it, petted it, yelled at it, kicked it, and would have taken a sledge hammer to it. But it was dead. We had told everyone in Fruit Heights that we would pick up their papers, and we were afraid if we waited, those papers would end up in Monday's trash.

"We've just got to go today, Brett. If we don't get those papers, the Bradleys might not have anything."

"Someone else might help them," I said, trying to be positive just in case the old truck had finally fallen victim to age.

"Maybe, but we can't be sure," Jason countered. "We've just got to get it working."

"Why today?" I growled, pounding helplessly on the steering wheel.

"Well, we sure aren't going to get it running this way," Jason said. "I'm getting some tools."

I pressed my lips together and shook my head. "Do you really think you can fix it? What will Dad say if you ruin it?"

"It's already ruined. I can't hurt it."

"I wish Dad were here," I moaned.

"Well, we'll have to do more than wish. Let's get to work."

Next to Dad, Jason was the best mechanic in the family, so if anyone could coax the truck into starting he could. I sat back and watched while he checked everything from the points to the gas pump. After an hour of grunting and experimenting, he dropped the hood, wiped a greasy hand across his forehead, and said optimistically, "Fire it up."

I whispered a prayer, turned the key, and pressed the starter. The truck groaned, coughed, sputtered, rattled, and finally purred. "Hop in," I commanded with a grin, "before she changes her mind."

Jason tossed the tools into the truck, wiped his hands on his pants, and jumped in just as we jerked away from the curb and headed for Fruit Heights.

The truck's miraculous resurrection was not our only surprise of the day. We soon discovered that our project had become contagious. A host of people in Fruit Heights had been pricked by the Christmas spirit. When we made our first stop a man shuffled out and asked, "Could this family you're helping use a trike? Our kids are too big for it now. It's just sitting in the garage gathering dust."

At another place we picked up an electric train set. A couple gave us a miniature table and chair set. We received a wagon and some Lincoln logs. A widower gave us a rocking chair.

When we stopped at the O'Briens', there was only a small pile of newspapers, hardly enough for the stop, but before we left, Mrs. O'Brien came out and asked, "Is there a little girl in this family?"

"Trina's four," Jason replied.

"I have a doll—one I bought years ago, thinking I'd have a girl. I had five boys instead." She smiled shyly. "Boys don't take to dolls. I've been meaning to do something with it." She left and came back with the biggest, prettiest doll I'd ever seen in my life. "It's never been used," she explained.

"Gee!" we gasped. "Are you sure you want to just give it away?"

She looked at the doll for a moment and wiped a tear from the corner of her eye. "I would have just given it to one of my girls had I had one." She sighed. "If Trina will like it, I want her to have it. I would like to see her face Christmas morning when she sees it." She took a deep breath and flashed a weak smile. "Oh, well. I guess Christmas morning I'll have to imagine what Trina is doing."

By the end of the day the old truck had made six trips and was about to die a second time after our rigorous demands, but we had collected just under 150 dollars worth of newspapers, not to mention the donated gifts we had received. We bought shoes and coats for the kids; a gift certificate for Sister Bradley; and two boxes of groceries, candies, and nuts for the stockings and Christmas dinner.

Christmas Eve everything was ready. Dad helped us fire up the old truck one more time. Jason and I filled it to overflowing and sputtered down the street to the Bradleys', coasting the last block so as not to announce our arrival.

It was starting to snow as we climbed out of the truck and sneaked to the Bradleys' front steps with our arms bulging with gifts. We could hear Sister Bradley and her three kids singing Christmas carols, and we paused for a moment in the shadows to listen before returning to the truck for the trike, the rocker, and the table and chairs.

When we had placed the last box of groceries

on the step, we rapped loudly on the door and then sprinted to a clump of bushes where we could observe unseen. Sister Bradley opened the door and peered into the darkness. She was beginning to close the door when she spotted our Christmas project all over her front steps. She gasped and looked up and down the street, then back at the pile of presents. Slowly she dropped to her knees and began to cry.

My vision blurred with tears, and something swelled up inside of me until I could hardly breathe. Starting from deep in my chest and finally reaching to the tips of my fingers and toes, a gratifying warmth overwhelmed me. Never in my life had I felt such an all-consuming fulfillment. I was sure I would burst, and I wondered why I had waited so long to discover this side of Christmas.

When we returned home, all the lights were off except those on the tree, and everyone but Dad was in bed. He was there waiting for us in the dim light next to an enormous package—addressed to Jason and me!

"Where'd that come from?" I asked as soon as I saw it.

Dad smiled and shrugged his shoulders. "Someone left it on the doorstep while you were over at the Bradleys'."

"Left it for us?" I groaned. He nodded. "You mean a Christmas package for us?" He shrugged again, obviously amused. "Well, we don't want it!" I flared. "That's exactly what we didn't want."

"They can just keep it," Jason rebelled. "I'm not opening it."

"It's an insult," I added. "I'm not taking anybody's care package."

Dad held up a restraining hand. "Talking isn't going to change a thing," I insisted, anticipating his argument. Dad motioned for us to sit down. We did, grumbling irritably. He waited for our protests to subside, and then he asked quietly, "Has this been a good Christmas?"

I looked over at Jason and he at me. "Yeah," I muttered, staring at the floor but avoiding the package.

"Why? What's so special about this Christmas?"

"Because . . . because we were giving something. We were making somebody happy."

"Does taking this package change that?"

"It's charity," I flared. "We don't want charity."

Dad nodded. "Do you know what charity is? Real charity? Love, pure love. This package is a token of someone's love, not of their ridicule or pity. It is the offspring of charity, of love, just as your gifts to the Bradleys sprang from love."

"But Dad," I protested.

Dad shook his head. "How would it have been had the Bradleys reacted to your gifts like you're reacting to this one?" He looked at Jason and me and waited for an answer, but all we could do was shrug our shoulders and stare at the anonymous package. "You know, sons, there can never be a giver without a receiver. Both are necessary and good."

He paused a moment. "When Luke went on his mission, I wanted to support him all by myself. I thought it only right that a father support his own son. My pride had a lot to do with it. I was being a little selfish. I didn't realize until I started getting secret contributions that there were those who wanted to give also. I came to understand that I didn't have the right to deny them the opportunity."

He looked at our package. "I don't know who left this for you. I wouldn't tell you even if I knew. But whoever it was has as much right to the joy of giving as you two. Unless you accept the gift, they can't enjoy the full satisfaction of giving." He placed his hands on our knees and concluded, "At Christmas time we give generously and receive graciously. That's the spirit of Christmas. When you can do those two things, equally well, you will have taken a giant step toward manhood."

Long after Dad went to bed, Jason and I stayed by the tree contemplating our unexpected gift. It was the hardest gift for us to accept, but we knew Dad was right.

"I wonder what's in it?" Jason finally mused.

We glanced at each other. A spark of curiosity glowed in our eyes. I looked around to determine whether we were alone. "We could always peek," I suggested furtively.

Jason nodded. "I never could wait till Christmas morning."

We both grinned, nodded our agreement, and then eagerly pulled the package toward us and began peeling off the wrapping. ✻

The Snow Is on the Land

S. Dilworth Young

The snow is on the land;
The hay is in the barn—
The cattle sheltered warm.
If any of thy people, Lord,
Are cold,
Lead thou them here
Where food and warming heart
Abound.
Around my hearth
May there be found
The needy poor.
What need at Christmas time
To have expensive gifts
From greater ones
If I can give
Thy blessed gifts of earth
To needy sons?

Unto the Least of These

Marilyn McMeen Miller Brown

I feel, almost, as though it were unfair
That I should have these memories
Of Christmas
And others less fortunate go
Never knowing
How it was—bouncing
Mother's baskets on our knees
During our journey through town
On the buckboard.
We had packed that food like children
Eternally hungry,
But those sweetbreads
Were for someone dearer than even we were dear:
The poor who needed
Turkey dinner almost as much as we
Needed to take it to them.
And so I think to myself how lucky I was
To have had these memories:
My mother's red jams sparkling from jars
Never opened or touched by one of us;
And a few round oranges,
Wrapped in paper, we got but once a year;
And all of us, eyes wide,
Wondering who it was special enough
To have the same at Christmas as we hoped to have.
These were moments I can only whisper with
    reverence:
Afraid my father's chimney hat would topple
While the horses clipped the streets
And he struck out toward the west of town,
And we all huddled down in quilts
And chattered, sang, and thought to ourselves,

If these are the least and they are the same
As though we'd done it unto Him,
He must be poor
And live in shacks lit sometimes only by the moon.
And many a Christmas night I've walked in radiant
    streets,
Not sharing half that joy I once felt then
To see the children laughing in the darkened doors
And father's bristling head of hair bowing low,
While he nearly dumped the biscuits on the floor.
We count ourselves among the lucky ones
Who listened for the Christ child
Year after year
And found him in our childhood close to home
And heard him in our prayers.
The answers topple from our memories now
As though the ends of waiting hurl like ribbons
Streaming into a patterned clasp.
Our woven images of life are spun from knowing
We once knew him
In our growing past.

To Springvale for Christmas

Zona Gale

....

W HEN PRESIDENT ARTHUR TILTON of Briarcliff
College, who usually used a two-cent stamp, said,
"Get me Chicago, please," his secretary was
impressed, looked for vast educational problems to
be in the making, and heard instead:

"Ed? Well, Ed, you and Rick and Grace and I
are going out to Springvale for Christmas. . . . Yes,
well, I've got a family too, you recall. But mother
was seventy last fall and—Do you realize that it's
eleven years since we all spent Christmas with her?
Grace has been every year. She's going this year.
And so are we! And take her the best Christmas she
ever had, too. Ed, mother was seventy last fall—"

At dinner, he asked his wife what would be a
suitable gift, a very special gift, for a woman of seventy. And she said: "Oh, your mother. Well, dear, I
should think the material for a good wool dress
would be right. I'll select it for you, if you like—"
He said that he would see, and he did not reopen
the subject.

In town on December twenty-fourth he timed
his arrival to allow him an hour in a shop. There he
bought a silver-gray silk of a fineness and a lightness
which pleased him and at a price which made him
comfortably guilty. And at the shop, Ed, who was
Edward McKillop Tilton, head of a law firm, picked
him up.

"Where's your present?" Arthur demanded.

Edward drew a case from his pocket and
showed him a tiny gold wristwatch of decent

manufacture and explained: "I expect you'll think
I'm a fool, but you know that mother has told time
for fifty years by the kitchen clock, or else the shield
of the black-marble parlor angel who never goes—
you get the idea?—and so I bought her this."

At the station was Grace, and the boy who
bore her bag bore also a parcel of great dimensions.

"Mother already has a feather bed," Arthur
reminded her.

"They won't let you take an automobile into
the coach," Edward warned her.

"It's a rug for the parlor," Grace told them.
"You know it *is* a parlor—one of the few left in the
Mississippi Valley. And mother has had that ingrain
down since before we left home—"

Grace's eyes were misted. Why would women
always do that? This was no occasion for sentiment.
This was a merry Christmas.

"Very nice. And Ricky'd better look sharp,"
said Edward dryly.

Ricky never did look sharp. About trains he was
conspicuously ignorant. He had no occupation.
Some said that he "wrote," but no one had ever
seen anything that he had written. He lived in
town—no one knew how—never accepted a cent
from his brothers, and was beloved of everyone,
most of all of his mother.

"Ricky won't bring anything, of course," they
said.

But when the train pulled out without him,
observably, a porter came staggering through the
cars carrying two great suitcases and following a
perturbed man of forty-something who said, "Oh,
here you are!" as if it were they who were missing,
and squeezed himself and his suitcases among
brothers and sister and rug. "I had only a minute to
spare," he said regretfully. "If I'd had two, I could

· 112 ·

have snatched some flowers. I flung 'em my card and told 'em to send 'em."

"Why are you taking so many lugs?" they wanted to know.

Ricky focused on the suitcases. "Just necessities," he said. "Just the presents. I didn't have room to get in anything else."

"Presents! What?"

"Well," said Ricky, "I'm taking books. I know mother doesn't care much for books, but the bookstore's the only place I can get trusted."

They turned over his books: fiction, travels, biography, a new illustrated edition of the Bible—they were willing to admire his selection. And Grace said confusedly but appreciatively: "You know, the parlor bookcase has never had a thing in it excepting a green curtain *over* it!"

And they were all borne forward, well pleased.

Springvale has eight hundred inhabitants. As they drove through the principal street at six o'clock on that evening of December twenty-fourth, all that they expected to see abroad was the popcorn wagon and a cat or two. Instead they counted seven automobiles and estimated thirty souls, and no one paid the slightest attention to them as strangers. Springvale was becoming metropolitan. There was a new church on one corner and a store building bore the sign "Public Library." Even the little hotel had a rubber plant in the window and a strip of cretonne overhead.

The three men believed themselves to be a surprise. But, mindful of the panic to be occasioned by four appetites precipitated into a Springvale ménage, Grace had told. Therefore the parlor was lighted and heated; there was in the air of the passage an odor of brown gravy which, no butler's pantry ever having inhibited, seemed a permanent savory. By the happiest chance, Mrs. Tilton had not heard their arrival nor—the parlor angel being in her customary eclipse and the kitchen grandfather's clock wrong—had she begun to look for them. They slipped in, they followed Grace down the hall, they entered upon her in her gray gingham apron worn over her best blue serge, and they saw her first in profile, frosting a lemon pie. With some assistance from her, they all took her in their arms at once.

"Aren't you surprised?" cried Edward in amazement.

"I haven't got over being surprised," she said placidly, "since I first heard you were coming!"

She gazed at them tenderly, with flour on her chin, and then said: "There's something you won't like. We're going to have the Christmas dinner tonight."

Their clamor that they would entirely like that did not change her look.

"Our church couldn't pay the minister this winter," she said, "on account of the new church building. So the minister and his wife are boarding around with the congregation. Tomorrow's their day to come here for a week. It's a hard life and I didn't have the heart to change 'em."

Her family covered their regret as best they could and entered upon her little feast. At the head of her table, with her four "children" about her, and father's armchair left vacant, they perceived that she was not quite the figure they had been thinking her. In this interval they had grown to think of her as a pathetic figure. Not because their father had died, not because she insisted on Springvale as a residence, not because of her eyes. Just pathetic. Mothers of grown children, they might have given themselves the suggestion, were always pathetic. But here was mother, a definite person, with poise and with ideas, who might be proud of her offspring, but who, in her heart, never forgot that they *were* her offspring and that she was the parent stock.

"I wouldn't eat two pieces of that pie," she said to President Tilton; "it's pretty rich." And he answered humbly: "Very well, Mother." And she took with composure Ricky's light chant:

> *"Now, you must remember, wherever you are,*
> *That you are the jam, but your mother's the*
>   *jar."*

"Certainly, my children," she said. "And I'm about to tell you when you may have your Christmas presents. Not tonight. Christmas Eve is no proper time for presents. It's stealing a day outright! And you miss the fun of looking forward all night long. The only proper time for the presents is after breakfast on Christmas morning, *after* the dishes are washed. The minister and his wife may get here any time from nine on. That means we've got to get to bed early!"

President Arthur Tilton lay in his bed looking at the muslin curtain on which the street lamp threw the shadow of a bare elm which he remembered. He thought: "She's a pioneer spirit. She's the kind who used to go ahead anyway, even if they had missed the emigrant party, and who used to cross the plains alone. She's the backbone of the world. I wish I could megaphone that to the students at Briarcliff who think their mothers 'try to boss' them!"

"Don't leave your windows open too far," he heard from the hall. "The wind's changed."

In the light of a snowy morning the home parlor showed the cluttered commonplace of a room whose furniture and ornaments were not believed to be beautiful and most of them known not to be useful. Yet when—after the dishes were washed—these five came to the leather chair which bore the gifts,

the moment was intensely satisfactory. This in spite of the sense of haste with which the parcels were attacked—lest the minister and his wife arrive in their midst.

"That's one reason," Mrs. Tilton said, "why I want to leave part of my Christmas for you until I take you to the train tonight. Do you care?"

"I'll leave a present I know about until then too," said Ricky. "May I?"

"Come on now, though," said President Arthur Tilton. "I want to see mother get her dolls."

It was well that they were not of an age to look for exclamations of delight from mother. To every gift her reaction was one of startled rebuke.

"Grace! How could you? All that money! Oh, it's beautiful! But the old one would have done me all my life. . . . Why, Edward! You extravagant boy! I never had a watch in my life. You ought not to have gone to all that expense. Arthur Tilton! A silk dress! What a firm piece of goods! I don't know what to say to you—you're all too good to me!"

At Ricky's books she stared and said: "My dear boy, you've been very reckless. Here are more books than I can ever read—now. Why, that's almost more than they've got to start the new library with. And you spent all that money on me!"

It dampened their complacence, but they understood her concealed delight and they forgave her an honest regret of their modest prodigality. For, when they opened her gifts for them, they felt the same reluctance to take the hours and hours of patient knitting for which these stood.

"Hush, and hurry," was her comment, "or the minister'll get us!"

The minister and his wife, however, were late. The second side of the turkey was ready and the mince pie hot when, toward noon, they came to the door—a faint little woman and a thin man with beautiful, exhausted eyes. They were both in some light glow of excitement and disregarded Mrs. Tilton's efforts to take their coats.

"No," said the minister's wife. "No. We do beg your pardon. But we find we have to go into the country this morning."

"It is absolutely necessary that we go into the country," said the minister earnestly. "This morning," he added impressively.

"Into the country! You're going to be here for dinner."

They were firm. They had to go into the country. They shook hands almost tenderly with these four guests. "We just heard about you in the post office," they said. "Merry Christmas—oh, Merry Christmas! We'll be back about dark."

They left their two shabby suitcases on the hall floor and went away.

"All the clothes they've got between them would hardly fill these up," said Mrs. Tilton mournfully. "Why on earth do you suppose they'd turn their back on a dinner that smells so good and go off into the country at noon on Christmas Day? They wouldn't do that for another invitation. Likely somebody's sick," she ended, her puzzled look denying her tone of finality.

"Well, thank the Lord for the call to the country," said Ricky shamelessly. "It saved our day."

They had their Christmas dinner; they had their afternoon—safe and happy and uninterrupted. Five commonplace-looking folk in a commonplace-looking house, but the eye of love knew that this was not all. In the wide sea of their routine they had found and taken for their own this island day, unforgettable.

"I thought it was going to be a gay day," said Ricky at its close, "but it hasn't. It's been heavenly!

Mother, shall we give them the rest of their presents now, you and I?"

"Not yet," she told them. "Ricky, I want to whisper to you."

She looked so guilty that they all laughed at her. Ricky was laughing when he came back from that brief privacy. He was still laughing mysteriously when his mother turned from a telephone call.

"What do you think?" she cried. "That was the woman that brought me my turkey. She knew the minister and his wife were to be with me today. She wants to know why they've been eating a lunch in a cutter out that way. Do you suppose—"

They all looked at one another doubtfully, then in abrupt conviction. "They went because they wanted us to have the day to ourselves!"

"Arthur," said Mrs. Tilton with immense determination, "let me whisper to you, too." And from that moment's privacy he also returned smiling, but a bit ruefully.

"Mother ought to be the president of a university," he said.

"Mother ought to be the head of a law firm," said Edward.

"Mother ought to write a book about herself," said Ricky.

"Mother's mother," said Grace, "and that's enough. But you're all so mysterious, except me."

"Grace," said Mrs. Tilton, "you remind me that I want to whisper to you."

Their train left in the late afternoon. Through the white streets they walked to the station, the somber little woman, the buoyant, capable daughter, the three big sons. She drew them to seclusion down by the baggage room and gave them four envelopes.

"Here's the rest of my Christmas for you," she

said. "I'd rather you'd open it on the train. Now, Ricky, what's yours?"

She was firm to their protests. The train was whistling when Ricky owned up that the rest of his Christmas present for his mother was a brand new daughter, to be acquired as soon as his new book was off the press. "We're going to marry on the advance royalty," he said importantly, "and live on—" The rest was lost in the roar of the express.

"Edward!" shouted Mrs. Tilton. "Come here. I want to whisper—"

She was obliged to shout it, whatever it was. But Edward heard, and nodded, and kissed her. There was time for her to slip something in Ricky's pocket and for the other goodbyes, and then the train drew out. From the other platform they saw her brave, calm face against the background of the little town. A mother of "grown children" pathetic? She seemed to them at that moment the one supremely triumphant figure in life.

They opened their envelopes soberly and sat soberly over the contents. The note, scribbled to Grace, explained: Mother wanted to divide up now what she had had for them in her will. She would keep one house and live on the rent from the other one, and "here's all the rest." They laughed at her postscript:

"Don't argue. I ought to give the most—I'm the mother."

"And look at her," said Edward solemnly. "As soon as she heard about Ricky, there at the station, she whispered to me that she wanted to send Ricky's sweetheart the watch I'd just given her. Took it off her wrist then and there."

"That must be what she slipped in my pocket," said Ricky.

It was.

"She asked me," he said, "if I minded if she

gave those books to the new Springvale Public Library."

"She asked me," said Grace, "if I cared if she gave the new rug to the new church that can't pay its minister."

President Arthur Tilton shouted with laughter.

"When we heard where the minister and his wife ate their Christmas dinner," he said, "she whispered to ask me whether she might give the silk dress to her when they get back tonight."

All this they knew by the time the train reached the crossing where they could look back on Springvale. On the slope of the hill lay the little cemetery, and Ricky said:

"And she told me that if my flowers got there before dark, she'd take them up to the cemetery for Christmas for father. By night she won't have even a flower left to tell her we've been there."

"Not even the second side of the turkey," said Grace, "and yet I think—"

"So do I," her brothers said. ※

Nearest and Dearest

Ruth Moench Bell

Look over my Christmas list, Richard, and see if you can suggest any changes."

With the expression of one on whom a long expected doom had fallen, Richard reached for the list. Then with masculine directness his eye took in the one important item: "Total $100."

Christine had hoped he would approach the sum by degrees and at the finish of a fascinating list of gifts be won over—gifts calculated to win enthusiasm even from a male creature. Reached in this way, Christine felt that the $100 would appear a paltry sum for so many entrancing items.

"What do you think of them?" Christine asked, to divert him from the appalling total. "Could you imagine anything more delightful for your sister Clara than a glass baking dish?" Christine smiled seductively as she pointed to the article for which her heart yearned.

"I don't know anything about those things," Richard sighed wearily. Then with simulated interest, "What was it you gave her last year?" he asked.

"One of those casserole baking dishes. And the year before I gave her an aluminum baking dish."

"Well, wouldn't they be enough of that sort of thing?"

"Oh, you see these glass baking dishes are the latest thing."

"I see. And the casserole was the latest thing last year. And aluminum was the latest the year before. Of course, it is all very well to have these latest things if one can afford them. But Tom's income is no larger than mine. Why not select something simple? Why not *make* her something?"

"Oh, I have so many things to make, loads and loads of aprons and handkerchiefs and guest towels. And they all have to be trimmed with hand crochet. It will take every minute till Christmas. And it makes me so nervous."

"Why do you keep up this silly custom?"

"They all give me something. I couldn't refrain from giving in exchange."

"I wish I could get hold of the bell-sheep," Richard smiled enigmatically, glancing up at the ceiling.

"I don't know what you mean."

"The gang leader."

"Women don't go in gangs," Christine, prettily indignant, flashed at him.

"Well then, the prototype of your particular clique."

"I do wish you would talk English, Richard, instead of slang and big words."

"My dear, somebody sets the pace. Some woman stronger minded and more original than the rest of you." Up in the air went Christine's nose and chin. But her husband in amused unconcern, appeared not to notice her indignation. In fact he was delighted that his arrow had gone true, straight into the heart of his wife's pride. "Women and men are like sheep. They all trail unconsciously in the wake of the bell-sheep. My word, I wish I could find her and persuade her to lead her band through another gap."

"You are delightfully complimentary," Christine snipped off. "I always flattered myself that I was the leader of our crowd."

"So did I, my dear, so did I," her husband agreed. "Then why don't you lead them where there is better picking. The husbands of this band are barren waste, picked-over stubble, shad scale, grease wood, buck brush." Richard's voice trailed off into a fit of laughter.

"I think you are just as disgusting as you can be," Christine tried hard not to laugh at her husband's absurd simile. "Besides your figure is an exceedingly faulty one. You surely are not suggesting that the band pick Jacob Morse's pockets in search of clover and wild peas or whatever fodder millionaire sheep seem to prefer."

Richard rocked with mirth over his wife's clever pursuit of his ridiculous comparison. And Christine, to conceal her merriment, flounced out of the house to visit with Richard's grandma.

"Richard has accused me of not being the bell-sheep. And he has appraised himself as very poor picking," Christine laughed as she sank into grandma's easy chair. "And all that after contemplating, unmoved, this list of adorable trifles for Christmas gifts. Do you see anything extravagant there, grandma?"

"Not a thing. Not a blessed thing," grandma smiled shrewdly. "Jacob Morse would scarcely notice an insignificant sum like that."

Jacob Morse was the one millionaire of the town. And as his wealth was the result of extortionate prices on an indispensable commodity, his name was an unsavory morsel in the mouth of everyone.

"By the way, did I ever show you my rubbish heap in the attic?" grandma mused.

"Never," Christine cried, "and I have been pining to see all those fascinating, old-fashioned things."

Up into the attic with a brace of candlesticks the twain hied.

"Why, what is thus?" Christine asked, holding up a dusty, battered object.

Grandma surveyed it with amusement. "That, my dear," she said with a twinkle, "is a joke."

"A joke?"

Grandma gazed at the object quizzically, and the ripple of amusement that had wreathed her features, gave place to sympathetic concern.

"On second thought," she said seriously, "it is a wrinkle producer."

"A wrinkle producer?" Christine knew that grandma was addicted to cryptic remarks; but this one was decidedly puzzling.

"They used to call them casters," grandma continued. "Every woman had to have one. I gave that one to Janet Wilson. She received two others for that Christmas. One was all that any woman could use; so mine went onto the what-not. And every other day Janet had the dismal task of dusting the vinegar bottle, the oil bottle, the pepper bottle, the salt bottle, the red-pepper bottle, and replacing them in the caster for which I yearned."

"If you gave it to Janet, I don't see how it came to be here," Christine asked.

"I got it by replevying it. You see, Janet had given me something she wanted very much for herself. A print of Rembrandt's portrait of his mother, it was. It did not mean as much to me as it had meant to Janet. And one day after she had endured the sight of it strung up on the wall so close to the ceiling that no one could possibly see the sweet, tender face, she burst out laughing. 'I don't believe you care very much for that print, do you, Mary?' she asked.

"'Not especially,' I confessed.

"'I have always longed to possess it,' she sighed. 'I wanted to enjoy it every day.

"'I guess you feel toward it as I felt toward the caster I gave you,' I laughed. 'And now you dust the caster, and I never look at the picture."

"'I'll tell you what,' she proposed, 'let's us trade presents.'

"And we did," grandma continued. "And what is more, we quit making each other expensive presents. A glass of jam or a piece of extra good fruit cake or some little occasional trifle expressed our good will toward each other quite as well, and lessened the sense of obligation an expensive gift imposes."

"That is what happened between Clara and me," Christine laughed. "I gave her a beautiful casserole last year. She had let it be known that she wanted one. Then Tom gave her one, and Edna gave her one. And she never uses all three. Sometimes I have felt like snatching it off her buffet and running home with it and serving Richard a delicious scollop in it."

"Why don't you?"

"Oh, I can't. And besides I'd rather have one of those glass baking dishes, now. The one I am getting for Clara. They are so much daintier."

"Then the casserole Richard worked so hard to pay for is already doomed to pass upward to the attic, a lonely, isolated companion for this caster which cost my husband so dearly."

"Is that what you meant by calling it a wrinkle-producer?" Christine asked.

"That is what I meant," grandma smiled. "Attics are full of wrinkle-producers. If women would visit their attics oftener, many of the things for which they long and for which their husbands strain to pay, would remain unbought, especially when they are to go to someone who knows what she wants better than anyone else can guess."

"It does look silly," Christine admitted. "But what can a person do? My relatives feel that they must give me something expensive."

"Which their husbands cannot afford," grandma supplemented.

"What do you suggest?" Christine begged.

"Why not take Richard's suggestions and be the bell-sheep? Lead the band into pastures of quiet and content."

"But how can I go about it?" Christine enquired.

"Just tell your friends that you are going to give no presents, hereafter, outside your immediate family. Tell them that you are going to consider the "nearest and dearest" this year, placing his peace of mind before all material gifts. Tell your friends that hereafter you will accept and give nothing but the gift supreme, the gift of the angels, good will."

Richard was growing uneasy. The Christmas season was drawing nearer and nearer. And yet no mention was made of the money for the gifts, the $100 so difficult to raise. Christine was kindness and consideration itself. At first Richard was restive and suspicious of the warmth of affection which proverbially bodes ill for a man's purse strings. When the days passed and no attack was made on the slim wallet, a grim fear clutched him.

The presents were being charged! The bills in that way would amount to considerably over the first cash estimate. Charged accounts always did. The extra affection was to prepare him for the January onslaught of bills. How deep these women were! Now a mere man—but what was the use?

Richard's hand went into his pocket. He drew out five ten-dollar bills. He had schemed and maneuvered to save them to pay on their accounts.

"We ought to square our accounts with these," he said as he handed them to his astonished wife. "But use them for those Christmas gifts. Don't charge anything," he added. "It is so easy to charge more than one would think of paying, if one paid for it at once."

Christine's eyes caught the worried look in her husband's face, and she yearned to press his boyish head in her arms and set his fears at rest. But no, she had made up her mind to wait till Christmas.

"You know we are not to give each other anything, this year," Christine volunteered as a partial concession.

Richard merely grunted. He had a distinct recollection of a similar remark made a certain Christmas before. A remark he had taken literally. And when he appeared that Christmas morning and found his sock filled to overflowing and caught Christine surreptitiously removing her empty stocking and weeping bitterly into it, he decided that the ways of women were past finding out. He registered this bit of Solomonesque wisdom deep in his consciousness: when a woman says, "Let us give each other nothing," come provided with the handsomest gift you can procure.

Richard made a mental note that he had better get a glass baking dish, like the one Christine had selected for Clara. He had already learned the feminine way of giving to each other the gift you desire for yourself.

He was not surprised Christmas morning when he surveyed the array of tissue-paper-covered parcels heaped about his place. With the usual masculine misgivings as to what impractical atrocity may be lurking within, Richard undid the first parcel.

He was interrupted by a cry of delight from Christine. "The very dish I was going to get Clara," she laughed. "But Richard, I thought we were not to get anything for each other this Christmas."

"I kept my promise as well as you did yours," he retorted as the first wrapper fell from the parcel.

Then a look of misery crossed his face as he read the card, "A wrinkle-eradicator for my dear husband."

Cold cream! She had bought him cold cream! Richard almost shuddered. Surely Christine knew how he loathed the touch or sight of cold cream or oil of any sort. Truly a man never knew what might happen to him after he married. He undid the second wrapper. Instead of a jar of cold cream, a roll of bills slipped out. Then she had charged the presents. Richard picked up the first one. It was marked paid. So were each of the others. They were the bills he had meant to pay with the fifty dollars he gave her.

Somewhat mystified, he glanced at his wife. But she was already by his side, her arms about his neck, her cheek against his. "I wanted you to be happy this Christmas, Sweetheart," she cried. "Peace in your heart and no worries on your brow. I have been the bell-sheep, too, as you suggested. All of our crowd have taken grandma's suggestion and considered first of all the one 'nearest and dearest.' But you haven't opened the other package I sent you."

With eager fingers, Richard undid the wrappings. After innumerable papers had been removed he found only a card on which was written: "This gift, I give to you, the gift of the angels, my unfailing, unwavering good will. Please God, it is to be yours forever. Never to be dusted or consigned to the attic. It implies no return favor unless you will, and I so merit it, your gift of good will toward me."

"It was the only gift I sent out," Christine cried as her husband folded her in his arms, "but I sent it to each of my friends. They say it is good to give gifts. It expands the spirit. If that is true, and I believe it is, surely the gift of good-will expands and enriches the soul more than any other gift: because more of ourselves goes into the giving. I used to worry over whether this or that present would please. I used to scheme and contrive to extract money from you to pay for things. Sometimes I even thought with resentment of the friends as I puzzled and stitched to please them. This Christmas season, to make good my gift, I have thought with the tenderest sympathy and warmest love of the many friends I wished to remember. I have pledged myself to allow no unkind thoughts to arise in my heart about them. I shall permit no ill-natured criticism of them to reach me unchallenged. And I like to hope that wherever they are today, each is sending her message of good will to me."

"I know one that is," Richard cried, deeply moved, "one whose love is deepened a thousand-fold. I believe good will is sometimes a rare gift from a wife to her husband and *vise versa*. And I'm prouder to have married the bell-sheep than I was to marry the belle of the balls we used to attend." ☀

A Christmas Thought

James Russell Lowell

The Holy Supper is kept, indeed,
In whatso we share, with another's need,—
Not that which we give, but what we share,—
For the gift without the giver is bare;
Who bestows himself with his alms feeds three,—
Himself, his hungering neighbor, and Me.

CHAPTER SEVEN

Service & Sacrifice

Our Pickle-Jar Christmas

Wilma M. Rich

WHEN I WAS A CHILD, it seemed to me that Christmastime always began the day Daddy brought home the Christmas tree. But the year I was five, Christmas for the family began much earlier.

Two months before Christmas on a cold October night, Mama rounded up her six children, including me, and sat us down in the long log room that served as kitchen, living room, and bedroom for the family.

She lifted three-year-old Benny and me onto the high bed with the crazy-patch quilt and gathered the four older children around us.

"Christmas is for surprises," she began. "How would each of you like to make this a special Christmas by surprising Daddy?"

Everyone agreed, and Benny and I squealed and clapped our hands at the prospect of treating Daddy, since he often had special surprises for us in his lunch bucket at the end of a workday.

"Sh! Let's talk quietly so Daddy won't hear. He's just on the other side of the door, remember." We could hear Daddy hammering and sawing in the new living room he was adding onto the room we presently lived in. He was working at home on nights when he worked day shift at the coal mine and mornings when he worked night shift, trying to finish the room before Christmas so we could have our Christmas tree there.

"You children know how hard Daddy works for us and how he worries about paying the bills?"

Mama asked. The Great Depression was drawing to a close, and though we didn't understand that, we did know that times were hard. The older children nodded, and taking a cue, I nodded, too, although I had no idea how much Daddy worked or worried. I didn't even know what a bill was.

Mama bent closer so she could speak quietly and make us all hear. "Since Daddy always makes Christmas so nice for us, I thought it would be fun to make this year Daddy's Christmas."

Getting into the spirit of things, we nodded. We loved keeping secrets, especially a Christmas surprise.

"What do you mean, Mama?" asked Sammy, who was two years older than I.

"You may not want to surprise Daddy when you find out what I have in mind," warned Mama.

"Yes we will!" promised Eva, the eldest and most magnanimous.

Mama continued, "Okay, but you don't have to decide until I explain." She quieted us again since we were beginning to fidget. "If this is going to be Daddy's Christmas, we'll all have to make a lot of sacrifices." Benny's eyes lit up; he loved to make things.

"Number one, none of the rest of us will receive any gifts or give presents to each other." As Mama watched to see everyone's reaction to this bombshell, the room became so still the sound of Daddy's hammer rang with clarity in the next room.

"No presents?" asked Marilyn and Jerry in unison. I watched Marilyn's tranquil countenance crumble and Jerry's green eyes enlarge, and I began to catch on. "That's right," said Mama, "nothing under the tree for any of us except Daddy." I saw the disappointment among my brothers and sisters, and I would have felt glum, too, except that I was sure Santa would bring each of us a gift on

Christmas Eve. Mama's lilting voice was gentle with understanding. "Remember the Christmas story? How the Wise Men traveled many days and nights to bring presents to baby Jesus?"

I loved all the stories about Christmas and snuggled into Mama's pillow, waiting to hear another one. "Remember the traditional story of the little shepherd boy who heard the angels singing 'Glory to the newborn King,' and gathered a tiny lamb to give as a gift to the King in the manger?"

While firelight danced through the holes in the front of our potbellied stove and Jack Frost painted pictures on the room's north window, Mama retold the story of the wondrous birth of our Savior.

When she finished, she held her arms as though cradling a child. "Jesus, who would someday make the greatest sacrifice of all, meant enough to the Wise Men for them to give up their greatest treasures to honor him."

I was enthralled, as I always was when Mama told this story. I looked at the rapture on the faces of the others and felt tingly inside. Sammy asked, "Didn't the Wise Men get any presents when they went back to their houses?"

"No, dear, only a peaceful feeling inside that made them feel happy."

"I don't care about not getting any presents," declared Eva after a moment, her eyes sparkling. The others agreed, although without complete conviction.

Mama studied our faces in the lamp's glow. "Does everyone agree, then?" One by one we nodded. "Are you sure you can all keep a secret?" Several looks were directed at Benny and me. "Will you and Benny promise not to tell Daddy?" Our heads bobbed up and down. "Here's what we're going to do."

As we listened, the chilly October wind whipped leaves against the windows, but we didn't care. Mama could make anything sound good.

The next morning, we started saving money for Daddy's Christmas surprise. Mama made economical foods for the children's school lunches instead of buying small treats for their lunches. She let Eva, Marilyn, Jerry, and Sammy put the saved quarters and nickels in a small pickle jar, then we all watched as she placed the jar on top of the tall kitchen cupboard in a corner of the room.

"That's a start," she said. "We'll see how fast it adds up."

And it did add up with each sacrifice we made. Those of us with piggy banks transferred our pennies into the pickle jar. Instead of buying treats with allowances or spending money when we went to town, we dropped our money into the jar.

Jerry and Sammy milked our black cow, Baby, and turned the handle on the separator while milk whirred into one container and cream into another. Then Eva and Marilyn churned the cream into butter to sell.

One Saturday, Mama took us to the livestock auction in our Model-A Ford truck. We sold our six runt lambs, now grown into fat, woolly sheep. Jerry and Sammy also sold their rabbits, dropping crisp dollar bills into the jar that night.

Each night after school, the bigger kids would hurry home to see how much Daddy had done on the new room, avidly watching the chinked railroad-tie walls go higher and higher. Then we would all help Mama with projects designed to help us earn or save money.

We cut quilt blocks while Mama sewed the blocks together on her treadle machine. We helped her make shirts for the boys from Daddy's old dress shirts and mittens from old woolen coats. We helped put patches on the knees of jeans and ruffles on skirts that were too short. My contribution was clipping thread and treadling the machine when Mama would let me.

Instead of buying new winter coats, Mama handed down what she could to younger ones and made over some old coats she found in a trunk for the others. When the school-age children said they needed new shoes, she asked them if they would rather have new shoes or Daddy's Christmas. Of course, they opted to polish and patch their old shoes and put the money they saved into the pickle jar.

We were enjoying the sight of the greenbacks and coins adding up. Each Saturday evening after our baths in the round metal tub, Mama would take down the jar from the cupboard, and we would count the money.

When the Sears and Roebuck catalog came a few weeks before Christmas, Mama told us we could each choose what we would like and cut the toys from the catalog to give to our paper dolls. Choosing, she pointed out, was as much fun as having.

Benny and I would save our treats from Daddy's lunchbox and let Mama send the cakes and cookies with him the next day, thereby saving the money she would have spent on more treats for Daddy. She would let us take pennies from her coin purse and drop them into the pickle jar.

November came and went, with Daddy putting up two-by-fours and planks for a roof on the new living room, then covering the boards with a tin roof. He laid the floor in early December and started plastering the walls two weeks before Christmas.

Making Christmas candy was always a special treat. This year, instead of buying sugar, syrup, canned milk, and nuts, we put the money away and made honey candy. While we stretched the hot candy like taffy, we sang Christmas carols.

Daddy worked almost through the night two nights before Christmas, putting the finishing touches on the new room and bringing in a stove for heat. He was eager to present the finished room to us as his Christmas gift to our family.

The next morning, the family—wrapped in quilts with heated rocks at our feet—loaded into Daddy's old truck and chugged through new-fallen snow to Clarks Valley to cut a Christmas tree. We chose a fragrant piñon tree with pine cones still clinging to its branches, and Daddy chopped the tree down while we kids romped in the snow and exchanged secret smiles.

All day Daddy quizzed Mama about Christmas gifts for the children, but Mama would just smile and say, "Don't worry, everything has been taken care of."

That night we wrapped Daddy's gift with bright red-and-green paper while Daddy made a stand for the tree. We trooped into the new room behind him as he carried the tree to a corner. In awe, we looked around us. The new living room seemed like a magnificent castle.

We decorated the tree with paper chains, popcorn, and our traditional Christmas angel. We sang Christmas carols and knelt around the tree for family prayer.

On Christmas morning, Daddy woke us with a boisterous, "Ho, ho, ho, Merry Christmas! Wake up, sleepyheads, and let's go see what's under the Christmas tree." We rubbed our eyes and smirked and giggled. We knew what was under the tree!

Daddy had put a big log in the stove the night before, and this morning the room was toasty warm and smelled of pine and new plaster.

Mama and her brood of little ones hurried into

the room ahead of Daddy, all of us thrilled with the new room he had built, and anxious to see his face when he noticed the tree.

"Whoa!" Daddy exclaimed as he studied the empty floor under the tree, empty except for one gaily wrapped package. "Where are the rest of the Christmas presents?"

"Under the tree, dear," replied Mama, her eyes glowing like Christmas lights.

"But I don't understand."

"Just read what's on the tag," instructed Mama, giving him a push.

"Yes, read it, Daddy!" exclaimed Sammy, whose curiosity was getting the best of him. "Read it! Read it! Read it!" shouted the rest of us.

Daddy picked up the gift and read aloud, "To Daddy on *your* Christmas, from all of us with love. Signed, Ellen (Mama), Eva, Marilyn, Jerry, Sammy, Wilma, and Benny."

"Surprise!" we shouted when Daddy took the wrapping from the present. Inside was a box, and inside the box was a neat stack of bills—some for building materials for the new room and some for groceries and utilities, bills that had mounted up during the years of the Depression—each marked "Paid in Full."

As Daddy thumbed through the papers, his eyes misted over, and he hugged and kissed each of us in turn, starting with Mama. "This is the best Christmas I've ever had," he declared. And we all knew it was the best one for us, too. ❄

Keeping Christmas

Henry Van Dyke

THERE IS A BETTER THING than the *observance* of Christmas day, and that is *keeping* Christmas. Are you willing to forget what you have done for other people and to remember what other people have done for you; to ignore what the world owes you and to think what *you owe the world;* to put your rights in the background and your duties in the middle distance and your chances to do a little more than your duty in the foreground; to see that your fellowmen are just as real as you are and try to look behind their faces to their hearts, hungry for joy; to own that probably the only good reason for your existence is not what you are going to get *out* of life, but what you are going to *give* to life; to close your book of complaints against the management of the universe and look around you for some place where you can sow a few seeds of happiness—Are you willing to do these things even for a day?

Then you can keep Christmas! ❄

The Year of the Flexible Flyers

Aney B. Chatterton

THE YEAR WAS 1932 and the nation's economy was at an all-time low. The disastrous crash of '29 had left its mark, and we were experiencing a time that was to become known as the Great Depression.

I was in the eighth grade, and we all started school that fall with few clothes and school supplies. There was no lunch program, and for many students there was no food to bring. So those of us who could bring something to eat shared whatever we had.

I remember that whenever any of us had an extra penny, we would put it in an envelope and hide it; when we had twenty pennies saved, we would take them to the store and buy two cans of Vienna sausages, a treat far better than candy. Then we would find a secluded area, put all our lunches together, open the cans of sausage, and divide everything equally. Those were special days.

As Christmastime approached that year, we didn't feel the excitement that usually comes with the holiday season. We understood about the Depression and knew there would be very little for any of us.

But there was one desire we all had, though none of us would have mentioned it to our parents. A new sled had appeared on the market called the Flexible Flyer. With its sleek finish, sharp runners, and smooth handlebars that steered it easily and gracefully, it was the Rolls Royce of all sleds.

We all marched to the hardware store one day after school to see the new wonder sled. "How much are the sleighs, Mr. Evans?" one of the boys asked.

"Well," he replied, "I think I can sell them for $4.98."

Our hearts sank. But that didn't stop us from dreaming the impossible dream.

School was finally dismissed for the holidays, and when Christmas Eve came we had our usual Christmas play and party. We returned to our homes, happy, yet sad, feeling keenly the weight of those depressed times.

I awoke early Christmas morning but was not anxious to get up. My mother finally called, so I dressed and we all went to the living room where the tree was. I was surprised to see that the tree had been redecorated and was more beautiful than ever. But the biggest surprise was still in store. There underneath the tree, with a big red ribbon tied around it, was a shiny new sled—a Flexible Flyer!

I let out a startled cry and dropped to the floor, sliding my fingers along the satiny finish, moving the handlebars back and forth, and finally cradling the precious sled in my arms. Tears rolled down my cheeks as I looked up at my parents and asked, "Where did you get the money for it?"

My mother wiped away a tear with the corner of her apron and replied, "Surely you believe in Santa Claus. Open your other present."

I opened another box and there was a beautiful dress, and though I loved it, my eyes were on the sled. I could only stand and gaze in awe. I was now the owner of a Flexible Flyer.

After our midday Christmas dinner, Mother announced, "Put on your boots and bundle up warm. We're going to town. We have another surprise for you." I didn't think anything could compare with the surprise I already had.

Dad hitched up the team to our big sleigh, I loaded in my new sled, and we went to town. As soon as we crossed the bridge I saw what the surprise was. Kids were everywhere, and so were Flexible Flyers. Main Street had been roped off so that we could start at the top of the hill and glide all the way down across the bridge without danger from cars. The entire community had turned out. Boys and girls were all jumping up and down, some were crying, most were throwing their arms around each other and shouting, "You got one too!"

Our parents finally got us calmed down long enough to listen to instructions. Three farmers with their horses and sleighs would take turns pulling us to the top of the hill where we would start. The older boys went first, running and then flopping "belly first," as we called it, onto their sleds. We watched as they glided effortlessly over the crusted snow. Faster and faster they went, crossing the bridge and coming to rest amid the cheers and clapping of parents. We all took turns, and as the day wore on we got braver and wilder. The boys discovered they could do tricks by dragging their feet in a certain way, causing their sleds to turn around and tip over. We all got caught up in this adventure, tumbling in a tangle of arms and legs, laughing helplessly as we slipped around, ending up in a pile of bundled bodies.

As night drew near, our parents called for us to stop—it was time to return home for chores. "No, no," we cried. "Please let us stay." Reluctantly they agreed, releasing us from chores for this one time only. When they returned it was dark, but the moon shone brightly, lighting the hill. The cold wind blew over our bodies; the stars seemed so brilliant and close, the hill dark and shadowy as we made our last run for the day. Cold and hungry, but happy, we

loaded our Flexible Flyers and returned home with memories that would last a lifetime.

Everywhere I went in the days that followed, my Flexible Flyer went with me. One night I decided to go to the barn, as I often did, just to watch Dad at work. I noticed that one of the stalls was empty, and I asked, "Where's Rosie? She isn't in her stall."

There was an awkward silence, and my dad finally replied, "We had to sell her. She cut her foot in the fence."

Sell Rosie? I thought. *Gentle, friendly Rosie?*

"But the cut would have healed," I said. "Why didn't you sell Meanie? She never does anything we want, but Rosie always leads the herd into the barn."

Dad didn't say anything, and suddenly I knew. Rosie had been sold to buy my Flexible Flyer. She was the best and would bring more money; and my parents had given the best they had—for me. I had always understood that my parents treasured me dearly, but until that moment I had never known a love so great. I ran from the barn in tears and hid myself behind the haystack.

I returned to the hill the next day and told my best friend about Rosie. "Yes, I know," she said. "My dad took ten bushels of apples from our cellar and took them to Pocatello and sold them door to door. He's never had to do that before. That's how I got my Flexible Flyer."

A growing amazement overtook me. "But how did they know?" I asked. "I didn't ask for a sled, so how did all the parents know we all wanted Flexible Flyers?"

Little by little we began to put the pieces together like a jigsaw puzzle. Everyone had a similar story to tell. Then we began to realize how the entire community had united in one monumental effort of sharing, trading, peddling, extra working, and, most of all, caring, to buy the Flexible Flyers. None of us ever had the slightest hint of what was going on right under our noses. That had to be the best-kept secret of all time in so small a community.

When school resumed and we marched into our classroom and stood by our desks waiting for the teacher to say those familiar words, "You may be seated," it seemed we all stood just a bit taller. Not that we had grown in stature, but we had grown in a different way. Nothing had really changed, yet everything had changed. The economy was still the same and we still shared our lunches and saved our pennies for the sausages, but inside we had all changed. We were happier, we played harder, and we studied more diligently. It was as if we had all committed ourselves to be the best we could be, to make our parents and community proud of us. It was the only way we knew to say "thanks."

When the snow finally melted and it was time to store the sleds, we were reluctant to part with them. We clung to them as a child clings to a favorite blanket. They had given meaning to our lives and provided us with a sense of identity. That terrible monster, the Great Depression, no longer seemed such a threat to us. Somehow we knew there would be better times, a brighter tomorrow, and a more prosperous future.

Many years later, long after I married, I asked my mother how they had pulled that secret off, and who started it. Her eyes twinkled. She gave me one of those warm, loving smiles that only a mother can give and replied, "My dear daughter, you must never stop believing in Santa Claus." ❋

The Christmas We Gave Away

Marilyn Ellsworth Swinyard

THE CHRISTMAS I REMEMBER BEST began with tragedy. It happened at 6 a.m. on one of those crisp Idaho Falls mornings the day before Christmas. Our neighbors, the Jesse Smith family, slept peacefully in their two-story home. The baby, barely six months cold, was in a crib next to her parents' room, and the three older children were upstairs.

Suddenly something jarred Jesse from his sleep. He thought he smelled smoke. Could a spark from the torch he'd defrosted the frozen water pipes with the day before have started a fire in the basement? Still half asleep, he stumbled to the bedroom door and flung it open. Clouds of black smoke poured into the room. "Lorraine!" he yelled. "Get the baby!" He ran toward the stairs and his sleeping children. The smoke was thicker as he gasped for breath. "Rick! Tom! Wake up!" The boys scrambled out of their beds. "Run, boys!" Tom grabbed his younger brother's hand, and they raced down the smoke-filled stairway to safety. His daughter's room was next. As Jesse groped through the heavy shroud of gray, he called, "Cindy! Cindy! Where are you?"

"Here, Daddy, here!" He followed the frightened cries, scooped up his daughter in his arms, and with his hand over her face, felt his way out the room and down through a narrow path of searing flames. They coughed, choked, gasped for breath, until they at last stumbled out the door where a relieved wife and three children stood shivering in the snow.

Now the family looked to the smoke and flames pouring out the roof of their home, the home that the night before had held all their earthly treasures. It had also held a promise of Christmas, mulled cider, homemade candy, and stockings waiting to be filled. They stood huddled in their nightclothes, barefoot in the biting cold, and watched their Christmas burn up along with their house.

The spell was broken by the sound of sirens piercing the icy air. Firemen leaped from the huge red trucks and turned their powerful hoses on the blaze. Seconds later, the bishop of the Smiths' ward drove up, bundled the family into his car, and took them to a home the ward elders quorum had just completed as a fund-raising project. They were not to witness the firemen's hopeless battle with the flames. For when the trucks finally pulled away, this time in silence, nothing stood of their house but its charred skeleton outlined against the sky.

And tomorrow was Christmas. At our house we were putting the last secret wrappings on the presents, making the last batch of popcorn for popcorn balls to go in our Christmas stockings. We three children were attempting dubious harmony with our favorite carols and breaking into giggles at the results.

Then Dad came in with the news. We sat with serious faces listening to him tell of the fire, the narrow escape, the house where the Smiths were spending Christmas Eve.

Why? Mother said. Why did this happen, just at Christmas? It isn't fair. They had children, just the same ages as ours, she said. Jesse and Dad were the closest friends; they even joked that they were so close they wore the same size shirt. The same size shirt! "Bill," Mother began hesitantly, "would you mind terribly if we gave Jesse one of the shirts I bought you for Christmas? You wear the same

size . . . " A hush fell on us all. We all seemed to be thinking the exact same thing. "I've got it!" my ten-year-old brother shouted. "We'll give the Smiths a Christmas! A Christmas for Christmas!" "Where could we get one?" my inquisitive little sister asked. "We'll give them ours," the others chorused in.

"Of course! We'll give them ours!" The house rang with excited voices, until Dad's stern command silenced us. "Hold it! Let's make sure we all want to do this. Let's take a vote. All in favor say aye."

"AYE!" chorused back at him. "All opposed?" was met with silence.

The hours that followed are ones we will never forget. First we sat around the tree and handed out presents. Instead of opening them, the giver would divulge their contents so the label could be changed to the appropriate Smith family member. My heart fell when Dad handed Kevin a box wrapped in gold foil and green ribbon. "It's a baseball glove, son," Dad told him, and a flash of disappointment crossed Kevin's face. I knew how he'd longed for that glove, and Dad wanted to say, "You keep it, son," but Kevin smiled as if he'd read our thoughts. "Thanks, Dad. It's just what Stan wanted, too," he replied.

"Look, here's the recipe holder I made for you, that is, for Sister Smith." We signed all the tags "From Santa," and the activity that followed would have put his workshop elves to shame.

They had presents, but what about a Christmas dinner? The turkey was cooked, pies baked, the carrots and celery prepared, and then all packed in a box. The Christmas stockings must be stuffed. Dad got a length of clothesline and some clothespins to hang the stockings with, but what about a tree? We looked at ours. Could we really part with it? "I know," Dad volunteered. "Let's decorate it with things they'll need." And so more things were added to the tree: a tube of toothpaste tied with red ribbon, a razor, comb, bars of soap nestled in the branches. Finally it was all ready.

It was a strange procession that silently paraded through the dark streets of Idaho Falls that night. Father led the way carrying a fully decorated tree. Mother followed with a complete Christmas dinner, down to the last dish of cranberry sauce. The three of us children pulled wagons and a sled piled with boxes of gifts. We waited until the last light was out in the Smiths' borrowed home, and then Mom and Dad stealthily carried each item in the door. When the last stocking had been hung, we turned again toward home.

All the way home I worried about what waited for my family at our home. What if the others were disappointed? All that was left were a few pine needles and paper scraps. I couldn't have been more wrong. The minute we were back inside we were more excited than ever. Every pine needle and paper scrap was a reminder of the magic of the evening, and we hadn't taken that to the Smiths. It was in our home as real as if you could see it. A happier family never went to bed on a Christmas Eve, and the next morning the magic was still there. For our celebration we wrote a promise to each person on a card and presented it around a spruce branch tied in a red ribbon.

"One shoe shine. To Father. Love Kevin." "This is good for two turns doing the evening dishes. Love, your husband Bill." And so it went.

Our Christmas dinner consisted of scrambled eggs and bacon, toast and sliced oranges. Somehow, I don't remember a better one. And I know we sang our carols that night with the same unconventional harmony, but it sounded sweeter than angels to me.

"Oh, Mommy," said my small sister as she snuggled up for her bedtime Christmas story, "I like

to give Christmases away." Tears blurred the book in my mother's hands, because she knew that none of us would ever forget this Christmas, the one when we gave our best gift. And as she read the story of the Baby born in a manger, it seemed our gift was but a small tribute to him who gave his best gift, his Son to us. ❊

The Christmas Letter

Charles M. Manwaring

MILES OF GRAY DESERT ended abruptly in a miragelike valley of green. A cluster of neat houses sparsely shaded by poplar and cedar trees flanked both sides of the road. Near the center of town stood a bank, a mini-supermarket, a hardware and general mercantile store, and a combination garage and service station.

A few strings of tinsel and pasteboard Santa Claus placards swung wearily in the hot breeze above the street. In the doubtful shade of a large cedar stood a small frame building with a weathered sign that read: U.S. POST OFFICE, DESERT CITY, ARIZONA, POPULATION 467. The cedar was decorated with colored bulbs and strands of red and green paper. Inside the post office a wreath of holly hung over a grilled window which boasted a faded sign: GENERAL DELIVERY . . . STAMPS.

Behind the window, Luke Jones sorted the mail without conscious thought or effort. After 30 years in Desert City there was little he didn't know about every resident—with one exception, the stranger who had arrived in town two days before. Luke shrugged, murmuring under his breath, "Curiosity killed the cat." His lips twitched into a wry grin. "Must be a mighty long trail of dead cats behind me."

Luke heard a scuffle of feet and turned toward the door. Mrs. Abbie Smithers walked in, and just behind her stood the stranger. Luke's eyes watched the stranger, but his words were to Mrs. Smithers. "Got a postcard for you, Abbie. From your sister in Colorado. She ain't going to get here for Christmas after all."

"For pity's sake!" Mrs. Smithers said. "I've cleaned house until the whole place shines like a new pin."

"Don't fret," Luke said calmly. "It's only a delay. Her little girl came down with the chicken pox. Here—you better read it yourself."

As Mrs. Smithers left the window, the stranger asked, "Anything for Bill Anders?"

Luke's sharp eyes studied him. He knew without looking that there was nothing, yet he turned and slowly sorted through some letters, his gaze darting sideways at the young man. "Ain't you the fellar whose car broke down here day before yesterday?"

"That's right."

"Too bad," Luke said. He looked directly at the serious-faced young man. "I hear it's costing you $70 to get it fixed." His glance was shrewd. "Garageman was in a while ago. Said it's been ready for you since yesterday."

"That's right. Have I got a letter?"

"Where you expecting this letter from?"

Anders's face flushed. "Look, I just want to know—"

"If I know where it's from," Luke interrupted, "maybe I can tell you when it'll be here."

Anders looked down at the floor. "It's coming from Los Angeles. I wrote airmail two days ago when my car broke down."

"Ain't here yet," Luke drawled.

Anders's face shadowed. He turned to leave.

"Should be in tomorrow," Luke said. "Mail gets in at 11:00."

Anders limped toward the door, and Luke noticed that he wore a heavy brace with a built-up shoe on one foot.

"Hey, Anders!"

The young man stopped and turned around.

"You clear broke?" An angry flush reddened Anders's face. "None of your business!"

Slyly Luke said, "You got money coming in that letter, ain't you?"

"What's it to you?" He stopped, took a deep breath, and said more quietly, "Yes, 100 dollars. Anything else you'd like to know?"

Without expression, Luke said, "From your folks, hey?"

Anders hobbled back to the window; his face was white. "Look, my folks are dead. A friend of mine in L.A. is sending me the money. At least, I asked him to send it, and I'm sure he will."

"Maybe," Luke said dryly, "maybe not."

"What do you mean?"

"Sometimes you find out you ain't got a friend when you ask for money."

Anders stared at him, then said, "Jim isn't that way."

Luke could sense an uncertainty behind the words. "Where you going from here if this Jim sends the money?"

Bill Anders's mood changed suddenly. He looked at Luke and grinned. "Darned if you aren't the most nosy, old . . . curious man I've ever seen."

"I've been told that."

Anders laughed. "All right, you might as well know. I've got a job waiting for me in Albuquerque that I've been trying to get since high school. A good job. A big chance for me." His voice lowered. "I've got to get there in time to begin work the day after Christmas. I've got to!" He turned abruptly and limped out to the street.

Luke rubbed his chin and stared after him.

At 11:30 the next morning Luke finished sorting the mail to the barely audible Christmas carols coming from the battered radio on the shelf. He examined again the letter addressed to Bill Anders. The postmark was smudged beyond recognition; the name and the address were typed. Luke held the envelope up to the light. He could see the outline of currency inside. He fingered the envelope. It crinkled like crisp, new greenbacks crinkle. Yes, it contained the 100 dollars Bill Anders was waiting for.

Luke's lips thinned a little. A hundred dollars could mean a lot to a person, even to a man in his position. It could mean that new fishing outfit he wanted for his next vacation. He smiled at the thought. A Christmas gift to himself. . .

He fondled the letter. What he would have given years ago for this money! It might have changed his whole life—marriage, children, grandchildren—but he had been unable to borrow the money. Friends—even relatives—had turned him down. He slammed the letter into the mail slot. Why should he worry about a crippled young man, a stranger he would never see again?

Luke heard dragging footsteps on the wood floor and turned around to see a subdued Bill Anders, a face lined with worry, yet eyes which still held a lurking hope.

Luke hesitated, and then he reached into the slot and pulled out the mail under the letter A. Deliberately he sorted through the letters; indecision still weighed upon him. He didn't have to give this letter to the boy. But if he didn't, could he ever live with himself? Could he look into a mirror without seeing the disappointment on the young man's face?

He held the letter away from the others.

"Is that for me?" Anders's voice was strained.

Luke held the letter up to the light. "Postmark's smudged. Can't tell where it's from."

"Is it for me?"

"Ain't got a return address on it," Luke drawled.

"It's from Jim! It must be!"

Luke watched the boy's face. It was transformed. His eyes were shining now, the lines of strain and worry vanished. Luke waited a moment longer, and then he tossed the letter through the iron grill.

Anders ripped open the envelope. Five crisp, 20-dollar bills fell out. There was no message. Carefully he picked up the money, handling each greenback almost with reverence. He glanced up at Luke. "Jim isn't one to write," he explained, "but when a guy needs help, he comes through."

"Guess you got a real friend, hey?" Luke said softly.

As he reached the door, his shoulders straight, Anders looked back and smiled. "Merry Christmas!"

Luke watched him limp down the street toward the garage. He sighed heavily and turned again to the mail rack. From the A slot he withdrew a postcard. It was postmarked Los Angeles and addressed to Bill Anders. The few scribbled words on the back were still fresh in Luke's memory. "Dear Bill: Sorry I can't help. Things are tight for me too, Jim."

Slowly Luke placed the card on the counter and stamped it "UNCLAIMED."

His voice was fretful as he muttered, "Curiosity cost more than a cat this time." But he was smiling as he turned back to his work.

From the battered radio came the soft strains of "Peace on Earth, Good Will to Men." ❋

Mom's Vacation

Elsie C. Carroll

WHEN UNCLE ANTHONY'S CHECK for two hundred dollars came with his characteristic note, "Have a merry Christmas," the Fishers decided to divide the money evenly among the four of them and each take a much desired Christmas vacation.

Tony, as a matter of course, would go to Glendon where Madge was at school. He had been considerably worried of late over frequent references in Madge's letters to a certain fascinating young football captain by the name of Ken Halliday. While Tony and Madge were not formally betrothed, he had been sure ever since they used to make mud pies in her Aunt Harriet's back yard, that some day they would keep house in reality.

Fifty dollars would take Nell to the district convention of the Business and Professional Women's clubs to be held in Montrose two days after Christmas. She had talked of that convention for weeks.

There were so many places Betty wanted to go that she wavered for several days, finally writing to Kate Donnel (whose cousin Phil she had met last summer who was to be a guest at the Donnel home) that she was pleased to accept her invitation.

When they asked Mom where she was going, she said that for years she had wanted to visit Janet Langton, an old school friend who continued to send her invitations each year. If she didn't go to Janet's she would run over to Aunt Grace's for a few days.

The check arrived on the fifteenth, and there was much excitement in the Fisher household from that time until the twenty-third, the date it happened that Tony and the girls would all leave for their trips. Mom would not go until the day before Christmas.

Tony asked the family to give him the amount they had intended to spend for his presents in cash. He explained that he had his eye on a nifty little diamond down in Kimbark's window that he could get for a thirty dollar deposit, and he was determined to put a stop to those perpetual allusions to that insufferable Ken Halliday in Madge's letters.

Nell gave him five dollars, explaining that she had intended to make him a silk shirt and that the material would have cost her about that much. Betty came through with another five, confessing that she was tempted to cut it in two because she would simply have to have a lot of new things for herself now she was going to Kate's. Mom, sensing the disappointment in Tony's eyes, supplied the other twenty dollars, figuring that if she went to Grace's instead of to Janet's she could make her old coat do until the spring sales.

Nell complained so much about her shabby traveling bag that Mom took back the beautifully bound volume of Keats she had paid six dollars for, for Nell's Christmas present, and bought instead an eighteen dollar bag, reasoning that she could sponge and press her brown crepe and with a new collar make it do a while longer. Nice things meant so much to Nell.

Betty's wants were so many that Mom, who couldn't bear to see the children disappointed, lay awake nearly all of two nights trying to devise ways and means for the new party dress with silver slippers and bag to match that anyone, according to Betty, would simply have to have at a house-party at the Donnel home.

Already Mom had spent more than her budget allowed for Christmas presents, and she had drawn practically all from her own clothing budget. But she still remembered so vividly how she had longed for a new gown that time, more than twenty years ago, when Betty's father had been coming to spend the holidays with her brother Anthony, that she felt as though nothing mattered quite so much as that Betty should have her outfit.

If only Richard could have been spared, these things that meant so much to the children would have been theirs by natural right. It was hard, trying to be father and mother both, but she had made a heroic effort to remain cheerful and courageous under the burden Richard's death had left upon her shoulders, and always there was the satisfying assurance that he was near her, loving her still and trying as best he could to comfort and sustain her.

Near dawn of the second sleepless night, the thought came to Mom that if she could endure the smoky, sagging paper on her room for one more year, Betty could have her things; and she went to sleep happy.

On the morning of the twenty-third Tony came downstairs just as Mom was breaking the eggs for the omelet. She gave a little start as he bounded into the kitchen with his customary, "Say, Mom, where's my _____?" This morning it was one of his military brushes that was missing. He wanted it to put in his bag he was packing. The thing that had startled Mom was the boy's likeness to his father. Every day he grew more like Richard. The sound of his voice, that quick little shrug of his shoulders, the way he had of tousling his hair when he was excited, that very, "Where's this or that?"— all these reminders hurt her; at the same time they thrilled her.

"Have you asked Betty if she borrowed your brush? She was cleaning her coat last night."

"Gosh, I might have thought of her." Tony started back to his packing, but he stopped at the foot of the stairs and after a moment's hesitation came back to the sink where his mother was working.

"Say, Mom, I guess you couldn't lend me a five or a ten until my next pay day could you? Things might come up that a fellow can't count on you know, and it's tough to have to crawfish before a crowd. I want to show that new bunch of Madge's that Ken Halliday's not the only squash in the garden. I may have enough dough; I have all I ought to spend; Manly gave me an extra ten for a present last night; but gosh I'd hate to be embarrassed. Just an extra five or ten would make me feel safe. It's only until my next pay you know. Could you spare it, Mom?"

Mom checked a sigh as she and answered a bit hesitantly, "Why, maybe I could spare that much."

She knew from past experiences that although Tony's intentions were perfectly good and honest in regard to paying her back when he received his next part-time salary, that there would be so many demands upon his check that she would probably say, as she had said so many times before, "Never mind, Son. That will be all right."

"It takes so gosh darned much to sport a girl," Tony apologized, as Mom wiped her hands and started toward her room for the money. "But Madge is worth it, don't you think, Mom?"

"She's a dear little girl, Tony. I have always loved Madge."

As she opened her dresser drawer and took out two of the five dollar bills from her vacation portion, she could hear Tony whistling contentedly as he whirled the egg-beater in the mixing bowl.

After breakfast while Nell was gone to get her credentials from the local president of the B.P.W.C.,

Betty came to the window where Mom was putting the last few stitches in the altered hem of the blue party dress. She had in her hand a tissue wrapped box.

"Isn't it the darlingest dress?" she exclaimed, touching the filmy material that matched her own shining eyes. "I'm just thrilled to death with it! And that bag is the dearest thing. You do have the best taste, Mumsy! I don't see how you could know just *exactly* what would suit me the way you do."

Mom smiled reminiscently. This might be the very dress of her seventeen-year-old dreams.

"Say, Mom," Betty's fingers were toying with the tinsel bow on the parcel she held in her hands. "I'm worried to death that Kate will give me something expensive for Christmas. You know I'd just feel too cheap for words to give her this little boudoir outfit if she gave me something big, you know. I was just wondering, Mom, if maybe you could lend me about ten dollars, so I could get something real nice there in Winchell while I'm waiting for connections. Just so I'd have it, you see, if she *should* give me something expensive."

Betty stood waiting, her eyes caressing the pink rosebuds on the blue girdle.

"You see, Mom," she continued, as her mother deliberated, "after Christmas there won't be so many things, and you can take it out of my school allowance next month or the next when I get caught up. I'd just be embarrassed to death to have Kate showing this dinky little present to her friends—and cousins—if she *had* given me something expensive."

"Why—maybe I can let you have the money," Mother answered slowly. "But I think that gift you made for Kate is lovely."

"So do I. But you can see, Mom, how it might be—can't you? You know her cousin Phil Ashton—

and a lot of other swell people will be there, and they'll all be giving her just wonderful gifts you see.

Nell did not get back until it was almost time for them to start to the station. She was very much excited.

"I met June Frandson coming over here. She had a telegram from her Aunt Laura in Orton telling her to bring one or two of her girl friends with her when she comes to spend the holidays. She has a great big house and is lonesome, June says. June wants me to go. She says she'll come back with me to the convention you see, and that will make another delegate for us. But the main thing is that I'll get to study that library cataloguing system they have in Orton and learn all the things I need to know so I can put the system in here.

"It would only cost twenty dollars more to go with June. Mom, couldn't you lend it to me? I know the library board will increase my wages as soon as I get that new system in operation, and here's my chance."

"Nell," called Betty from the head of the stairs. "Don't you know it's time we're off?"

"Couldn't you, Mom? It's a real chance, isn't it?"

"Go on and get your things while I get you the money," Mother said, and Nell rushed up the stairs for her bag and wraps.

Their mother stood on the porch and waved the three of them goodbye as the whistle of the approaching train sounded from down the gully. At the gate each of the children in turn halted a moment and called back a final goodbye.

"Have a good time, Mom."

"Don't worry about us."

"We'll see you next year."

Mrs. Fisher stood watching them until they were out of sight. Even then she did not move. She stood until the puffing of the train had subsided at the station, and until a shriller whistle and renewed puffings announced that her children were off on their Christmas vacations.

At last she slowly turned back into the house, shivering a little as she closed the door.

How still it was! The clock seemed fairly to shout at her.

She picked up the paper from the floor where Tony had dropped it when he had finished breakfast. She removed Betty's sweater from the living room couch and hung it on the hall tree. She glanced through the kitchen door at the panful of unwashed dishes in the sink.

Somehow the stillness of the house and that queer feeling of being alone seemed to recall all the Christmases she and her family had spent in this home which had never seemed so still before. There had been the first one with just herself and Richard making as merry as two children; the next one with Baby Nell; and others and others with the happiness of childhood expectancy making a glamor over mere commonplaceness; the last one before Richard left them—and the five since that time when she had tried so hard to do the things he would have done—and now this one—and she was alone.

The clock seemed to be shouting that word at her: "Alone! alone!" it kept saying.

Her eyes began to blur, so with her customary resolution she started toward the sink. She had found that work usually sent the blues scampering.

As she passed her bedroom door, however, the sight of her open dresser drawer caught her eye. She went in to close it.

She picked up the one lone ten dollar bill that remained of her brother's gift. Her unshed tears seemed to make it dance mockingly in her hand.

Suddenly a wave of overwhelming bitterness swept over her.

She was tired. She wanted a rest and a change as much as the children did. What did they care for her? It was always give, give, give! Her whole life had been made up of doing for and giving to her children. Did they appreciate it? No! What did it matter to them that they had taken her Christmas money—that she didn't even have enough to go to Aunt Grace's? What did it matter to them that she who loved pretty clothes as much as Betty must go on wearing her shabby coat and frayed dress, for months. Or that she who loved beautiful things about her as much as Nell must go on sleeping in this room with its soiled paper? What did anything matter to them just so they had what they wanted?

Suddenly she felt that motherhood, that life itself, was empty and futile.

She threw herself upon her bed and began to sob. Each sob intensified her feeling of self-pity, and the more she pitied herself the harder she wept. As she recalled all the sacrifices and hardships of her years of motherhood, she wondered how she had endured them. There had been the winter when Betty was three that all the children had had whooping cough. For weeks she had not known a night's rest. There had been Tony's operation with the complications afterwards and the months and months of anxiety and expense—bills that had cramped them for years. The year of the influenza epidemic seemed like a nightmare to her. Then had come Richard's sickness and the paralyzing shock of his death—and new worries and responsibilities.

She had never concerned herself with the financial side of their life while Richard was with them. In his blind consideration he had shielded her from that. It had meant mistakes and scheming and terrifying worries after he had gone.

There had been other agonizing experiences as well. She shuddered as she recalled Nell's infatuation two years ago for that middle-aged man from the East who had pretended to be an artist—and how near it had threatened to ruin her life. Some of Tony's gang escapades made her go cold when she recalled them, and Betty's impetuous love affairs with every Tom, Dick, and Harry of their own and neighboring towns.

Always it had been work and sacrifice and anxiety on her part. And what had she been given in return for it all—nothing but thoughtless selfishness of which today was a typical example. What did she mean to her children anyway but a drudge, a source to be drained for their pleasure. They hadn't even cared enough about her to realize that they had taken, with everything else she had given, her Christmas vacation.

Once Mom had given vent to her feelings, the bitterness against her lot grew more and more intense. She cried until her head and throat ached and her mouth was dry and parched. She thought of the sink full of dishes and the disordered rooms she knew the children had left upstairs; but she made no movement to get up. What did it matter how the house looked? What did anything matter? She wished she could lie right there and die, leaving the dishes and the disorder for the children to find when they came back. Maybe they would appreciate her when she was dead.

Then suddenly she was aware of a presence in the room. She hadn't heard anyone come in, and yet there was someone standing beside her bed. She sat up to see if it were one of her neighbors; but it was neither Bertha Shober nor Angie Hartley. She didn't know the woman and yet she seemed strangely familiar.

As she was looking at her, trying to recall

where they had met, the woman asked quietly, "Are you ready?"

"Ready?" Mom repeated. "Ready for what?"

"Your trip."

"But I'm not going. There isn't enough money. I gave it to the children."

"But I came to take you. Come!"

With a vague feeling that she should have washed the dishes and tidied the house before going away, she followed her visitor.

Almost instantly they were entering a home she had never seen before. Suddenly she gave a little cry.

"Why—there is—Richard in the other room and the ch—No! Why—it's—it's Tony—and Madge!"

"Yes. And those are their children. See how happy they are."

"What a fine man Tony is. How much he is like Richard. I must speak to him and to those lovely children."

"Not now. We must go."

Reluctantly she followed her guide. While she was still wondering who this woman could be, they entered a large white building. On all sides of the long room the walls were lined with books. People were seated at tables reading. In a little alcove off from the main room a group of men and women sat talking.

"Why, there is Nell," exclaimed Mom. "What is she doing here?"

"She is having a meeting with the board of directors of the new library. She is presenting her plan for a rural circulation of books that will bring the best reading to be had to every home in the land."

How fine she looks—how contented. I must tell her—"

Almost in the next breath they were in a lovely home. Beautiful music came to their ears. It was Schubert's Serenade and recalled to Mom the thrill she had felt the time Betty played it the night she was promoted from junior high school. How proud she had been and thankful she had made the necessary sacrifices for Betty to keep on with her music. Through an open door could be seen a dark haired boy at a piano, with another boy standing near with a violin. Beside them was a beautiful woman directing them.

"Betty! It is my Betty! What is she doing here?"

"She belongs here. This is her home. Those are her sons!"

"How wonderful! And I used to be so afraid she was going to throw herself away on that good-for-nothing Pete Granger."

"We must go now." Reluctantly Mom followed the guide out from the loveliness in which she had been reveling. A moment more and—

Mom opened here eyes. For a moment she stared about in bewilderment. Where was she now?

A corner of smoked, sagging paper convinced her she was in her own room. A damp greenback crumpled in her hand made her sit up and rub her eyes. It was only for a second, then she remembered.

She sat on the edge of the bed for a few moments staring at the money in her hand. Finally she addressed the bill with conciliation in her voice.

"I expect you think I'm a great baby, don't you? Even if you are not big enough to take me to Janet Langton's or to Grace's, you're big enough to help me have a good time right here at home. Let's see—I know. You are big enough to help me make a real Christmas for that bunch of motherless Thompsons down the gulch. And I guess I'd better get busy giving you a chance to do your Christmas service. I'll bring those kiddies right here. The house won't seem so lonesome, and I won't have time to worry about how abused I am." Mom got to her feet with a new determination shaping itself in her mind. "It's time right now that I begin to understand that it is instinctive and natural for children to seem selfish and ruthless as they go after the things that mean their own future happiness and success. The world is built that way. Parents should know better than to expect their children to *pay them* for their work and sacrifice. The way that debt is paid is by the children passing on what their parents have done for them to the next generation—to their children. I ought to have had sense enough to see that all the time. I guess Nell and Tony and Betty aren't the monsters I was trying to make out to myself they are; they're spoiled some by my— what is it some writer called it—'smother love'—but mostly they're just natural."

This new philosophy gave Mom something interesting to think over as she went about her work getting ready for the Thompson children's Christmas party. Soon she was her busy, contented self—outwardly, though there still lingered the ghost of a longing for at least a little sign that her children recognized what she was doing for them.

Her recompense came Christmas morning in the form of a night letter, a telegram, and a special delivery. The first was from Nell. It read:

"The Orton librarian will give me three days next week. That twenty dollars means my whole future. You're a treasure, Mom."

Tony's was a ten-word slang masterpiece:

"Sparkler put skids on Halliday. Your twenty bucks saved day."

Betty's was a five-page diary of thrills. It ended:

"And Mumsy, Kate's cousin—listen while I whisper this in your ear—He's the *real prince*

charming I've always dreamed about. How could I ever have looked at Pete Granger. He thinks my blue dress is a dream, and I wish you could have heard him rave over my good taste in the plaque I gave Kate. (Thanks to your ten dollar loan.) Mumsy, you're the darlingest dear in the whole world! Tony and Nell and I were talking about it on the train, and we all made a pre-New Year's resolution that we're going to be worth all you are doing for us. If you don't believe it, just ask Old Lady Future." ❄

A Special Christmas

S. Dilworth Young

ONE CHRISTMAS SEASON when I was about five, I saw in a store window a jigsaw puzzle with a picture of an old fire engine going full speed down the street. The horses pulling it were galloping, smoke from the engine chimney was blowing out behind, and dogs were barking. I passed that store window many times and glued my eyes on that picture. I wanted that puzzle for Christmas more than I wanted a sled or skates or anything else.

When Christmas morning finally came, I found hung on my chair a stocking full of good things. But right off I spotted my puzzle. It was wrapped in bright paper, but I could tell by the shape what it was. I quickly opened the box and was soon lost in the pleasure of putting the puzzle together.

Before long my father came into the room and explained to my younger brother, older sister, and me that the Jensen family down the street had recently come from Denmark. He said the father had no job and no money, and then he suggested that we take our Christmas dinner to them. He also asked each of us to select our most loved toy and give it to a child in the Jensen family.

Father said we would leave at eleven forty-five and were to be ready then with our toys.

Before we left for the Jensens', I spent three happy hours playing with and enjoying my puzzle. I thought about giving something else, but I knew deep down that there was only one gift to give.

At eleven forty-five we all started out. Father carried the turkey on a platter. Mother and my sister Emily followed with potatoes, gravy, dressing, cran-berries, and dessert. And under my arm, carefully rewrapped, was my fire engine puzzle.

When we entered the Jensen home, Father placed the turkey on the small bare table in the corner, and the others followed.

Each one of us in turn then gave his present. Emily gave her beautiful doll to the girl. I stepped forward and looked at the boy about my age. "Here," I said as I pushed the puzzle at him. He took it from me and smiled. Next my brother gave his offering to the smallest child. And then we returned home.

It was strange, but somehow as I walked the block between our house and the Jensens', it seemed as if my feet didn't touch the ground. I felt as though I were floating on clouds of good feeling, for I knew I had made someone else happy.

Even our Christmas dinner of canned beans, bread, butter, and bottled fruit had a special and unforgettable meaning on that special Christmas Day! ❄

The Joy They Shared

Juanita Sadler

CHRISTMAS EVE in the Philippines was a bright, sun-drenched day. The evidence that it was Christmas boomed from the jeepney radios as we made our way along the crowded streets to the barrio where our investigators, the Juguilons, lived.

They were not only our investigators; they were our friends. We were going to share Christmas Eve with them. They didn't have much, but they wanted to share what they did have. We found that the Filipinos were very generous: you could never give them something without them wanting to give you much more. As missionaries in the Philippines we were always receiving from the kindly people we served. The Juguilons were such a family. Their home was modest, but it was filled with love, love they were always willing to give away.

Their home was one of the smallest in the barrio; its one room was clean and tidy. All of the family's belongings were tied in neat little bundles which hugged the walls. When we came to teach the gospel we sat on the floor with the family.

Our meetings with the family were wonderful and productive. Brother and Sister Juguilon worked hard to understand all that we were telling them. They read the Book of Mormon we gave them. They had to read from our Bible because they could not afford to buy their own. They were diligent; they listened and studied and prayed so they could become a part of the Lord's true church.

When we arrived on Christmas Eve, the room was almost filled by two borrowed, king-sized wooden chairs. We were invited to sit while our friends sat at our feet.

Sitting in the middle of the circle of children was a scraggly little Christmas tree which had been delivered anonymously to the Juguilon home that evening. Underneath it was a gift for each of the children. With beaming faces our friends shared their joy with us. The small, green symbol of Christmas was, to this family, the world's most beautiful. It boasted of widely spaced branches draped with candy-filled ornaments and a popcorn garland which hung lazily from its limbs.

Six pairs of children's eyes focused lovingly on the tiny tree. A small hand lifted to touch a branch, as if to confirm its reality. Another softly coaxed a hanging ornament into gentle movement. We all enjoyed watching the children until the Christmas festivity began. This festivity was a quiet, yet joyful one.

With grateful reverence, Sister Juguilon placed a white box in front of her. Each of us waited in anticipation as she knelt and carefully began to unfold the sides of the box. Even the Christmas tree could not hold the children's attention now. Inside were swirls of snow-white frosting that blanketed the enticing Christmas feast—it was a cake, a beautiful, store-bought cake. For the Juguilon family this was a most unusual and rare treat.

All eyes were turned upon us as we received the first pieces. No one else ate, just us. We were their guests; they waited to eat until they were certain that we desired no more. Their joy came in giving.

Together we celebrated the birth of our Savior. We left filled with the joy they shared. However, their story continued in our absence on Christmas Day.

Mealtime on that Christmas Day was attended

by Brother Juguilon, but not partaken of. Finally Sister Juguilon asked her husband why he would not eat that day. He quietly answered that this day was, for him, a day of fasting, and a day of thanksgiving. Knowing that it was Christmas she agreed that it was a day for thanksgiving. "But fasting?" she asked.

Quietly he answered. "This year was different. This year each of our children received a gift for Christmas." This, to him, was cause to return thanks to God. ✳

Christmas, Second Time Around

Steve D. Hanson

As WE PLANNED our ward's youth calendar for the year 1978–79, we wanted to emphasize service. So in that spirit it was decided that this year our Young Men-Young Women Christmas party would be replaced by a service project—that of providing Christmas for some needy family. A youth committee was organized and an LDS family outside of our ward selected.

A needier family could not have been chosen. The mother, who was divorced, was a recent convert to the Church and lived with her three children and her own aged mother in a small, one-bedroom house that was scarcely bigger than most people's living room. There was no furniture to speak of, and the family's sole source of entertainment and relaxation came from a small black-and-white television set. The woman worked nights to provide a meager sustenance for her family, with no surplus to purchase either a Christmas tree or presents for her children and their grandmother.

Our youth committee set to work planning this very special Christmas activity. They wanted to go all out—a Christmas tree, Christmas dinner, and presents for each member of the family. Each Young Men and Young Women class was assigned a specific area: the Explorers would purchase the Christmas tree and buy presents for the young boy; the Laurels would provide the food, including a turkey for Christmas dinner; the Venturers would buy presents for the mother; and on it went until each class had an assignment. A super Christmas for a deserving family was assured.

To make this an even more meaningful experience for our young people, we asked them to earn the money they would be contributing. Mother and dad's money would not be acceptable on this project. It was gratifying to see how positively the majority of the youth responded to the challenge.

The gifts, beautifully wrapped, the tree, and the food were all taken by the youth committee to this special family several days before Christmas. The young people were touched by the sincere, emotional appreciation expressed by this mother on behalf of her family. And we adult leaders felt a real lesson had been learned. But this experience was to have a greater impact on the youth than we knew.

Christmas morning, as I was ushering my family into the car to go over to my brother's for our traditional Christmas dinner, our Young Men president pulled up in front of the house.

"Did you hear what happened to the family we provided the Christmas for?" he asked.

Before I could reply, he went on: "While the mother was working Christmas Eve, someone broke into the house and stole all their Christmas presents—even took their old TV set."

It seemed impossible! After all that work, how could this happen? My heart ached for that family as I thought how disappointing this must have been for them. Then I noticed that his car was filled with presents. Smiling, he continued:

"That's the second batch of presents going over to the family this morning. When we found out about the robbery, we called a few kids in the ward, and before we knew it, they had contacted others—and all these kids and their families donated their own Christmas presents to our 'Christmas family.'"

Sitting on top of the pile of presents was a small TV set. He saw me looking at it, and as he began to get into his car, he said, "One of our fourteen-year-old men donated his own TV set."

He drove off, and I got into our car with my family.

"What was that all about, dad?" one of my children asked.

After a pause, and feeling very grateful for my association with these young people, I replied, "I've just learned a lesson in charity. Let me tell you a story about the true spirit of Christmas." ✳

The Gift of the Magi

O. Henry

ONE DOLLAR AND EIGHTY-SEVEN CENTS. That was all. And sixty cents of it was in pennies. Pennies saved one and two at a time by bulldozing the grocer and the vegetable man and the butcher until one's cheeks burned with the silent imputation of parsimony that such close dealing implied. Three times Della counted it. One dollar and eighty-seven cents. And the next day would be Christmas.

There was clearly nothing to do but flop down on the shabby little couch and howl. So Della did it. Which instigates the moral reflection that life is made up of sobs, sniffles, and smiles, with sniffles predominating.

While the mistress of the home is gradually subsiding from the first stage to the second, take a look at the home. A furnished flat at $8 per week. It did not exactly beggar description, but it certainly had that word on the lookout for the mendicancy squad.

In the vestibule below was a letter-box into which no letter would go, and an electric button from which no mortal finger could coax a ring. Also appertaining thereunto was a card bearing the name "Mr. James Dillingham Young."

The "Dillingham" had been flung to the breeze during a former period of prosperity when its possessor was being paid $30 per week. Now, then the income was shrunk to $20, the letters of "Dillingham" looked blurred, as though they were thinking seriously of contracting to a modest and unassuming D. But whenever Mr. James Dillingham Young came home and reached his flat above he was

called "Jim" and greatly hugged by Mrs. James Dillingham Young, already introduced to you as Della. Which is all very good.

Della finished her cry and attended to her cheeks with the powder rag. She stood by the window and looked out dully at a grey cat walking a grey fence in a grey backyard. Tomorrow would be Christmas Day, and she had only $1.87 with which to buy Jim a present. She had been saving every penny she could for months, with this result. Twenty dollars a week doesn't go far. Expenses had been greater than she had calculated. They always are. Only $1.87 to buy a present for Jim. Her Jim. Many a happy hour she had spent planning for something nice for him. Something fine and rare and sterling—something just a little bit near to being worthy of the honour of being owned by Jim.

There was a pier-glass between the windows of the room. Perhaps you have seen a pier-glass in an $8 flat. A very thin and very agile person may, by observing his reflection in a rapid sequence of longitudinal strips, obtain a fairly accurate conception of his looks. Della, being slender, had mastered the art.

Suddenly she whirled from the window and stood before the glass. Her eyes were shining brilliantly, but her face had lost its colour within twenty seconds. Rapidly she pulled down her hair and let it fall to its full length.

Now, there were two possessions of the James Dillingham Youngs in which they both took a mighty pride. One was Jim's gold watch that had been his father's and grandfather's. The other was Della's hair. Had the Queen of Sheba lived in the flat across the airshaft, Della would have let her hair hang out the window some day to dry just to depreciate Her Majesty's jewels and gifts. Had King Solomon been the janitor, with all his treasures piled up in the basement, Jim would have pulled out his watch every time he passed, just to see him pluck at his beard from envy.

So now Della's beautiful hair fell about her, rippling and shining like a cascade of brown waters. It reached below her knee and made itself almost a garment for her. And then she did it up again nervously and quickly. Once she faltered for a minute and stood still while a tear or two splashed on the worn red carpet.

On went her old brown jacket; on went her old brown hat. With a whirl of skirts and with the brilliant sparkle still in her eyes, she fluttered out the door and down the stairs to the street.

Where she stopped the sign read: "Mme. Sofronie. Hair Goods of All Kinds." One flight up Della ran, and collected herself, panting. Madame, large, too white, chilly, hardly looked the "Sofronie."

"Will you buy my hair?" asked Della.

"I buy hair," said Madame. "Take yer hat off and let's have a sight at the looks of it."

Down rippled the brown cascade.

"Twenty dollars," said Madame, lifting the mass with a practiced hand.

"Give it to me quick," said Della.

Oh, and the next two hours tripped by on rosy wings. Forget the hashed metaphor. She was ransacking the stores for Jim's present.

She found it at last. It surely had been made for Jim and no one else. There was no other like it in any of the stores, and she had turned all of them inside out. It was a platinum fob chain simple and chaste in design, properly proclaiming its value by substance alone and not by meretricious ornamentation—as all good things should do. It was even worthy of The Watch. As soon as she saw it she knew that it must be Jim's. It was like him. Quietness and value—the description applied to both. Twenty-one

dollars they took from her for it, and she hurried home with the 87 cents. With that chain on his watch Jim might be properly anxious about the time in any company. Grand as the watch was, he sometimes looked at it on the sly on account of the old leather strap that he used in place of a chain.

When Della reached home her intoxication gave way a little to prudence and reason. She got out her curling irons and lighted the gas and went to work repairing the ravages made by generosity added to love. Which is always a tremendous task, dear friends—a mammoth task.

Within forty minutes her head was covered with tiny close-lying curls that made her look wonderfully like a truant schoolboy. She looked at her reflection in the mirror long, carefully, and critically.

"If Jim doesn't kill me," she said to herself, "before he takes a second look at me, he'll say I look like a Coney Island chorus girl. But what could I do—oh! what could I do with a dollar and eighty-seven cents?"

At seven o'clock the coffee was made and the frying-pan was on the back of the stove hot and ready to cook the chops.

Jim was never late. Della doubled the fob chain in her hand and sat on the corner of the table near the door that he always entered. Then she heard his step on the stair away down on the first flight, and she turned white for just a moment. She had a habit of saying little silent prayers about the simplest everyday things, and now she whispered: "Please God, make him think I am still pretty."

The door opened and Jim stepped in and closed it. He looked thin and very serious. Poor fellow, he was only twenty-two—and to be burdened with a family! He needed a new overcoat and he was without gloves.

Jim stopped inside the door, as immovable as a

setter at the scent of quail. His eyes were fixed upon Della, and there was an expression in them that she could not read, and it terrified her. It was not anger, nor surprise, nor disapproval, nor horror, nor any of the sentiments that she had been prepared for. He simply stared at her fixedly with that peculiar expression on his face.

Della wriggled off the table and went for him.

"Jim, darling," she cried, "don't look at me that way. I had my hair cut off and sold it because I couldn't have lived through Christmas without giving you a present. It'll grow out again—you won't mind,will you? I just had to do it. My hair grows awfully fast. Say 'Merry Christmas!' Jim, and let's be happy. You don't know what a nice—what a beautiful, nice gift I've got for you."

"You've cut off your hair?" asked Jim, laboriously, as if he had not arrived at that patent fact yet even after the hardest mental labour.

"Cut it off and sold it," said Della. "Don't you like me just as well, anyhow? I'm me without my hair, ain't I?"

Jim looked about the room curiously.

"You say your hair is gone?" he said, with an air almost of idiocy.

"You needn't look for it," said Della. "It's sold, I tell you—sold and gone, too. It's Christmas Eve, boy. Be good to me, for it went for you. Maybe the hairs of my head were numbered," she went on with a sudden serious sweetness, "but nobody could ever count my love for you. Shall I put the chops on, Jim?"

Out of his trance Jim seemed quickly to wake. He enfolded his Della. For ten seconds let us regard with discreet scrutiny some inconsequential object in the other direction. Eight dollars a week or a million a year—what is the difference? A mathematician or a wit would give you the wrong answer. The magi brought valuable gifts, but that was not among them. This dark assertion will be illuminated later on.

Jim drew a package from his overcoat pocket and threw it upon the table.

"Don't make a mistake, Dell," he said, "about me. I don't think there's anything in the way of a haircut or a shave or a shampoo that could make me like my girl any less. But if you'll unwrap that package you may see why you had me going a while at first."

White fingers and nimble tore at the string and paper. And then an ecstatic scream of joy; and then, alas! a quick feminine change to hysterical tears and wails, necessitating the immediate employment of all the comforting powers of the lord of the flat.

For there lay The Combs—the set of combs, side and back, that Della had worshiped for long in a Broadway window. Beautiful combs, pure tortoise shell, with jeweled rims—just the shade to wear in the beautiful vanished hair. They were expensive combs, she knew, and her heart had simply craved and yearned over them without the least hope of possession. And now, they were hers, but the tresses that should have adorned the coveted adornments were gone.

But she hugged them to her bosom, and at length she was able to look up with dim eyes and a smile and say: "My hair grows so fast, Jim!"

And then Della leaped up like a little singed cat and cried, "Oh, oh!"

Jim had not yet seen his beautiful present. She held it out to him eagerly upon her open palm. The dull precious metal seemed to flash with a reflection of her bright and ardent spirit.

"Isn't it a dandy, Jim? I hunted all over town to find it. You'll have to look at the time a hundred times a day now. Give me your watch. I want to see how it looks on it."

Instead of obeying, Jim tumbled down on the couch and put his hands under the back of his head and smiled.

"Dell," said he, "let's put our Christmas presents away and keep 'em a while. They're too nice to use just at present. I sold the watch to get the money to buy your combs. And now suppose you put the chops on."

The magi, as you know, were wise men—wonderfully wise men who brought gifts to the Babe in the manger. They invented the art of giving Christmas presents. Being wise, their gifts were no doubt wise ones, possibly bearing the privilege of exchange in case of duplication. And here I have lamely related to you the uneventful chronicle of two foolish children in a flat who most unwisely sacrificed for each other the greatest treasures of their house. But in a last word to the wise of these days let it be said that of all who give gifts these two were the wisest. Of all who give and receive gifts, such as they are wisest. Everywhere they are wisest. They are the magi. ✳

CHAPTER EIGHT

Worship & Joy

Christmas Legends

Denis A. McCarthy

Christmas morn, the legends say,
Even the cattle kneel to pray,
Even the beasts of wood and field
Homage to Christ the Saviour yield.
Horse and cow and woolly sheep
Wake themselves from their heavy sleep,
Bending heads and knees to Him
Who came to earth in a stable dim.
Far away in the forest dark
Creatures timidly wake and hark,
Feathered bird and furry beast
Turn their eyes to the mystic East.
Loud at the dawning, chanticleer
Sounds his note, the rest of the year,
But Christmas Eve the whole night long
Honouring Christ he sings his song.
Christmas morn, the legends say,
Even the cattle kneel to pray,
Even the wildest beast afar
Knows the light of the Saviour's star.

All Are Vocal with His Name

Phillips Brooks

The silent skies are full of speech
    For who hath ears to hear;
The winds are whispering each to each,
The moon is calling to the beach,
And stars their sacred wisdom teach
    Of faith and love and fear.

But once the sky the silence broke
    And song o'erflowed the earth;
The midnight air with glory shook,
And angels mortal language spoke,
When God our human nature took
    In Christ, the Savior's birth.

And Christmas once is Christmas still;
    The gates through which he came,
And forests' wild and murmuring rill,
And fruitful field and breezy hill,
And all that else the wide world fill
    Are vocal with his name.

Shall we not listen while they sing
    This latest Christmas morn;
And music hear in everything,
And faithful lives in tribute bring
To the great song which greets the King,
    Who comes when Christ is born?

The Joys of Christmas

Ezra Taft Benson

I LOVE CHRISTMASTIME! And I find great joy in remembering Christmases past. Perhaps it is the emotion of the season that makes this time of year seem particularly poignant and meaningful. And especially memorable.

Many events of almost nine decades of Christmases, dating back to my childhood on the Whitney, Idaho farm where I was reared, are still clear in my mind and among some of the most enjoyable memories I have.

As a boy I loved going to the canyon to cut our Christmas tree, and I always tried to get one that reached to the ceiling.

Though we received only a few gifts, our stockings were filled with fruit, nuts and candy, and Santa always left something.

Like all children, we suffered terrible anticipation at Christmastime—until, that is, we happened onto the Santa Claus costume in the bottom of an old trunk. Suddenly the secret was out. So that was why Father was always out doing chores when Santa came on Christmas morning. The following December it occurred to me that if Father had been playing Santa all those years, he and Mother must be hiding our gifts somewhere on the farm. I couldn't stifle my inquisitive mind, and in no time I'd led my younger brothers on a search that turned up several gifts buried in the wheat in the granary.

I'm told that I was a bit of a tease during my youth. I do remember coming in on my sister Margaret while she was balancing on a stepladder to decorate the tree. Sensing an opportunity to tease

her, I feigned danger by giving the ladder a little shake. Margaret, who was not amused, ordered me out of the room and then tossed in my direction a dustpan that caught me on the lip. I still have a scar to remember that little prank by.

One of my favorite winter—and especially holiday—activities was taking out the big two-horse bobsleigh with bells on the horses. In those days, "Jingle Bells" was not only a song, it was a thrilling experience. There's nothing quite like riding through country lanes with the sleighbox filled with straw and a group of friends singing Christmas carols. In more recent decades my wife, Flora, and I have made many happy Christmas trips to visit family in Calgary, Alberta, Canada. The highlight of each visit is a ride in a horse-drawn cutter or bobsleigh. It's exhilarating to get hold of the lines of a good team drawing a bobsleigh or two-seat cutter and ride out into the Canadian open.

In Whitney on Christmas Day our family visited our grandparents, and we almost always traveled to their homes by bobsleigh. These were such happy occasions. Our grandparents were very musical and always provided entertainment of various kinds. There were recitations, skits, original poems, music, and dancing. Grandma Dunkley, a convert to the Church from Scotland, would dance the Highland Fling for us, and we loved that.

As with these recollections of childhood Christmases, warm memories fill my mind of the traditions Flora and I have enjoyed with our own family.

Our home was always decorated with holly and mistletoe and a beautiful tree. Flora and the girls baked delicious cakes and cookies—enough, it seemed at times, to feed a small army. One of our cherished Christmas possessions was a sturdy set of sleigh bells that had jingled each winter from Flora's father's cutter. When our children were young, we rang the bells outside their bedroom windows to signal that Santa Claus was coming. In later years we hung the bells on the front door, and the jingle of the bells when the door opened brought back a parade of pleasant memories.

On Christmas Eve we would read together Luke's recounting of the Savior's birth, and sometimes Dickens' *A Christmas Carol* as well, and sing carols and hymns. Then, following the custom my parents observed when I was a boy, our children lined up a row of chairs, one for each child, and hung their stockings over the backs. Once the children were safely tucked in bed, Flora and I filled the stockings with candy, nuts, and fruit, and laid their gifts from Santa on and under their chairs.

I still remember those Christmas Eve nights when our youngest daughter crawled into bed with us in the middle of the night and tried to convince us it was time to get up. (I'll admit that at least once we gave in and let her take a peek at the tree and its treasures before coaxing her back to sleep.) But by 5:30 or so when we awoke to excited whispers and the sound of bare feet on the floor, we knew there was no keeping any of the children in bed any longer. Soon we would shepherd them into the kitchen for a glass of milk and a roll. Then they would line up, youngest to oldest, and march into the living room. We loved their expressions of delight at their gifts.

Ours were really just ordinary Christmases—if peace and joy and togetherness can ever be called ordinary.

Flora always went to great lengths to make our home a wonderful place during the holidays. Her efforts were well described, I thought, by Sister Marjorie Hinckley after she and her husband, President Gordon B. Hinckley, visited us during the 1964 holiday season in Frankfurt, Germany, where I was serving as mission president. Sister Hinckley wrote Flora: "After going through the Orient and across Asia, where there was so little evidence of Christmas, and then to suddenly find ourselves in your beautiful home with the Christmas tree and the lights, and music and the red-ribboned staircase, and . . . most of all, the sweet spirit and peace of a Latter-day Saint home, was something that will always remain with us."

Flora was so anxious to spread the holiday spirit that, on a visit to Salt Lake City, she returned to Germany carrying a suitcase full of frozen turkeys and cranberry sauce so that she could have a traditional holiday dinner for the missionaries. Truly, Flora has always radiated the spirit of Christmas.

In addition to warm memories about our family Christmas traditions and activities, my thoughts about Christmases past include a number of significant events that have taken place during the holiday season.

I'll never forget one Christmas, the Christmas of 1923. I returned home on Christmas Eve to my parents and ten brothers and sisters after serving two-and-a-half years as a missionary in England. Earlier that day, while traveling through Salt Lake City, Church Patriarch Hyrum G. Smith conferred upon me a blessing in which he counseled me to be devoted to the Lord, and then promised that, in turn, the Lord would make me equal to my labors.

Then it was on to Whitney for a joyful reunion with my family. That evening Mother and Father took me into their confidence, letting me help them fill the stockings after going to the granary and elsewhere to gather presents they had hidden. This took a good part of the night. We spent the rest visiting, with me reporting on my mission and Mother and

Father telling me what had happened while I was away. It was a choice evening.

My brothers and sisters arose early Christmas morning. After having a glass of milk and a piece of bread in the kitchen, they hurried into the living room to see what goodies Santa had brought them. It was a happy morning. I couldn't hold back the tears as I felt the joy and love in our home. It seemed that we were hugging and kissing each other throughout the entire day. It was a wonderful reunion. Being away from home had only intensified my deep feelings for my noble parents and my dear brothers and sisters.

Such experiences are sweet and binding, and tend to remind us of the things that are really important. It was just over two decades later that the holiday season again figured prominently in my departure to and subsequent return from Europe. December of 1945 and 1946 will forever live in my memory. Just three days before Christmas in 1945 President George Albert Smith convened a special meeting of the First Presidency and the Council of the Twelve. With World War II finally over, President Smith announced it was time for the Church to reestablish contact with the Saints in Europe and distribute much-needed welfare supplies. In that meeting I was called to go to Europe as president of the European Mission to handle those assignments.

The call came as a complete surprise. Because of conditions in Europe, it was not possible to take my family with me. I had no idea what I would find when I got there, how I would arrange for travel throughout a continent that had been devastated by war, or how long the First Presidency would require me to stay. I was told that I should prepare to leave as soon as possible. This unexpected development affected greatly our preparations for Christmas and

created an unusually sentimental and loving atmosphere in our home. Flora and I realized we would be separated for a period of time, and our feelings were tender at the prospect.

How grateful I was for her support, and for the knowledge we shared that this was the Lord's will for our family at this time. As the Christmas season drew to a close, I recorded in my journal: "The next year will no doubt be spent, in large measure and possibly in its entirety, abroad. It will mean some sacrifice of material comforts. I will miss my wife and sweet children and the association of the brethren and the visits to the stakes. I go, however, with no fear whatsoever, knowing that this is the Lord's work and that He will sustain me. I am grateful for the opportunity and deeply grateful that my wife, who is always most loyal, feels the same way. God bless them while I am away."

The following ten-and-a-half months were among the most challenging and yet rewarding I or my family had known. The separation tested our faith and endurance and physical energy to the limit, but helped us grow as never before.

I'll never forget the thrill of stepping off the airplane in Salt Lake City the following December, in 1946, and finding Flora waiting for me. That Christmas was among the most poignant I have ever spent. Perhaps there had been no year in my life when my soul had been so stirred or when I had faced such challenges. I had been forced to rely completely upon the Lord, and my gratitude for His goodness and watchcare filled my soul and brought me easily to tears. I had come to love deeply the Saints in Europe, and leaving them had been a bittersweet experience.

But being home again brought such deep and fulfilling joy. While the separation had been difficult for us all, we had grown even closer to one another.

And as we realized how many blessings the Lord had given us throughout the year, tears flowed freely. After the children had opened their presents on Christmas Day, I wrote in my journal, "The children were most happy and appreciative. There has not been an unkind word all day. In fact, we seldom hear arguments in our home. But this day has been especially blessed. It has been such a joy to sit with my angel wife and review the past, devoid of regrets, anticipate the future joyously, and count our many blessings gratefully. I shall never forget this glorious Christmas."

Of course, we have many other wonderful Christmas-related memories. Our family lived for eight years during the 1950s in Washington, D.C., while I served in the Cabinet of President Dwight D. Eisenhower. That unusual setting provided unusual experiences.

So much of what we did in Washington turned out to be a family affair. Certainly that was the case each Christmas as my wife and children pitched in to participate in the staff party held in the Department of Agriculture, where I served as Secretary. I delivered a spiritual message, our daughters usually sang, and Flora made many of the arrangements and often recited a favorite poem. It seemed that whenever she recited Edgar A. Guest's "It Takes a Heap O Livin' in a House to Make It Home" the press made particular mention of it in their reports.

Almost every year we held a Christmas fireside in our home. Sometimes over a hundred young people crowded inside and sat on the floor, steps, or anywhere they could find a place. My wife and our daughters prepared wonderful refreshments for everyone, and I was honored to talk about the Savior and His divine mission. It was some of these simple occasions that brought greatest satisfaction.

Just four days before Christmas in 1954, our family had a special opportunity. President Eisenhower knew our custom of having a family hour one night during the week, and he expressed a wish to see how it was done. President and Mrs. Eisenhower and our family gathered that evening in the home of Bill and Allie Marriott for an evening of holiday fun and entertainment. Our sons performed comic skits and other readings, the girls sang, Flora recited a reading, and I did my part by leading the whole group in singing "John Brown's Baby Had a Cold upon Its Chest." It was plain, old-fashioned, homespun entertainment. The President and his party participated and seemed to enjoy it all. For our part, we were delighted with the opportunity to share an evening with the President.

Another holiday season, some two decades later, brought an event of much different proportions. In 1973, Sister Benson and I enjoyed a very restful, contemplative Christmas Day with relatives and friends from near and far away remembering us with cards, phone calls, and gifts. The holiday had been a peaceful one.

The following evening I received a phone call from President Spencer W. Kimball bringing me word of the sudden passing of President Harold B. Lee. President Lee and I had been boyhood friends dating back to our Idaho youth. We had even attended the same high school. I wrote in my journal, "It seemed impossible. He has been so well and I have felt that he would be the last President of the Church I would know in mortal life. Some relief came as I knelt in prayer alone in my study, but I found it impossible to sleep until well after midnight."

Beyond my shock and deep sorrow for the loss of a dear friend was the realization that his death would have direct impact upon the course of my life. I wrote, "This places a grueling load upon President Spencer W. Kimball and a load upon me, which I know I cannot carry without the rich blessings of the Lord. I know this is the Lord's work and I know that He knows the direction this work should take. The work will not fail. . . . [But] it is almost overwhelming as I contemplate the possibility of my being called to serve as the President of the Twelve. With all my heart I will seek the inspiration of heaven and the blessings of our Heavenly Father." Perhaps one of the most telling aspects of that holiday season was the poignant realization of how completely I must rely upon the Lord to help me do His will.

All of these Christmas memories, from the joyful to the sublime, from the excitement of opening packages to the serenity of tender reunions with loved ones, cause me to reflect on what Christmas really means and what impact the observance of the Savior's birth can have in our lives.

The real purpose of Christmas is to worship Him whose birth is commemorated during this season. How might we do that? By giving. Certainly there are genuine feelings of love and friendship wrapped up in the beautiful packages we exchange with those dear to us. But I'm concerned about another kind of giving. Considering all that the Savior has given and continues to give us, is there something we might give Him in return this Christmastime?

Christ's great gift to us was His life and sacrifice. Should that not then be our small gift to Him—our lives and sacrifices, not only now but in the future?

Men and women who turn their lives over to God will discover that He can make a lot more out of their lives than they can. He will deepen their joys, expand their vision, quicken their minds, strengthen their muscles, lift their spirits, multiply their blessings, increase their opportunities, comfort their souls, raise up friends, and pour out peace. Whoever will lose his life in the service of God will find eternal life.

Sacrifice is truly the crowning test of the gospel. We are tried and tested in this mortal probation to see if we will, in fact, turn our lives over to God. If we will put first in our lives the kingdom of God. (See Matthew 6:33.) To gain eternal life, we must be willing, if called upon, to sacrifice all things for the gospel and for the Lord.

Just as when one loses his life in the service of God, he really finds the abundant life, so also when one sacrifices all to God, then God in return shares all He has with him.

Try as we may, we simply cannot put the Lord in our debt. For every time we try to do His will, He simply pours out more blessings upon us. Sometimes the blessings may seem to be a little slow in coming—perhaps this tests our faith—but come they will, and abundantly. It has been said, "Cast your bread upon the waters, and after a while it shall come back to you toasted and buttered."

Each week we make a solemn covenant to be like Him, to always remember Him in everything, and to keep all of His commandments. In return, He promises to give us His Spirit.

We once knew well our Elder Brother and our Father in Heaven. We rejoiced at the prospects of earth life, which would make it possible for us to have a fulness of joy. We could hardly wait to demonstrate to our Father and our Brother, the Lord, how much we loved them and how we would be obedient to them in spite of the earthly opposition of the evil one.

Now we are here. Our memories are veiled. We are showing God and ourselves what we can do.

Nothing is going to startle us more when we pass through the veil to the other side than to realize how well we know our Father and how familiar His face is to us.

God loves us. He is watching us. He wants us to succeed. We will know someday that He has not left one thing undone for the eternal welfare of each of us. If we only knew it, heavenly hosts are pulling for us—friends in heaven that we cannot now remember who yearn for our victory. This is our day to show what we can do—what life and sacrifice we can daily, hourly, instantly make for God. If we give our all, we will get His all from the greatest of all.

Perhaps one of the greatest blessings of this wonderful Christmas season we celebrate is that it increases our sensitivity to things spiritual, to things of God. It causes us to contemplate our relationship with our Father and the degree of devotion we have for God.

It prompts us to be more tolerant and giving, more conscious of others, more generous and genuine, more filled with hope and charity and love— all Christlike attributes. No wonder the spirit of Christmas touches the hearts of people the world over. Because for at least a time, increased attention and devotion are turned toward our Lord and Savior, Jesus Christ.

This Christmas, as we reflect upon the wonderful memories of the past, let us resolve to give a most meaningful gift to the Lord. Let us give Him our lives, our sacrifices. Those who do so will discover that He truly can make a lot more out of their lives than they can. Whoever will lose his life in the service of God will find eternal life.

Without Christ there would be no Christmas, and without Christ there can be no fulness of joy. It is my testimony that the Babe of Bethlehem, Jesus the Christ, is the one perfect Guide, the one perfect Example. Only by emulating Him and adhering to His eternal truth can we realize peace on earth and good will toward all. There is no other way. He is the Way, the Truth, and the Light.

Not many years hence Christ will come again. He will come in power and might as King of kings and Lord of lords. And ultimately every knee will bow and every tongue confess that Jesus is the Christ.

But I testify *now* that Jesus is the Christ and that *He lives.* ❄

There's a Song in the Air

Josiah G. Holland

There's a song in the air!
  There's a star in the sky!
There's a Mother's deep prayer,
  And a Baby's low cry!
And the star rains its fire while the beautiful sing,
For the manger of Bethlehem cradles a King.

There's a tumult of joy
  O'er the wonderful birth,
For the Virgin's sweet Boy
  Is the Lord of the earth.
Ay! the star rains its fire while the beautiful sing,
For the manger of Bethlehem cradles a King!

In the light of that star
  Lie the ages impearled;
And that song from afar
  Has swept over the world.
Every heart is aflame, and the beautiful sing
In the homes of the nations that Jesus is King!

We rejoice in the light,
  And we echo the song
That comes down through the night
  From the heavenly throng.
Ay! we shout to the lovely evangel they bring,
And we greet in His cradle our Saviour and King!

In the Bleak Mid-Winter

Christina Georgina Rossetti

In the bleak mid-winter
  Frosty wind made moan,
Earth stood hard as iron,
  Water like a stone;
Snow had fallen, snow on snow,
  Snow on snow,
In the bleak mid-winter
  Long ago.

Our God, Heaven cannot hold him
  Nor earth sustain;
Heaven and earth shall flee away
  When he comes to reign:
In the bleak mid-winter
  A stable-place sufficed
The Lord God Almighty
  Jesus Christ. . . .

What can I give him,
  Poor as I am?
If I were a shepherd
  I would bring a lamb,
If I were a Wise Man
  I would do my part,—
Yet what I can I give him,
  Give my heart.

Friend to Friend

S. Dilworth Young

At Christmas time a home is sweeter far;
The cattle quiet in the barn,
The children nestled safe from harm,
The kettle on the fire-crane sings.
There's time for friend to call on friend
To wish the joy that Christmas brings.
Because the Christ was born on earth
There'll be no end to heavenly things.

Brightest and Best of the Sons of the Morning

A. C. Smyth

Brightest and best of the sons of the morning
Dawn on our darkness and lend us thine aid;
Star of the east, the horizon adorning,
Guide where our infant Redeemer is laid.

Cold on His cradle the dew drops are shining,
Low lies His head with the beasts of the stall;
Angels adore Him in slumber reclining.
Maker, and Monarch, and Savior of all.

Say, shall we yield Him, in costly devotion,
Odors of Edom, and offerings divine?
Gems of the mountain and pearls of the ocean,
Myrrh from the forest or gold from the mine?

Vainly we offer each ample oblation;
Vainly with gifts would His favor secure,
Richer by far is the heart's adoration;
Dearer to God are the prayers of the poor.

Uncle Kees' Christmas Rebellion

Pierre Van Paassen

Dᴜʀɪɴɢ ᴍʏ ʙᴏʏʜᴏᴏᴅ in Holland, Christmas was by no means a joyous celebration. Our spiritual leaders clung to the interpretation handed down by that gloomiest of men, John Calvin. Even the singing of carols was considered tantamount to blasphemy, and festive candles and gaily decorated fir trees were deemed pagan abominations.

But one old-fashioned Calvinist Christmas lingers in my mind with delight. It was bitter cold in the great church that morning, for the vast nave and transept were unheated. Worshipers pulled the collars of their overcoats up around their chins and sat with their hands in their pockets. Women wrapped their shawls tightly around their shoulders. When the congregation sang, their breath steamed up on faint white clouds toward the golden chandeliers. The preacher that day was a certain Dr. van Hoorn, who was a representative of the ultra-orthodox faction.

The organist had sent word to my Uncle Kees that he was too ill to fulfill his duties. Kees, happy at the opportunity to play the great organ, now sat in the loft peering down through the curtains on the congregation of about 2,000 souls. He had taken me with him into the organ loft.

The organ, a towering structure, reached upward a full 125 feet. It was renowned throughout the land and indeed throughout all Europe. Its wind was provided by a man treading over a huge pedal consisting of twelve parallel beams.

In his sermon Dr. van Hoorn struck a pessimistic note. Christmas, he said, signified the descent of God into the tomb of human flesh, "that charnel house of corruption and dead bones." He dwelt sadistically on our human depravity, our utter worthlessness, tainted as we were from birth with original sin. The dominie groaned and members of the congregation bowed their heads in awful awareness of their guilt.

As the sermon progressed Kees grew more and more restless. He scratched his head and tugged at his mustache and goatee. He could scarcely sit still.

"Man, man," he muttered, shaking his head, "are these the good tidings, is that the glad message?" And turning to me he whispered fiercely, "That man smothers the hope of the world in the dustbin of theology!"

We sang a doleful psalm by way of interlude, and the sermon, which had already lasted an hour and forty minutes, moved toward its climax. It ended in so deep a note of despair that across the years I still feel a recurrence of the anguish I then experienced. It was more than likely, the minister threw out by way of a parting shot, that of his entire congregation not a single soul would enter the kingdom of heaven. Many were called, but few were chosen.

Kees shook with indignation as the minister concluded. For a moment I feared that he could walk off in a huff and not play the Bach postlude, or any postlude at all. Down below, Dr. van Hoorn could be seen lifting his hands for the benediction. Kees suddenly threw off his jacket, kicked off his shoes, and pulled out all the stops on the organ. When the minister had finished there followed a moment of intense silence.

Kees waited an instant longer while the air poured into the instrument. His face was set and grim and he looked extremely pale. Then throwing his head back and opening his mouth as if he were going to shout, he brought his fingers down on the keyboard. *Hallelujah! Hallelujah! Hallelujah!*

The organ roared the tremendous finale of Handel's chorus of *Messiah*. And again with an abrupt crashing effect, as if a million voices burst into song, *Hallelujah! Hallelujah! Hallelujah!* The music swelled and rolled with the boom of thunder against the vaulted dome, returning again and again with the blast of praise like breakers bursting on the seashore.

Kees beckoned to me. "More air!" he called out.

I ran into the bellows chamber, where Leendert Bols was stamping down the beams like a madman, transported by the music, waving his arms in the air.

"More air!" I shouted. "He wants more air!"

"Hallelujah!" Leendert shouted back. "Hallelujah!" He grabbed me by the arm and together we fairly broke into a trot on the pedal beams.

Then the anthem came to a close. But Kees was not finished yet. Now the organ sang out sweetly the Dutch people's most beloved evangelical song: "The Name above Every Name, the Name of Jesus," sung to the tune very similar to "Home, Sweet Home."

We sang it with all our heart, Leendert and I, as did the congregation on its way out.

It was a tornado of melody that Kees had unleashed. Mountains leaped with joy. The hills and the seas clapped their hands in gladness. Heaven and earth, the voices of men and angels, seemed joined in a hymn of praise to a God who did not doom and damn, but who so loved, loved, loved the world. ❊

The Oxen

Thomas Hardy

Christmas Eve, and twelve of the clock.
"Now they are all on their knees,"
An elder said as we sat in a flock
By the embers in hearthside ease.

We pictured the meek mild creatures where
They dwelt in their strawy pen,
Nor did it occur to one of us there
To doubt they were kneeling then.

So fair a fancy few would weave
In these years! Yet, I feel,
If someone said on Christmas Eve,
"Come; see the oxen kneel,

"In the lonely barton by yonder coomb
Our childhood used to know,"
I should go with him in the gloom,
Hoping it might be so.

A Christmas Carol

Christina Georgina Rossetti

Before the paling of the stars,
　Before the winter morn,
Before the earliest cock-crow
　Jesus Christ was born:
　Born in a stable,
　Cradled in a manger,
In the world His hands had made
　Born a stranger. . . .

Jesus on His mother's breast
　In the stable cold,
Spotless Lamb of God was He,
　Shepherd of the fold:
Let us kneel with Mary maid,
　With Joseph bent and hoary,
With saint and angel, ox and ass,
　To hail the King of Glory.

The Joy of Christmas

Charles Dickens

CHRISTMAS TIME! That man must be a misanthrope indeed in whose breast something like a jovial feeling is not roused, in whose mind some pleasant associations are not awakened by the recurrence of Christmas. There are people who will tell you that Christmas is not to them what it used to be; that each succeeding Christmas has found some cherished hope or happy prospect of the year before dimmed or passed away; that the present only serves to remind them of reduced circumstances and straightened incomes—of the feasts they once bestowed on hollow friends and of the cold looks that meet them now in adversity and misfortune. Never heed such dismal reminiscences. There are few men who have lived long enough in the world who cannot call up such thoughts any day in the year. Then do not select the merriest of the 365 for your doleful recollections. ✵

A Warm and Gracious Christmas

Marion D. Hanks

ONE DAY NEAR CHRISTMAS SEASON, I drove by a large grocery store in Salt Lake City. It was late afternoon, and the streets were crowded. This accentuated the pain and anxiety obviously being suffered by a young woman who stood at the rear of a car that was half backed out of some diagonal parking places opening to the street. The automobile protruded into traffic so that I and others had to carefully find our way around her. There was a long line of vehicles behind me so I could not stop, but I was concerned enough about the circumstance to travel around the block and come up on the inside lane and stop behind her. She had as yet no evident help, and she looked increasingly apprehensive.

I could detect the odor of a flooded engine and found that there were not only groceries in the car but also a youngster shouting lustily in the back seat, and another slightly older child on the front seat. The engine had refused to start, as engines sometimes perversely do, and she was now in tears. No one had stopped to help.

Since the front of the car was on a slight incline, I backed it down carefully so it stood just a little in front of my automobile. I then gave her specific instructions on how to start the car as I pushed it (the car was an old-fashioned one like mine in which you can still choose your gear), turned on the ignition for her, had her depress the clutch while I watched, carefully established some signals about

pushing her, and went back to my automobile to prayerfully and hopefully begin the process. Thankfully, she let the clutch out at the agreed-upon signal, the engine caught, and she roared away in the now-functioning car. She did not turn at the first corner as I anticipated but went on up the street, frantically waving her gratitude. With some concern for the safety and welfare of other drivers and pedestrians, I turned another direction. I did not know her and to my knowledge have not seen her again.

The pleasant thing that I remember is that I went home that night joyful and at ease with this challenging world. I had enjoyed the blessing of offering a little help to someone who needed it. What made me shake my head a bit ruefully, and caused me to smile as I arrived home and greeted my wife and children cheerfully, was the thought of others who passed us by without stopping or without any apparent interest in helping. Before they could see what we were doing, or perhaps not caring what we were doing, a number of the drivers had honked their horns angrily, and some had even leaned out the window to emit growling and nasty noises, or to offer a rude gesture, because their progress had been impeded for a split second. I wondered what their families had been subjected to when they got home.

"Christmas is for loving; Christmas is for giving; Christmas is for helping," in the spirit of him who showed us the way and gave us the plan for happy life here and eternal life in the world to come.

The Love of Christmas

I love the alchemy of this special, wonderful, holy-day season. I love its lights, its sounds, and its scents. I love the tenderness it evokes, the gratitude and generosity, the sensitivity to thanks and to giving, the acts of kindness and of love, the effect on family. I love what it does to release friendliness and goodwill between one person and another, kept by most of us under pretty rigid control the rest of the year. There are occasions, of course, when those carefully reserved feelings come forth naturally and spontaneously, as for instance, when we're caught under an awning in a downpour, or waiting behind a snowplow, or joined together in distress or action in the face of some calamity or personal difficulty. But of all these occasions, Christmas seems to be chief among those that bring out from good folks, and maybe some of us less good, those repressed emotions of brotherliness and kindliness.

Spirit and Memories

I love the spirit and memories of Christmas. It was at Christmas long ago that a tiny girl nestled snugly in my arms in the middle of the night and sighed with relief. She had been upchucking, perhaps from a slight overdose of excitement and anticipation, mixed with the season's largess of goodies. "Daddy," she said, "for a while I was afraid I was going to lose the Christmas spirit."

And I love to remember the little hand on my knee as we rode through soft flakes of snow to our grandmother's on Christmas morning. We had been singing with the carolers on the radio when she asked, "What does it mean to adore him?"

I worked at an answer, but every attempt engendered more questions and further efforts to explain until finally, compassionately, she laid that tiny hand on my knee and said, "I guess to adore him just means to love him."

Theme and Variations

Consider three themes, or one theme and two variations, in expressing our love for the season. The theme is centered in a few words in a very familiar song. These are the words. Have you *heard* them as well as *sung* them?

> *Joy to the world, the Lord is come;*
> *Let earth receive her King!*
> *Let ev'ry heart prepare him room,*
> *And Saints and angels sing.*
>
> (*HYMNS*, NO. 201.)

More than seven hundred years before he came, Isaiah sang a sweet psalm of his coming:

> *The people that walked in darkness have seen a great light: they that dwell in the land of the shadow of death, upon them hath the light shined. . . . For unto us a child is born, unto us a son is given: and the government shall be upon his shoulder: and his name shall be called Wonderful, Counsellor, The mighty God, The everlasting Father, The Prince of Peace.*
>
> (ISAIAH 9:2, 6.)

Christ Is Born

His advent, of course, had been long anticipated. In God's plan there was need and place for a sacrifice, an atoning sacrifice for sin. And so he came in due season, not as man anticipated but as God directed. There wasn't any pomp; there were no blaring trumpets, no parade or ceremony, no army, no array of great ones ushering in the King. There were a crowded inn, a manger, a mother and a baby, some shepherds and some wise men, unconscious of their different stations. There were angels and a message for those who had ears to hear.

> *They were all looking for a king*
> *To set them free and lift them high;*
> *Thou camest, a little baby thing*
> *To make a woman cry.*
>
> (ADAPTED FROM GEORGE MACDONALD.)

He grew, served, taught, "learned he obedience by the things which he suffered," and did, as he had been sent to do, the will of his Father. (See Hebrews 5:8.)

He Is Crucified

When the appointed time came, he was accused, mocked, arrayed in a purple robe. They plaited a crown of thorns and put it about his head. They smote him with a reed and took him to be crucified. He was lifted up on the cross by man that he might, as he said, "draw all men unto me, that as I have been lifted up by men even so should men be lifted up by the Father, to stand before me, to be judged of their works, whether they be good or whether they be evil." (3 Nephi 27:14.)

On the cross he comforted those who suffered with him, he invoked the forgiveness of his Father for those who took his life, and in anguish he cried out to the God whose face for the moment may have been turned away from the awful scene—who knows, perhaps to wipe a tear. "Truly this was the Son of God," said the centurion. (Matthew 27:54.) He rose, as we know, at the appointed time from the tomb in which he had been tenderly laid—the first that should rise. Resurrected, he companied for many days with his apostles and others, ascended to heaven as they watched him, visited his people in the American hemisphere and taught them, appeared to Paul and to Stephen, and, in the last dispensation, with his Father, revealed himself to a boy prophet. As he promised, he will come again. For all of that I give thanks. I bear testimony that it is true. He will come again.

A Thanksgiving Time

My first variation on the theme is Thanksgiving. Christmas, and every other important holiday, it occurs to me, is a *thanksgiving time:* to parents, to the founders of our country and the fathers of our free society, to those who have offered their lives to keep it free, to our loved ones departed, and at Christmas (always and every day, of course, but especially at Christmas) to God our Father and his holy Son, Jesus Christ. The past year has been full of perplexing problems; the possibilities ahead are certainly sobering in prospect. Yet the Christmas season brings to our hearts the spirit of thanks and of giving.

Wholesome, Hallowed, Gracious

With Christ and gratitude and giving in our minds, then let me share the third part, or the second variation. It comes from another source, from another time. From *Hamlet* we read:

> *Some say that ever 'gainst that season comes*
> *Wherein our Saviour's birth is celebrated,*
> *This bird of dawning singeth all night long;*
> *And then, they say, no spirit dare stir abroad,*
> *The nights are wholesome, then no planets*
> *   strike,*
> *No fairy takes, nor witch hath power to charm,*
> *So hallowed and so gracious is that time.*
> (Hamlet, I.i.158–64.)

Wholesome, hallowed, gracious—what wonderful words. I love them. They represent to me all that Christmas and the season may mean. Think of them for a moment.

How to make the season *wholesome?* Why, by glancing healthfully inward for a moment. By seeking to bring ourselves more nearly to that measure of wholeness, of integrity, of unity with loftiest desires, of congruence with richest spiritual feeling, of harmony with that person I would fondly like to be.

Many years ago a great man who taught at Brigham Young University and was editor of the *Improvement Era* gave us a vision of the importance of that harmony. When I graduated from high school, I wanted to attend Brigham Young University, with his name and face and strengths in mind. I really had in mind Harrison R. Merrill and BYU, in that order. If you know it well, rejoice with me; if not, be introduced to one of his greatest poems. He called it "Christmas Eve on the Desert":

Tonight, not one alone am I, but three—
The Lad I was, the Man I am, and he
Who looks adown the coming future years
And wonders at my sloth. His hopes and fears
Should goad me to the manly game
Of adding to the honor of my name.
I'm Fate to him—that chap that's I, grown old.
No matter how much stocks and land and gold
I save for him, he can't buy back a single day
On which I built a pattern for his way.

I, in turn, am product of that Boy
Who rarely thought of After Selves. His joy
Was in the present. He might have saved me
*   woe*
Had he but thought. The ways that I must go
Are his. He marked them all for me
And I must follow—and so must he—
My Future Self—Unless I save him!

*   Save?—Somehow that word,*
Deep down, a precious thought has stirred
Savior?—Yes, I'm savior to that "Me."
That thoughtful After Person whom I see!—
The thought is staggering! I sit and gaze
At my two Other Selves, joint keepers of my
*   days!*

Master of Christmas, You dared to bleed and
*   die*
That others might find life. How much more I
Should willingly give up my present days
To lofty deeds; seek out the ways
To build a splendid life. I should not fail
To set my feet upon the star-bound trail
For him—that After Self. You said that he
Who'd lose his life should find it, and I know
You found a larger life, still live and grow.
Your doctrine was, so I've been told, serve man.
I wonder if I'm doing all I can
To serve? Will serving help that Older Me
To be the man he'd fondly like to be?

*   Last night I passed a shack*
Where hunger lurked. I must go back
And take a lamb. Is that the message of the Star
Whose rays, please God, can shine this far?

Tonight, not one alone am I, but three—
The Lad I was, the Man I am, and he
Who is my Future Self—nay, more:
I am His savior—that thought makes me four!
Master of Christmas, that Star of Thine shines
*   clear—*
Bless Thou the four of me—out here!

(In Dusk on the Desert [Provo, Ut.: Utah Academy of Sciences, Arts, and Letters, 1938], pp. 6–7.)

Wholesome, hallowed, gracious. The angelic message was, "Peace on earth, goodwill to men." We do not despair of peace; yet we know something of history and something of the scriptures and something of present complexities, and we know that no one of us nor all of us together can govern the world of men and their decisions. There *is* something we can do about peace in our lives and peace between us and our families and our neighbors—

something. But we cannot control an insatiable world and the decisions of many men. But goodwill to men, what of that? Many of you are already experts in that adventure, but perhaps others have yet to learn that goodwill, like love, is more than language.

Do you know the words of Edna St. Vincent Millay?

Love is not all; it is not meat nor drink,
Nor slumber nor a roof against the rain;
Nor yet a floating spar to men that sink.

(IN *INTERNATIONAL THESAURUS OF QUOTATIONS*
[NEW YORK: HARPER AND ROW, 1970].)

Loving—and Giving

God so loved that he gave. Christ so loved that he gave. What of us? I remember the impressive words of Bonhoeffer, who said of Jesus that he was a *man for others;* and the words of Luther, who in his great speech on good works talked of Mary, who, having heard the *announcement*, went about her life preparing, not retired from the active scene because she had such knowledge but involved in giving and growing and preparing.

For *graciousness*, how do you like the marvelous, simple story of the little boy who saw the bright, new automobile and said to its owner, walking about it on Christmas Eve:

"Is this your car, Mister?"
Paul nodded. "My brother gave it to me for Christmas."
The boy looked astounded. "You mean your brother gave it to you and it didn't cost you nothing? Gosh, I wish . . . "
He hesitated, and Paul knew what he was going to wish. He was going to wish that he had a brother like that. But what the lad said jarred

Paul all the way down to his heels. "I wish," the boy went on, "that I could be a brother like that."

Paul looked at the boy in astonishment, then impulsively he said, "Would you like a ride in my automobile?"

"Oh, yes, I'd love that!"

After a short ride, the urchin turned, and with his eyes aglow said, "Mister, would you mind driving in front of my house?"

Paul smiled a little. He thought he knew what the lad wanted. He wanted to show his neighbors that he could ride home in a big automobile. But Paul was wrong again.

"Will you stop right where those two steps are?" the boy asked.

He ran up the steps. Then, in a little while Paul heard him coming back, but he was not coming fast. He was carrying his little polio-crippled brother. He sat him down on the bottom step, then sort of squeezed up against him, and pointed to the car.

"There she is, Buddy, just like I told you upstairs. His brother give it to him for Christmas, and it didn't cost him a cent, and some day I'm gonna give you one just like it; then you can see for yourself all the pretty things in the Christmas windows that I've been trying to tell you about."

Paul got out and lifted the little lad to the front seat of his car. The shining-eyed older brother climbed in beside him and the three of them began a memorable holiday ride.

That Christmas Eve Paul learned what Jesus meant when He said: It is more blessed to give . . .

(C. ROY ANGELL, *BASKETS OF SILVER*
[NASHVILLE: BROADMAN PRESS, 1955], P. 96.)

Entertaining Angels Unawares

And I would like to tell you another thing I love very much about Christmas. I love to remember what the scripture says, and perhaps you are well aware of it: "Let brotherly love continue. Be not forgetful to entertain strangers: for thereby some have entertained angels unawares." (Hebrews 13:1–2.)

There was a night when we had the blessing of having in our home a stranger, sorely afflicted. After all these years I have some hesitance to mention the incident, lest anyone know or connect her with it. She was from far away. She was away from her family. She had been a patient in an institution, had been released to go to her parents in another state also far away, but, after a period of little progression and apparently with little hope in sight, had been relieved of her restraints there. Having affiliation with the Church, she found her way to Salt Lake City, to Temple Square, which she thought to be the heart of the Church, and sat across the desk from me, hopeless, her eyes blank, talking about her children, talking intermittently also about the voices she heard. She was ill. There was no appropriate place to send her, so we took her home.

Our holiday season was impaired a bit, as I now impair the memory by telling of it. That didn't matter much. We missed a few parties; we felt someone should be with her, because she was obviously seriously ill. We didn't know the professional therapy; we knew how to pray to God, and she joined us with our then very little family. The days went by. Christmas arrived. That morning she arose with us. She sat in a chair and watched as the presents were given and received. For every one received around the circle, she also received a gift. I fancied I saw the curtain over her mind going up a little. I watched a tear come trickling, and then, without premedita-

tion and certainly without instruction, a little girl climbed onto her knee, put her arms around her neck, and said, "Sarah, I love you." And the tears gushed and the curtain rose and the woman and mother came through. She wept, then talked freely about her little ones, about her husband at home, about her problems.

A little later I made a telephone call. I spoke to a man who was agonizing through the day. He didn't want her away, but her illness had made it too difficult for the children to have her home. I talked with him of her present circumstance. He said, "We'd like to get her home." We found a way. There was an airplane and gracious people who made arrangements, and a lady who got nervously aboard and soon thereafter arrived home to the arms of her own loved ones. She wrote us over the years to thank us for a simple gift of caring at a special time.

Oh, I love the words, *wholesome, hallowed, gracious.* Among the many wonderful things I am warmed to remember is a brief statement from a great book written long ago. It is about a slave who lived in Christ's time and watched him on a certain special Sunday in the midst of a multitude.

> *Suddenly, for no reason at all that Demetrius could observe, there was a wave of excitement. It swept down over the sluggish swollen stream of zealots like a sharp breeze. Men all about him were breaking loose from their families, tossing their packs into the arms of their overburdened children, and racing forward toward some urgent attraction. Far up ahead the shouts were increasing in volume, spontaneously organizing into a concerted reiterated cry; a single, magic word that drove the multitude into a frenzy. . . .*

· 170 ·

"Do you know what is going on?" said Demetrius. [He was talking to another Greek slave.]

"They're yelling something about a king. That's all I can make of it." . . .

"You think they've got somebody up front who wants to be their king? Is that it?"

"Looks like it. They keep howling another word that I don't know—Messiah. The man's name, maybe." . . .

Standing on tiptoe for an instant in the swaying crowd, Demetrius caught a fleeting glimpse of the obvious center of interest, a brown-haired, bareheaded, well-favored Jew. A tight little circle had been left open for the slow advance of the shaggy white donkey on which he rode. . . . There had been no effort to bedeck the pretender with any royal regalia. He was clad in a simple brown mantle with no decorations of any kind, and the handful of men—his intimate friends, no doubt—who tried to shield him from the pressure of the throng, wore the commonest sort of country garb. . . .

It was quite clear now to Demetrius that the incident was accidental. . . . Whoever had started this wild pandemonium, it was apparent that it lacked the hero's approbation.

The face of the enigmatic Jew seemed weighted with an almost insupportable burden of anxiety. The eyes, narrowed as if in resigned acceptance of some inevitable catastrophe, stared straight ahead toward Jerusalem. . . .

Gradually the brooding eyes moved over the crowd until they came to rest on the strained, bewildered face of Demetrius. Perhaps, he wondered, the man's gaze halted there because he alone—in all this welter of hysteria—refrained from shouting. His silence

singled him out. The eyes calmly appraised Demetrius. They neither widened nor smiled; but, in some indefinable manner, they held Demetrius in a grip so firm it was almost a physical compulsion. The message they communicated was something other than sympathy, something more vital than friendly concern; a sort of stabilizing power that swept away all such negations as slavery, poverty, or any other afflicting circumstance. Demetrius was suffused with the glow of this curious kinship. Blind with sudden tears, he elbowed through the throng and reached the roadside. The uncouth Athenian, bursting with curiosity, inopportunely accosted him.

"See him—close up?" he asked.

Demetrius nodded. . . .

"Crazy?" persisted the Athenian.

"No."

"King?"

"No," muttered Demetrius, soberly—"not a king."

"What is he, then?" demanded the Athenian.

"I don't know," mumbled Demetrius, in a puzzled voice, "but—he is something more important than a king."

(LLOYD C. DOUGLAS, *THE ROBE* [BOSTON: HOUGHTON MIFFLIN CO., 1975], PP. 71–74.)

All who love him should enjoy a happy Christmas.

Joy to the world, the Lord is come;
Let earth receive her King!
Let ev'ry heart prepare him room,
And Saints and angels sing.

(*HYMNS*, NO. 201.)

Through God's blessing, we may have a wholesome, hallowed, gracious, special time. Jesus Christ is the Son of God. He lives, he governs, he inspires and directs, he will come again. God help us to worship him in all the wonderful ways there are this wholesome, hallowed, gracious season. ✳

My Gift

Eugene Field

Nor crown, nor robe, nor spice I bring
As offering unto Christ, my King.
Yet have I brought a gift the Child
May not despise, however small;
For here I lay my heart today,
And it is full of love to all.
Take Thou the poor but loyal thing,
My only tribute, Christ, my King!

The Earth Has Grown Old

Phillips Brooks

The Earth has grown old with its burden of care
    But at Christmas it always is young;
The heart of the jewel burns lustrous and fair,
And its soul, full of music, breaks forth on the air
    When the song of the angels is sung.

It is coming, Old Earth, it is coming tonight!
    On the snowflakes which cover thy sod
The feet of the Christ-child fall gentle and white
And the voice of the Christ-child tells out with
        delight
That mankind are the children of God.

Thou Whose Birth

A. C. Swinburne

Thou whose birth on earth
Angels sang to men,
While the stars made mirth,
Saviour, at thy birth
This day born again.

As this night was bright
With thy cradle-ray,
Very light of light,
Turn the wild world's night
To thy perfect day.

Bid our peace increase
Thou that madest morn,
Bid oppressions cease;
Bid the night be peace
Bid the day be born.

The Christmas Peace

F. H. Sweet

Sing holly now and mistletoe,
    And all resentment from your heart;
Sing the accessories which show,
    And in this joyous day have part;
Sing help to him who fain would wrong,
    And good to him who would deride;
Lift up your heart in joy and song
    And sing the Christ back to your side.

Ever 'gainst That Season

William Shakespeare

Some say that ever 'gainst that season comes
Wherein our Saviour's birth is celebrated,
The bird of dawning singeth all night long;
And then, they say, no spirit can walk abroad;
The nights are wholesome; then no planets strike,
No fairy takes, nor witch hath power to charm,
So hallow'd and so gracious is the time.

Holiday on the Bus

Tracine Hales Parkinson

THE YEAR I WAS NINETEEN I was invited to spend
the Christmas holidays working tours for the Hilton
Hotel in Los Angeles with my cousin. We would be
able to visit all the main attractions in the L.A. area
and get paid for it too. I called for plane reservations far too late, and the only transportation still
available to get me to L.A. was the bus. I would
leave Logan, Utah, on Christmas Day at noon. My
sister dropped me off at the Greyhound stop and I
waited for the bus to come. When it arrived I
remember feeling quite festive and happy because of
the day and the prospect of the adventure. As I
boarded the bus and looked about I saw only a few
riders. They all seemed preoccupied with something
outside the window. No one looked up and nobody
smiled.

I took my seat. Several stops later we picked up
two little girls. They were totally laden with recently
opened gifts, and I was delighted when they sat
down across the aisle from me. I was feeling a little
lonely that it was Christmas Day and there hadn't
been anyone to talk with. I was to learn that their
names were Trisha and Debbie and they were on
their way for their annual Christmas visit with their
grandparents in St. George, Utah. At the time they
were in the third and fifth grades. One by one they
pulled out their treasures and showed me each gift
they had received.

The day progressed and soon the early evening
was upon us. We stopped in a little town for a supper break. As I was exiting the bus I noticed that
the only street lamp that was lit was the one above

the stop. The night was very dark, and there seemed to be a million stars in the sky. The small crowd of people from the bus ate quietly, and I felt let down that it was Christmas and everyone seemed void of the spirit. As I looked back I wonder now if all those folks were just sad to be apart from the people they love on Christmas Day.

I had been doing my student teaching with some fourth graders that quarter at Utah State University, and I had taught them the song "Silent Night" in sign language. As we sat and waited to be beckoned back to the bus, I asked the girls if they would like to learn it. They enthusiastically said yes and I began teaching it to them. The signs to the first verse are very simple, and they had it all learned before we boarded the bus.

After we settled back into our seats, Trisha said to her sister, "Debbie, we should practice our song so we can show it to Grandma and Grandpa when we get to St. George." Debbie agreed and they spread their coats onto the floor of the bus and settled down facing each other to practice. I glanced up to see that several of the other passengers on the bus were visiting quietly and some of the overhead lights were on. People seemed to have relaxed a little. Now that Christmas was coming to a close, maybe they were feeling better about having spent it on a bus.

The girls started singing, "Silent Night, Holy Night, All is calm, All is bright . . . " After finishing the song they began again. I glanced up. Having been so totally involved with coaching them, I hadn't noticed that all the lights in the bus had been turned off. The only light that remained on was the one above the girls' seats. As my eyes adjusted to the darkness I could see the eyes of the other passengers upon us. They were looking over their seats and down the aisle of the bus. The only

sound was the hum of the bus and voices of the two girls clear and strong. The light above their seats reflected off their hands and emphasized the signs. The quiet that came over the bus was not the empty one I had been feeling throughout that day. It was one of peace and joy.

The true spirit of Christmas came through to all of us who had the opportunity to be riding that bus that night. It was not connected with gift giving or even with family. I was overwhelmed at the realization that I had been searching for the spirit of Christmas at the mall, at the theater, under the tree, and in dozens of busy holiday functions, and all the time it could be found in the humblest of situations. Here it was with all its power and mystery on a bus full of strangers headed for St. George, Utah.

I wondered if Trisha and Debbie were aware of the wonderful gift they gave to those of us riding the bus that night. Each Christmas since then they write to me and talk of the first Christmas when we met. Perhaps they too felt the warmth that permeated through the crowd that night. I find myself searching each year for that very same feeling that rushed through my soul that night and filled me with a love for other people and for the Savior. ✳

CHAPTER NINE

Home & Family

The Old Blue Bike

Joel R. Bryan

It was a Christmas when my three older sisters were 12, 10, and 7 just after my father, a young engineer, had accepted a transfer from Schenectady, New York, to Los Angeles, California. On Christmas Eve, my mother made preparations for the traditional Christmas dinner the next afternoon. My sisters took turns trying to keep me and my three-year-old brother from playing baseball with the shining Christmas tree ornaments. Mother found time to tend our new baby sister.

Amid the bustle of the Christmas Eve excitement, my father was preoccupied. His thoughts kept returning to the used bicycle hidden carefully in the garage rafters. Next to it lay the boxes holding two brand-new, shining black, matching three-speed bikes which he had purchased for my two older sisters. The budget strains of Christmas had prevented Dad from buying a third black three-speed for Leanne. Instead, he set about restoring the old single-speed, fat-tired bike the older two no longer rode. Scouring pads and elbow grease made the rusty spokes shine. The inner tubes were patched, and a new coat of paint erased the battle scars of collisions and neglect. A replacement set of hand-grips made the handlebars look almost new.

My father realized Leanne would probably recognize the old war horse, but he was sure she could be happy just having her own bike. And in a year or two, when she outgrew this one, he would be able to buy her a brand-new one. Leanne had already received a big share of hand-me-downs from her older sisters. Many of her clothes, toys, and books had been previously used.

This Christmas Eve, as my mother tucked all of us in bed, Dad commenced his marathon toy and bicycle assembly projects. When he finished the new, black bicycles, he placed them side by side near the Christmas tree. He then carefully rolled out and placed the rejuvenated old bike next to the new ones. The stark contrast of the old half-sized, blue, thick-tubed bike against the sleek, black beauties made the revamped two-wheeler suddenly look small and old-fashioned. Dad reconsidered. Had he made a mistake in trying to redo the old bike for Leanne? Would she feel slighted? Leanne was too young to understand the economics of family finances, but she would be quick to spot this injustice perpetrated by Santa Claus: new bikes for her sisters, the old war horse for her.

A gradual panic swept over Dad as he realized he'd slipped up. Better run to the store and buy a matching bike, quick! But on Christmas Eve? It was already 11:30 P.M., and the stores would probably be closed. A few hurried telephone calls confirmed the worst. Everything was closed.

My grandmother, who was visiting for the holidays, tried to comfort Dad. "Don't worry, Ray. She'll love the bike. You've made it look just like new."

Dad was not comforted. He kept imagining the disappointed look on Leanne's face as she recognized the old hand-me-down. Though it was very late when he finished the last stocking and exhausted as he was from his assembly projects, Dad did not sleep well that night.

Early Christmas morning, we were poised in our annual positions in the hall—all in a row, youngest to the oldest. It was still dark outside, but we were already hopping with that special excitement of children on Christmas morning. Dad was in the living room making the movie camera and lights ready to record our grand entrance. Finally he yelled, "Okay, come on in," and we blazed through the doorway like a shot. In a matter of minutes, the beautiful array of packages and ornaments was transformed into a mountain of strewn boxes, wrappings, and ribbons. My older sisters spotted their black beauties, gave them the once over with due praise and admiration, and moved on to the Christmas tree to locate more presents. Amid the chaos and clutter, Leanne stood firmly next to the old blue bike. She was touching every part and talking aloud, "Look, it has new grips and new paint! A *brand-new* seat! Just look at those pedals, and it's my very own, my very own bike."

Leanne didn't seem to notice there were other presents for her under the tree. She stayed near the bike and repeated the same speech several times, though no one was listening, no one, that is, except my father. He stood silently on the other side of the room, oblivious to the rest of the children, the movie camera held low at his side, listening to Leanne. Tears of joy streamed down his face as he witnessed this perfect acceptance of his imperfect gift.

It has been a long time since the black beauties were worn out and discarded. Even the old war horse was sent to the glue factory years ago. But the image of my father's tear-streaked face on Christmas Day reminds me still of the warmth of a Christmas gift well given and well received. ❉

Christmas Reminiscences

Joseph F. Smith, from a letter to a son

My BELOVED SON:—Your most refreshing and welcome letter of Christmas eve, came to my hand yesterday, and I read and re-read it with pleasure, mingled with grateful tears.

Your letter also took me back not only to the boyhood days of my own boys and girls, but also to those of my very own. From 1846 to 1848 and 9 I knew no Christmas, and no holiday; and, indeed, if we had a Christmas or a New Year celebration at all before 1846—or until after I was married, for the life of me, at this moment, I cannot remember it. I was teamster, herd-boy, plow-boy, irrigator, harvester, with scythe or cradle, wood-hauler, thresher, winnower (by the half-bushel measure or fanning-mill, later), general roustabout, and a fatherless, motherless, and almost friendless missionary, and withal, always penniless.

I say *almost friendless.* I had one true friend, a widow, frail, aged—but oh! so true! She was my never-to-be-forgotten and ever-to-be-loved and remembered Aunt Mercy R. Thompson. She, like my own precious mother, never forgot me while they lived. But in their time, they had very little, and it was a continuous struggle just to live!

Then when, after these dreary experiences, my own precious cherubs began to come along, we were existing on $3 per day for each working day employed, and that in tithing products at high prices. Well, I cannot tell you how we managed to live at all, but we did! God must have helped us, for

I did not *steal* nor defraud my neighbor. I did not owe any man, woman, or child one cent, except it was my gracious Aunt Mercy who, as often as she could, slipped a favor in my way. I owed no man through all those days, and I *had* to work—I could not be idle.

Now again to the Christmas holidays: There [was] . . . not a dollar in cash, with which to buy one thing for Christmas. I could draw a few pounds of flour, or meat, a little molasses, or something of that kind, ahead, at the general Tithing Office and pay up at the end of the month with tithing scrip, received in payment of my labor which more than often began at 6 A.M. and ended at 11 P.M., at $3 per day in tithing pay, which was not cash.

I saw many reveling in luxuries, with means to lavish on their every *want,* which were far more than their needs—riding in buggies, on prancing horses, enjoying their leisure, while *I—we all!* were on foot and of necessity tugging away with all our mights to keep soul and body together. Under these spiritless conditions, one day just before Christmas, I left the old home with feelings I cannot describe. I wanted to do something for my chicks. I wanted something to please them, and to mark the Christmas day from all other days—but not a cent to do it with! I walked up and down Main Street, looking into the shop windows—into Amussen's jewelry store, into every store—everywhere—and then slunk out of sight of humanity and sat down and wept like a child, until my poured-out grief relieved my aching heart; and after awhile returned home, as empty as when I left, and played with my children, grateful and happy . . . for them. . . .

After these trials, my pathway became more smooth. I began to pick up; by hard work, rigid economy, self-denial, and the love of God, I prospered. Little openings were presented, and I improved them. . . . Oh! let God be praised. I bless you, my son, and all of you. May the Lord God bless my sons. ✳

A Family Affair

Lucy Parr

It was the day before the day before the day before—well, anyway, there were only five days until Christmas. Stevie had demanded the latest count-down before he would begin dressing for breakfast. Only five days! And that simply was not enough time for all that remained to be done.

Ellen Reid, constantly on the verge of jumping to her feet, forced herself to remain seated, out-wardly calm. "Mealtime must be calm and pleas-ant." How often she had reminded the children of that fact. "It takes no longer to finish a meal at the table than on the wing."

Oh, how many things she needed to be doing this very minute, things far more important than eating. But if she got up, the children would believe that that excused them, and what voluminous little storehouses their memories were for the least infrac-tion.

"Mom! That's mustard!" Mike yelped, bring-ing Ellen from the depths of her reverie.

And so it was —spread thickly over her break-fast toast.

"How in the world—?" she cried.

"You put the jar on the table yourself," Denna giggled. "Didn't she, Daddy? We've all been waiting to see how soon you'd catch on. But Mike spoiled the fun."

"Well, I should hope so. Your own mother!"

Denna grew serious. "Is my own mother going to remember about finishing my costume for the school program tonight?"

"Oh, no!" Ellen groaned. "It's a good thing

you reminded me. I've more than a jillion other things to do today."

"Put that on the top of the pile, huh, Mom? I simply have to look good." Such a vain, lovely crea-ture she was becoming at ten. "You know, Trudi Dale's mother is buying her costume, and I have to stand right next to Trudi all evening. So be sure it's good, huh?"

Attempting to keep impatience from her voice, wondering how they would find time even to attend the program, Ellen promised, "I'll try. I'll try, and try, and try—"

"Hey, Ma! Your needle's stuck," Mike teased.

At 13, Mike was slightly impertinent, though actually a good boy, not a troublemaker as were many other boys his age.

As Jim pushed his chair back from the table, Ellen glanced up quickly. "Dear, check as closely as you can, discreetly, how many from the office will be dropping in for the open house Christmas after-noon. I need some idea how many to plan for."

"Better count on the whole outfit," Jim laughed. "The fame of your buffets has spread far and wide."

"Oh, and I must remember those strange little crackers that Mr. Bennett always expects." Ellen popped from her chair now, as if suddenly released when Jim's rising had disturbed the family circle.

Reaching for dishes to place in the sink even as she rose, Ellen turned back to Mike. "Come on, tiger. Better get that food inside. The school bus arrives in ten minutes. And as the ads say—'it's best to brush after every meal.'"

"But I have to take time to chew," he protested.

"Then chew!" Ellen snapped, catching Jim's good-bye kiss somewhere in the region of her right ear.

"Try to take it a little easy, honey," Jim urged.

"Uh-huh!" she grimaced. "It's Christmas time, remember?"

"How could I ever forget, around here. The original wall-to-wall Christmas." He smiled warmly and repeated, "But do take it easy, Ellie. Christmas will come, even if you don't have the last perfect bow on every package."

"Oh, that reminds me," Ellen said. "That's one thing I must get today. I'll have to rewrap the packages for Les and Arda—they clash so. I should have done them at the same time."

Turning to the sink once more, she barely caught the wink exchanged by Jim and Mike as Jim departed. Great conspirators, those two were. But they both enjoyed the fruits of her "fuzzing and fruming," as five-year-old Stevie called the rush and excitement.

"There's the bus, half a minute early," Ellen called, but Mike was gone.

She caught sight of him pounding down the walk and up the steps into the snapping jaws of the yellow monster that, after the briefest of pauses, went on around the corner. Any day now Mike was going to misjudge Hank Leeds' reaction time on that bus door, and there would be two Mike Reids, snapped neatly down the center—and most school mornings one Mike Reid was almost more than she could contend with.

Ellen let her breath out in a whoosh of relief at this one more safe deliverance and turned back to the dishes. She rushed through the most essential of the morning chores, deciding to leave Denna's costume until afternoon. It would be best to get her trip to town finished early.

What a gem Jim was, she thought, to leave her the car, when it meant he must make a bus transfer each way. She should have been more patient with him this morning—in fact, with all of them. She should at least have given him a proper kiss.

But it wasn't quite fair, the way they all ganged up to tease her that way just because she was deep in the rush of Christmas preparations. Maybe she was a perfectionist; maybe she did wear herself out making everything just right. But, oh, they did have a good Christmas—not just a good one, but a beautiful one. Everyone said so, even Jim and the children.

"Ours is the prettiest house on the whole street," Denna had said in awe last year.

"Perhaps even the prettiest in the entire world," Jim had added. "And we have the tiredest mother in captivity." But his smile had said it was lovely, and lovable of her to make it this way for them.

It was—well, it had almost become a tradition with her. "Ellen's house is the warmest, the brightest, the most beautiful." In her extra care of selection and imaginative wrappings, she made up for the fact that her gifts were not as expensive as the ones Arda and Madeline always brought. She simply had to send the small packages of remembrance to the out-of-town aunts, both hers and Jim's, not to mention the myriad of cards, with letters in many of them.

Jim had scolded again this year. "What do you care if Anna Mae's boy wears braces on his teeth? Or that Joan's kids had the flu for three days last October? Or that Sara's Becky is well on the way to becoming a child prodigy at the piano? You haven't seen any of them in over ten years. Maybe you wouldn't recognize any one of them."

But she did care. And she wrote a real letter to them just once a year.

"Then write sometime other than the rushed holiday season," Jim had reasoned.

"Oh, but it's somehow more special now," she had insisted.

And she had done it—as always. And now there was all this shopping to be finished, and baking to begin, and Denna's costume—as always.

Ellen rushed Stevie into his coat and cap, impatient at the way he wanted to dawdle over the Christmas coloring book she had bought last week. What a boon that had been, keeping him from incessantly asking, "Whatcha doing now, Mamma? Whatcha making now, huh?"

"See how far I got now, Mamma," he boasted. "See, I got all the toys and the elf pictures finished. I got Santa almost ready to come down the chimney now."

"That's fine, dear," she answered, absentmindedly. "Come on."

Stevie held back, a challenge in his eyes and voice. "You didn't even see!"

"I will later. I'll take a long time to look through your whole book soon. But we have to go now." Her voice rose at the end, and with an effort Ellen pulled it down to normal. "Please, Stevie. This is no time to be stubborn. We'll have so much fun later, when everything is ready."

If everything is ever ready, she added to herself, as he followed reluctantly.

They dashed from one store to another, frantically marking items off the endless list, having to backtrack for things that Ellen couldn't decide on until she had compared at other shops.

Stevie had long since grown quiet and listless, and Ellen couldn't help wishing they were through. She'd like to call it quits too. Denna's costume hung over her mind like the sword of Damocles. Already she had run past the time she should have allowed for this shopping, but she simply couldn't make time for a trip to town tomorrow.

She was irritable and tense by the time they pushed through the door at Maybanks. "'Tis the season to be jolly. . . ." The words rang out from a loudspeaker overhead.

"And we will—we will," she promised, "in just a few days."

Ellen caught a sharp breath, quickly stepping behind a display. She hadn't time for a long discussion with Jan Parry today, as much as she ordinarily enjoyed her friend's eager prattling. But she needn't have worried. Jan was as rushed and distracted as she. It was with a feeling of shocked recognition that Ellen saw the frown on Jan's face, the impatience with which the other woman grasped four-year-old Lisa's hand and pulled her away from the nearby toy display.

"We haven't time!" Jan snapped.

They moved away, but not before Ellen heard the little girl's plaintiff cry, "Haven't we got time to wish for what Santa will bring? Not even time for that, Mommy?"

There was no joy in the child's face, only defeat. And Ellen felt an answering ache in her own heart.

Not even time for the fun of Christmas, the anticipation?

What did all the rest mean without that, at least to a child?

She had been robbing Stevie and the older ones as surely as if she had taken something of theirs with no intention of returning it, for she never could replace these childhood Christmases once they were gone.

Promises. . . . She continually offered them promises for the future in place of the fun that should be a part of *now*.

Ellen stood very still, striving for control of the tumult within her.

"Mamma? Mamma, are you all right?" There was real concern in Stevie's voice.

With an effort, Ellen forced a smile to her lips. "Oh, honey, I'm just fine." She hugged him close. "Maybe I'm finer than for a long, long time."

He wouldn't understand that, but he did understand when she said, "I'm tired of shopping." There was one twinge of regret about the several items that still remained on her list, but impatiently she pushed that aside.

Stevie's hand was warm in her own. "Let's just watch the trains go swishing around their twisty little tracks until we're tired of that," she suggested. "Then we'll go home and finish Denna's costume."

"That old costume will have to wait a jillion minutes," he giggled. "'Cause I sure do like to watch the trains—now that you're not cross any more."

His hand pressed tightly against Ellen's as they walked among the toys. She did not need to see his face to know the joy it would be mirroring. And as she held close to her son's childish eagerness, she planned.

The tree—there was no reason why the children could not help trim that. They would enjoy sharing in that part of Christmas. Their fun would more than make up for a few misplaced ornaments.

Mike could make the big wreath for the front door. He had shown a definite creative ability since starting at junior high—at least Miss Adams said so, and it hadn't sounded like mere PTA chatter.

They might even get out that dog-eared book. They had read from it often when the first two were little. "'Twas the night before Christmas, when all through the house. . . ." Stevie would like that, and the others were not too old, either, not when it was a family affair.

A family affair, she thought eagerly.

Perhaps Jim was right, and Christmas *would* come. And if the packages for Les and Arda did clash, they could just be placed at opposite sides of the tree.

Much later, after Denna's costume was finished, the older children had been clued in on the new rules of Christmas, and a fine dinner had been eaten before time to leave for Denna's program. Ellen found herself humming, "'Tis the season to be jolly. . . ."

"'Tis indeed! 'Tis indeed!" she laughed.

This unfamiliar giddiness!—might she be catching something?

At that moment Jim appeared, with the three children wedged in the doorway around him.

"See, I told you, Daddy," Stevie crowed. "We're all going to be part of Christmas this time. Mamma said so herself."

"Well, well, well," Jim marveled. "So 'tis truly to be a merry Christmas for one and all—even for Santa's busiest helper herself."

"It could be an awful failure," Ellen cautioned. "Without all that 'fuzzing and fruming,' everything might fall apart."

"Then we'll all help put Humpty Dumpty back together again," Jim laughed. "But for now we'll worry about the present." He turned to the children. "I vote to keep it just the way it is this minute—with your mother prettier than she's ever been."

"Aye, aye," Mike shouted. And Denna agreed.

"I do, too," Stevie added. "I like for merry Christmas to be at our house."

She had been catching something, all right, Ellen thought in wonder—an advanced case of Christmas spirit, an epidemic that had spread to all of them. ❄

Christmas at Sea

Robert Louis Stevenson

The sheets were frozen hard, and they cut the naked hand;
The decks were like a slide, where a seaman scarce could stand;
The wind was a nor'-wester, blowing squally off the sea;
And cliffs and spouting breakers were the only things a-lee.

They heard the surf a-roaring before the break of day;
But 'twas only with the peep of light we saw how ill we lay.
We tumbled every hand on deck instanter, with a shout,
And we gave her the maintops'l, and stood by to go about.

All day we tacked and tacked between the South Head and the North;
All day we hauled the frozen sheets, and got no further forth;
All day as cold as charity, in bitter pain and dread,
For very life and nature we tacked from head to head.

We gave the South a wider berth, for there the tide-race roared;
But every tack we made we brought the North Head close aboard.
So's we saw the cliff and houses and the breakers running high,
And the coastguard in his garden, with his glass against his eye.

The frost was on the village roofs as white as ocean foam;
The good red fires were burning bright in every longshore home;
The windows sparkled clear, and the chimneys volleyed out;
And I vow we sniffed the victuals as the vessel went about.

The bells upon the church were rung with a mighty jovial cheer;
For it's just that I should tell you how (of all days in the year)
This day of our adversity was blessèd Christmas morn,
And the house above the coastguard's was the house where I was born.

O well I saw the pleasant room, the pleasant faces there,
My mother's silver spectacles, my father's silver hair;
And well I saw the firelight, like a flight of homely elves,
Go dancing round the china plates that stand upon the shelves.

And well I knew the talk they had, the talk that was of me,
Of the shadow on the household and the son that went to sea;
And O the wicked fool I seemed, in every kind of way,
To be here and hauling frozen ropes on blessèd Christmas Day.

They lit the high sea-light, and the dark began to fall.
"All hands to loose topgallant sails," I heard the captain call.
"By the Lord, she'll never stand it," our first mate, Jackson, cried.
. . . "It's the one way or the other, Mr. Jackson," he replied.

She staggered to her bearings, but the sails were new and good,
And the ship smelt up to windward just as though she understood;
As the winter's day was ending, in the entry of the night,
We cleared the weary headland, and passed below the light.

And they heaved a mighty breath, every soul on board but me,
As they saw her nose again pointing handsome out to sea;
But all that I could think of, in the darkness and the cold,
Was just that I was leaving home and my folks were growing old.

The Year We Discovered Tradition

Jay A. Parry

Ross LAID A SHOCKER on us at mealtime. We had talked about it but hadn't decided: "I don't think we'll have Christmas decorations or anything this year," he said. "All the kids are grown—except you, Marsha, and you don't mind, do you?"

Marsha mumbled something—her mouth was full of whole wheat bread at the moment—but her response didn't seem to be one of trauma. And when I thought about it, I didn't really mind, either.

Christmas was different with all of our children gone, anyway. Marsha was fifteen, and she had grown up almost as an only child. For years some of our three other children had come home for Christmas holidays. But then they gradually married and began to have children. This year every one had written that they wanted to celebrate Christmas in their own homes, establishing their own traditions.

After her bite was chewed and swallowed Marsha looked at Ross for a minute and then said, "Well, Dad, if we aren't going to have a tree or anything, what *will* we have?" Her face was a little red, and she looked bothered.

Ross just laughed and took her hand and mine and said, "Each other, of course. We'll have each other."

Marsha didn't look too sure. But finally she nodded and took another bite. "Ah gus thas oakay," she said.

"Don't talk with your mouth full. What did you say?" I said.

She swallowed and then smiled and said, "I said, 'I guess that's okay.' Okay that we'll just have each other." Then she looked at her plate and took another bite.

I wondered if she really meant it. Didn't she care at all about the traditions we had established and followed all these years? I was a little disappointed.

The next two weeks were always the busiest—and therefore the most hectic—of any month of the year. As chorister, I had to prepare for the Primary presentation at the ward party every year. This year we were going to have the children learn "Jingle Bells," "O Little Town of Bethlehem," and "I Wonder When He Comes Again." It wouldn't have been such a big job except that I agreed to specially coach any children who were having particular problems with learning the songs. Next year I'll do my special coaching in groups!

Then I supervised our yearly candy-making project, an important tradition in our family that we couldn't let go. We make big batches of several kinds and take them anonymously to different families we know, all of whom pretend they don't know who gave it.

Marsha always enjoyed helping in that project—she's one of the few people I know who can eat candy at will and seem to suffer no adverse effects—and we were just finishing up a special batch of caramel-filled peanut clusters when I said, talking loud to be heard over the Christmas music, "You know we're going to give presents to each other, don't you?"

She was eating some caramel-covered peanuts at the time—something *my* body has indicated it would really rather I would not do—and had to swallow before she could answer. "Mom," she finally said, "whatever in the world makes you say that?"

She was so casual about it that I wondered if it reflected her true feelings. But she didn't stop there. I must have looked upset, because she said, "Well, just because we aren't going to have a tree or lights doesn't mean we aren't going to give presents. Nobody said we weren't."

My throat felt kind of dry. Did she really not care about not having a tree? I asked her. "Honey, doesn't it bother you that we aren't going to have a tree or lights?"

She shrugged and didn't answer for a moment. Then she looked at me. "No, I don't care about that. We're doing everything else that's Christmasy. Why waste money on the kid stuff?"

"That's right—the really important traditions we'll still keep, because if we didn't, it wouldn't feel like Christmas."

Somehow it felt as if I said that for my own benefit rather than Marsha's.

Marsha nodded and said no more about it. But I caught myself snitching a little more chocolate than usual and realized I was upset. I'm being over-sensitive, I thought. What matters is that we don't let her down in the things she *does* care about.

Then it was Christmas Eve. Ross came in from work a little late—they had the day off at noon, but he was working on a tough project with a tight deadline and he didn't think he should leave. "Hi, girls," he said, when he came in the door. "All ready for the big day tomorrow?"

I laughed and said, "Of course" (trying to be cheerful, I guess), but Marsha didn't say anything.

"What's the matter, Marsh?" Ross said. "Did you just learn that Santa Claus isn't real?"

She looked a little disgusted and said, "Oh,

Daddy," and went back to her book. She had just discovered Tolkien's *Lord of the Rings* trilogy, and it was all we could do to drag her away from it.

So Ross sat down with the paper; then I served meat loaf sandwiches in the living room while Ross and I watched a special on TV about Christmas in other lands and Marsha tried to ignore it to read. After the program, Ross read us the story of Christ's birth out of Luke, we had family prayer, and then Marsha went down to her room. In a few minutes she was back with an armload of presents. "Merry Christmas!" she said, and plunked the gifts down on our coffee table. "Don't stay up too late or Santa won't come!" Then she said goodnight and went down the stairs.

I looked over at that pile of presents. They looked so lone and bare sitting on that table. I got out of my chair and took my rubber plant off the little end table in the corner and put it next to her presents. "There, that's better," I said.

Ross yawned and stretched and said he'd like to go to bed to read, but I stopped him. "Do you think Marsha feels okay about a treeless Christmas?" I asked.

He laughed. "Don't you think she'd tell us if she didn't? When has she ever *not* told us when she had something to say?"

"I guess you're right," I said. But it just didn't feel right.

We had prayer and Ross went to bed to read while I puffed by the bed doing my exercises. But my heart wasn't in it. I somehow still felt uncom-fortable with our decision. Finally I dismissed it and went to bed. When had she ever *not* told us when she had something to say?

We slept in late on Christmas morning. Finally I got up and took the rest of our gifts out of our closet into the living room. The rubber plant needed a little water so I gave it a drink. I fixed some pancakes and hot syrup and kept them warm on the stove.

It was 9:30.

Ross was finally awake.

There was no sign of Marsha. And she *never* slept in late like that. "Ross, could you go down and tell Marsha that breakfast is ready?" I hollered down the hall. If she wasn't up by now, there was no reason not to wake her by yelling.

Ross clumped down the stairs, especially cooperative because it was Christmas.

But he didn't come back up.

"Hey, you guys, breakfast is going to get cold," I yelled down the stairs. "And I want to open presents."

No response.

I was not pleased, to say the least. Here I had gotten up early for them and fixed a nice hot (and tasty) breakfast, and they didn't even have the courtesy to come when it was ready. I started down the stairs, and with each step I felt more upset. I had to fix breakfast every day for them. And now I did it on a holiday as a special indication of my love and desire to take good care of my family, and they didn't even have the decency to respond. Well, if they were going to be rude, so would I.

Marsha's door was shut. I wouldn't even knock. I turned the knob and pushed it open, my mouth forming the words "How thoughtless—!"

But I didn't say it. There in the far corner of the room was a tree. It was a small Christmas tree, covered with lights and tinsel and glass ornaments. It was scrawny and misshapen. It was beautiful.

Sitting next to it on the floor, looking very sheepish, was Ross. And sitting on the bed, her legs tucked under her, was Marsha.

She smiled and blushed and said, "Like it, Mama?"

I shut the door and leaned against it—and saw that all the Christmas cards we had received that year were arranged on the wall in the shape of a wreath, with an especially colorful one with Jesus on it in the center.

On her dresser was a nativity scene, with little plastic figures and a cardboard backing. It must have cost a dollar at Woolworth's.

I swallowed hard and tried to speak, but I couldn't. I swallowed again and tears came into my eyes. "When did you—why?" was all I could say.

Marsha came up to me and put her arm around my shoulders. "Now, Mama, don't feel bad. You and Daddy were doing what you thought would be best for us all, and I really thought it would be all right, too. But I just couldn't take it—you know? So the Benson boys said they'd pick me up a tree and I collected all the cards and bought a nativity set—I couldn't find ours—but it's all right."

Her saying "It's all right" only made me feel worse. I thought—for the first time, I'm afraid—of how I would have felt at fifteen if my parents had suddenly dropped some of our cherished traditions.

Ross stood up and put his arms around both of us. I could tell he felt bad, too. But he squeezed us both close to him for a minute, then squeezed us again, and stepped around us to the door. "I need to get the gifts," he said. "We can't let this lovely tree go to waste." And he ran up the stairs.

I looked at Marsha for a moment and then my eyes filled with tears. I wasn't sure if it was because I felt bad about misjudging Marsha's needs or because I was relieved that she cared about our traditions after all.

She hugged me and started patting me on the back and saying, "It's all right, Mama."

Then Ross came down with an armful of presents—with the rubber tree balanced precariously on top—and with a pancake hanging out of his mouth like a huge tongue. He put everything down on the floor next to Marsha's little tree and then turned to us and took the pancake out of his mouth.

"Look! It bounces!" he said, and dropped the pancake on the floor. Then he laughed and put his arms around us again. "Someone turned them into rubber while we were distracted down here," he said.

I looked over at the tree with its little pile of gifts, and down at the pancake lying forlornly there on the carpet, and I had to smile in spite of myself. Breakfast was ruined and the morning was half shot, but what did I care? We were having a *real* family Christmas after all—our traditional Christmas—and nothing else seemed to matter. ❋

CHAPTER TEN

Celebration & Fun

Christmas Every Day

William Dean Howells

THE LITTLE GIRL came into her papa's study, as she always did Saturday morning before breakfast, and asked for a story. He tried to beg off that morning, for he was very busy, but she would not let him. So he began:

"Well, once there was a little pig—"

She put her hand over his mouth and stopped him at the word. She said she had heard little pig stories till she was perfectly sick of them.

"Well, what kind of story *shall* I tell, then?"

"About Christmas. It's getting to be the season. It's past Thanksgiving already."

"It seems to me," argued her papa, "that I've told as often about Christmas as I have about little pigs."

"No difference! Christmas is more interesting."

"Well!" Her papa roused himself from his writing by a great effort. "Well, then, I'll tell you about the little girl that wanted it Christmas every day in the year. How would you like that?"

"First-rate!" said the little girl; and she nestled into comfortable shape in his lap, ready for listening.

"Very well, then, this little pig—Oh, what are you pounding me for?"

"Because you said little pig instead of little girl."

"I should like to know what's the difference between a little pig and a little girl that wanted it Christmas every day!"

"Papa," said the little girl, warningly, "if you don't go on, I'll *give* it to you!" And at this her papa darted off like lightning, and began to tell the story as fast as he could.

Well, once there was a little girl who liked Christmas so much that she wanted it to be Christmas every day in the year; and as soon as Thanksgiving was over she began to send postal cards to the old Christmas Fairy to ask if she mightn't have it. But the old Fairy never answered any of the postals; and, after a while, the little girl found out that the Fairy was pretty particular, and wouldn't even notice anything but letters, not even correspondence cards in envelopes; but real letters on sheets of paper, and sealed outside with a monogram—or your initial, any way. So, then, she began to send her letters; and in about three weeks—or just the day before Christmas, it was—she got a letter from the Fairy, saying she might have it Christmas every day for a year, and then they would see about having it longer.

The little girl was a good deal excited already, preparing for the old-fashioned, once-a-year Christmas that was coming the next day, and perhaps the Fairy's promise didn't make such an impression on her as it would have made at some other time. She just resolved to keep it to herself, and surprise everybody with it as it kept coming true; and then it slipped out of her mind altogether.

She had a splendid Christmas. She went to bed early, so as to let Santa Claus have a chance at the stockings, and in the morning she was up the first of anybody and went and felt them, and found hers all lumpy with packages of candy, and oranges and grapes, and pocket-books and rubber balls and all kinds of small presents, and her big brother's with nothing but the tongs in them, and her young lady sister's with a new silk umbrella, and her papa's and mamma's with potatoes and pieces of coal wrapped up in tissue paper, just as they always had every Christmas. Then she waited around till the rest of the

family were up, and she was the first to burst into the library, when the doors were opened, and look at the large presents laid out on the library-table—books, and portfolios, and boxes of stationery, and breast-pins, and dolls, and little stoves, and dozens of hand-kerchiefs, and ink-stands, and skates, and snow-shovels, and photograph-frames, and little easels, and boxes of watercolors, and Turkish paste, and nougat, and candied cherries, and dolls' houses, and waterproofs—and the big Christmas-tree, lighted and standing in a waste-
basket in the middle.

She had a splendid Christmas all day. She ate so much candy that she did not want any breakfast; and the whole forenoon the presents kept pouring in that the expressman had not had time to deliver the night before; and she went 'round giving the presents she had got for other people, and came home and ate turkey and cranberry for dinner, and plum-pudding and nuts and raisins and oranges and more candy, and then went out and coasted and came in with a stomach-ache, crying; and her papa said he would see if his house was turned into that sort of fool's paradise another year; and they had a light supper, and pretty early everybody went to bed cross.

Here the little girl pounded her papa in the back, again.

"Well, what now? Did I say pigs?"

"You made them *act* like pigs."

"Well, didn't they?"

"No matter; you oughtn't to put it into a story."

"Very well, then, I'll take it all out."

Her father went on:

The little girl slept very heavily, and she slept very late, but she was wakened at last by the other children dancing 'round her bed with their stockings full of presents in their hands.

"What is it?" said the little girl, and she rubbed her eyes and tried to rise up in bed.

"Christmas! Christmas! Christmas!" they all shouted, and waved their stockings.

"Nonsense! It was Christmas yesterday."

Her brothers and sisters just laughed. "We don't know about that. It's Christmas today, any way. You come into the library and see."

Then all at once it flashed on the little girl that the Fairy was keeping her promise, and her year of Christmases was beginning. She was dreadfully sleepy, but she sprang up like a lark—a lark that had overeaten itself and gone to bed cross—and darted into the library. There it was again! Books, and port-folios, and boxes of stationery, and breast-pins—

"You needn't go over it all, Papa; I guess I can remember just what was there," said the little girl.

Well, and there was the Christmas-tree blazing away, and the family picking out their presents, but looking pretty sleepy, and her father perfectly puzzled, and her mother ready to cry. "I'm sure I don't see how I'm to dispose of all these things," said her mother, and her father said it seemed to him they had had some-thing just like it the day before, but he supposed he must have dreamed it. This struck the little girl as the best kind of joke; and so she ate so much candy she didn't want any breakfast, and went 'round carrying presents, and had turkey and cranberry for dinner, and then went out and coasted, and came in with a—

"Papa!"

"Well, what now?"

"What did you promise, you forgetful thing?"

"Oh! oh, yes!"

Well, the next day, it was just the same thing over again, but everybody getting crosser; and at the end of a week's time so many people had lost their tempers that you could pick up lost tempers everywhere; they perfectly strewed the ground. Even when people tried to recover their tempers they usually got somebody else's, and it made the most dreadful mix.

The little girl began to get frightened, keeping the secret all to herself; she wanted to tell her mother, but she didn't dare to; and she was ashamed to ask the Fairy to take back her gift, it seemed ungrateful and ill-bred, and she thought she would try to stand it, but she hardly knew how she could, for a whole year. So it went on and on, and it was Christmas on St. Valentine's Day, and Washington's Birthday, just the same as any day, and it didn't skip even the First of April, though everything was counterfeit that day, and that was some little relief.

After a while, coal and potatoes began to be awfully scarce, so many had been wrapped up in tissue paper to fool papas and mammas with. Turkeys got to be about a thousand dollars apiece—

"Papa!"

"Well, what?"

"You're beginning to fib."

"Well, two thousand, then."

And they got to passing off almost anything for turkeys—half-grown humming-birds, and even rocs out of the "Arabian Nights"—the real turkeys were so scarce. And cranberries—well, they asked a diamond apiece for cranberries. All the woods and orchards were cut down for Christmas-trees, and where the woods and orchards used to be, it looked just like a stubble-field, with the stumps. After a while they had to make Christmas-trees out of rags, and stuff them with bran, like old-fashioned dolls; but there were plenty of rags, because people got so poor, buying presents for one another, that they couldn't get any new clothes, and they just wore their old ones to tatters. They got so poor that everybody had to go to the poor-house, except the confectioners, and the fancy store-keepers, and the picture-booksellers, and the expressmen; and they all got so rich and proud that

they would hardly wait upon a person when he came to buy; it was perfectly shameful!

Well, after it had gone on about three or four months, the little girl, whenever she came into the room in the morning and saw those great ugly lumpy stockings dangling at the fire-place, and the disgusting presents around everywhere, used to just sit down and burst out crying. In six months she was perfectly exhausted; she couldn't even cry any more; she just lay on the lounge and rolled her eyes and panted. About the beginning of October she took to sitting down on dolls wherever she found them—French dolls, or any kind—she hated the sight of them so; and by Thanksgiving she was crazy, and just slammed her presents across the room.

By that time people didn't carry presents around nicely any more. They flung them over the fence, or through the window, or anything; and, instead of running their tongues out and taking great pains to write "For dear Papa," or "Mamma," or "Brother," or "Sister," or "Susie," or "Sammie," or "Billie," or "Bobby," or "Jimmie," or "Jennie," or whoever it was, and troubling to get the spelling right, and then signing their names, and "Xmas, 188—," they used to write in the gift-books, "Take it, you horrid old thing!" and then go and bang it against the front door. Nearly everybody had built barns to hold their presents, but pretty soon the barns overflowed, and then they used to let them lie out in the rain, or anywhere. Sometimes the police used to come and tell them to shovel their presents off the sidewalk, or they would arrest them.

"I thought you said everybody had gone to the poor-house," interrupted the little girl.

"They did go, at first," said her papa; "but after a while the poor-houses got so full that they had to send the people back to their own houses. They tried to cry, when they got back, but they couldn't make the least sound."

"Why couldn't they?"

"Because they had lost their voices, saying 'Merry Christmas' so much. Did I tell you how it was on the Fourth of July?"

"No, how was it?" And the little girl nestled closer, in expectation of something uncommon.

Well, the night before, the boys stayed up to celebrate, as they always do, and fell asleep before twelve o'clock, as usual, expecting to be wakened by the bells and cannon. But it was nearly eight o'clock before the first boy in the United States woke up, and then he found out what the trouble was. As soon as he could get his clothes on, he ran out of the house and smashed a big cannon-torpedo down on the pavement; but it didn't make any more noise than a damp wad of paper, and, after he tried about twenty or thirty more, he began to pick them up and look at them. Every single torpedo was a big raisin! Then he just streaked it upstairs, and examined his firecrackers and toy-pistol and two-dollar collection of fireworks and found that they were nothing but sugar and candy painted up to look like fireworks! Before ten o'clock, every boy in the United States found out that his Fourth of July things had turned into Christmas things; and then they just sat down and cried—they were so mad. There are about twenty million boys in the United States, and so you can imagine what a noise they made. Some men got together before night, with a little powder that hadn't turned into purple sugar yet, and they said they would fire off one cannon, *any way. But the cannon burst into a thousand pieces, for it was nothing but rock-candy, and some of the men nearly got killed. The Fourth of July orations all turned into Christmas carols, and when anybody tried to read the Declaration, instead of saying, "When in the course of human events it becomes necessary," he was sure to*

sing, "God rest you, merry gentlemen." It was perfectly awful.

The little girl drew a deep sigh of satisfaction. "And how was it at Thanksgiving?" she asked. Her papa hesitated. "Well, I'm almost afraid to tell you. I'm afraid you'll think it's wicked." "Well, tell, any way," said the little girl.

Well, before it came Thanksgiving, it had leaked out who had caused all these Christmases. The little girl had suffered so much that she had talked about it in her sleep; and after that, hardly anybody would play with her. People just perfectly despised her, because if it had not been for her greediness, it wouldn't have happened; and now, when it came Thanksgiving, and she wanted them to go to church, and have a squash-pie and turkey, and show their gratitude, they said that all the turkeys had been eaten up for her old Christmas dinners, and if she would stop the Christmases, they would see about the gratitude. Wasn't it dreadful? And the very next day the little girl began to send letters to the Christmas Fairy, and then telegrams, to stop it. But it didn't do any good; and then she got to calling at the Fairy's house, but the girl that came to the door always said "Not at home," or "Engaged," or "At dinner," or something like that; and so it went on till it came to the old once-a-year Christmas Eve. The little girl fell asleep, and when she woke up in the morning—

"She found it was all nothing but a dream," suggested the little girl.

"No, indeed!" said her papa. "It was all every bit true!"

"Well, what *did* she find out then?"

"Why, that it wasn't Christmas at last, and wasn't ever going to be, any more. Now it's time for breakfast."

The little girl held her papa fast around the neck.

"You shan't go if you're going to leave it *so!*"

"How do you want it left?"

"Christmas once a year."

"All right," said her papa; and he went on again.

Well, there was the greatest rejoicing all over the county, and it extended clear up into Canada. The people met together everywhere, and kissed and cried for joy. The city carts went around and gathered up all the candy and raisins and nuts, and dumped them into the river; and it made the fish perfectly sick; and the whole United States, as far out as Alaska, was one blaze of bonfires, where the children were burning up their gift-books and presents of all kinds. They had the greatest time!

The little girl went to thank the old Fairy because she had stopped it being Christmas, and she said she hoped she would keep her promise, and see that Christmas never, never came again. Then the Fairy frowned, and asked her if she was sure she knew what she meant; and the little girl asked her, why not? and the old Fairy said that now she was behaving just as greedily as ever, and she'd better look out. This made the little girl think it all over carefully again, and she said she would be willing to have it Christmas about once in a thousand years; and then she said a hundred, and then she said ten, and at last she got down to one. Then the Fairy said that was the good old way that had pleased people ever since Christmas began, and she was agreed. Then the little girl said, "What're your shoes made of?" And the Fairy said, "Leather." And the little girl said, "Bargain's done forever," and skipped off, and hippity-hopped the whole way home, she was so glad.

"How will that do?" asked the papa.

"First-rate!" said the little girl; but she hated to have the story stop, and was rather sober. However,

her mamma put her head in at the door, and asked her papa:

"Are you never coming to breakfast? What have you been telling that child?"

"Oh, just a moral tale."

The little girl caught him around the neck again.

"*We* know! Don't you tell *what*, Papa! Don't you tell *what!*"

The Ghost of Christmas Present

FROM *A Christmas Carol*

Charles Dickens

A WAKENING IN THE MIDDLE of a prodigiously tough snore, and sitting up in bed to get his thoughts together, Scrooge had no occasion to be told that the bell was again upon the stroke of One. He felt that he was restored to consciousness in the right nick of time, for the especial purpose of holding a conference with the second messenger dispatched to him through Jacob Marley's intervention. . . . He got up softly and shuffled in his slippers to the door.

The moment Scrooge's hand was on the lock, a strange voice called him by his name, and bade him enter. He obeyed.

It was his own room. There was no doubt about that. But it had undergone a surprising transformation. The walls and ceiling were so hung with living green, that it looked a perfect grove; from every part of which, bright gleaming berries glistened. The crisp leaves of holly, mistletoe, and ivy reflected back the light, as if so many little mirrors had been scattered there. . . . Heaped up on the floor, to form a kind of throne, were turkeys, geese, game, poultry, brawn, great joints of meat, sucking-pigs, long wreaths of sausages, mince-pies, plum-puddings, barrels of oysters, red-hot chestnuts, cherry-cheeked apples, juicy oranges, luscious pears, immense twelfth-cakes, and seething bowls of punch, that made the chamber dim with their delicious steam. In easy state upon this couch, there sat a jolly Giant, glorious to see; who bore a glowing torch, in shape not unlike Plenty's horn, and held it up, high up, to shed its light on Scrooge, as he came peeping round the door.

"Come in!" exclaimed the Ghost. "Come in! and know me better, man!"

Scrooge entered timidly, and hung his head before this Spirit. He was not the dogged Scrooge he had been; and though the Spirit's eyes were clear and kind, he did not like to meet them.

"I am the Ghost of Christmas Present," said the Spirit. "Look upon me!"

Scrooge reverently did so. . . .

"Touch my robe!"

Scrooge did as he was told, and held it fast.

Holly, mistletoe, red berries, ivy, turkeys, geese, game, poultry, brawn, meat, pigs, sausages, oysters, pies, puddings, fruit, and punch, all vanished instantly. So did the room, the fire, the ruddy glow, the hour of night, and they stood in the city streets on Christmas morning, where (for the weather was severe) the people made a rough, but brisk and not unpleasant kind of music, in scraping the snow from the pavement in front of their dwellings, and from the tops of their houses, whence it was made delight to the boys to see it come plumping down into the road below, and splitting into artificial little snow-storms.

The house fronts looked black enough, and the windows blacker, contrasting with the smooth white sheet of snow upon the roofs, and with the dirtier snow upon the ground. . . . The sky was gloomy, and the shortest streets were choked up with a dingy mist. . . . There was nothing very cheerful in the climate or the town, and yet there was an air of cheerfulness abroad that the clearest summer air and brightest summer sun might have endeavoured to diffuse in vain.

For the people who were shovelling away on the house-tops were jovial and full of glee; calling out to one another from the parapets and now and then exchanging a facetious snowball—better-natured missile far than many a wordy jest—laughing heartily if it went right and not less heartily if it went wrong. The poulterers' shops were still half open, and the fruiterers' were radiant in their glory. . . . The customers were all so hurried and so eager in the hopeful promise of the day, that they tumbled up against each other at the door, crashing their wicker baskets wildly, and left their purchases upon the counter, and came running back to fetch them, and committed hundreds of the like mistakes, in the best humour possible; while the Grocer and his people were so frank and fresh that the polished hearts with which they fastened their aprons behind might have been their own, worn outside for general inspection, and for Christmas daws to peck at if they chose.

But soon the steeples called good people all, to church and chapel, and away they came, flocking through the streets in their best clothes, and with their gayest faces. And at the same time there emerged from scores of bye-streets, lanes, and nameless turnings, innumerable people, carrying their dinners to the bakers' shops. The sight of these poor revellers appeared to interest the Spirit very much, for he stood with Scrooge beside him in a baker's doorway, and taking off the covers as their bearers passed, sprinkled incense on their dinners from his torch. And it was a very uncommon kind of torch, for once or twice when there were angry words between some dinner-carriers who had jostled each other, he shed a few drops of water on them from it, and their good humour was restored directly. For they said, it was a shame to quarrel upon Christmas Day. And so it was! God love it, so it was!

In time the bells ceased, and the bakers were shut up; and yet there was a genial shadowing forth of all these dinners and the progress of their cooking, in the thawed blotch of wet above each baker's oven; where the pavement smoked as if its stones were cooking too.

"Is there a peculiar flavour in what you sprinkle from your torch?" asked Scrooge.

"There is. My own."

"Would it apply to any kind of dinner on this day?" asked Scrooge.

"To any kindly given. To a poor one most."

"Why to a poor one most?" asked Scrooge.

"Because it needs it most." . . .

By this time it was getting dark, and snowing pretty heavily; and as Scrooge and the Spirit went along the streets, the brightness of the roaring fires in kitchens, parlours, and all sorts of rooms, was wonderful. Here, the flickering of the blaze showed preparations for a cosy dinner, with hot plates baking through and through before the fire, and deep red curtains, ready to be drawn to shut out cold and darkness. There all the children of the house were running out into the snow to meet their married sisters, brothers, cousins, uncles, aunts, and be the first to greet them. Here, again, were shadows on the window-blind of guests assembling; and there a group of handsome girls, all hooded and fur-booted, and all chattering at once, tripped lightly off to some near neighbour's house; where, woe upon the single man who saw them enter—artful witches, well they knew it—in a glow!

But, if you had judged from the numbers of people on their way to friendly gatherings, you might have thought that no one was at home to give them welcome when they got there, instead of every house expecting company, and piling up its fires half-chimney high. Blessings on it, how the Ghost exulted! How it bared its breadth of breast, and opened its capacious palm, and floated on, out-pouring, with a generous hand, its bright and harm-less mirth on everything within its reach! The very lamplighter, who ran on before, dotting the dusky street with specks of light, and who was dressed to spend the evening somewhere, laughed out loudly as the Spirit passed, though little kenned the lamp-lighter that he had any company but Christmas!

And now, without a word of warning from the Ghost, they stood upon a bleak and desert moor, where monstrous masses of rude stone were cast about, as though it were the burial-place of giants; and water spread itself wheresoever it listed, or would have done so, but for the frost that held it prisoner; and nothing grew but moss and furze, and coarse rank grass. Down in the west the setting sun had left a streak of fiery red, which glared upon the desolation for an instant, like a sullen eye, and frowning lower, lower, lower yet, was lost in the thick gloom of darkest night.

"What place is this?" asked Scrooge.

"A place where Miners live, who labour in the bowels of the earth," returned the Spirit. "But they know me. See!"

A light shone from the window of a hut, and swiftly they advanced towards it. Passing through the wall of mud and stone, they found a cheerful company assembled round a glowing fire. An old, old man and woman, with their children and their children's children, and another generation beyond that, all decked out gaily in their holiday attire. The old man, in a voice that seldom rose above the howling of the wind upon the barren waste, was singing them a Christmas song—it had been a very old song when he was a boy—and from time to

time they all joined in the chorus. So surely as they raised their voices, the old man got quite blithe and loud; and so surely as they stopped, his vigour sank again.

The Spirit did not tarry here, but bade Scrooge hold his robe, and passing on above the moor, sped—whither? Not to sea? To sea. To Scrooge's horror, looking back, he saw the last of the land, a frightful range of rocks, behind them; and his ears were deafened by the thundering of water, as it rolled and roared, and raged among the dreadful caverns it had worn, and fiercely tried to undermine the earth.

Built upon a dismal reef of sunken rocks, some league or so from shore, on which the waters chafed and dashed, the wild year through, there stood a solitary lighthouse. Great heaps of sea-weed clung to its base, and storm-birds—born of the wind one might suppose, as sea-weed of the water—rose and fell about it, like the waves they skimmed.

But even here, two men who watched the light had made a fire, that through the loophole in the thick stone wall shed out a ray of brightness on the awful sea. Joining their horny hands over the rough table at which they sat, they wished each other Merry Christmas in their can of grog; and one of them: the elder, too, with his face all damaged and scarred with hard weather, as the figure-head of an old ship might be: struck up a sturdy song that was like a Gale in itself.

Again the Ghost sped on, above the black and heaving sea—on, on—until, being far away, as he told Scrooge, from any shore, they lighted on a ship. They stood beside the helmsman at the wheel, the look-out in the bow, the officers who had the watch; dark, ghostly figures in their several stations; but every man among them hummed a Christmas tune, or had a Christmas thought, or spoke below his breath to his companion of some bygone Christmas Day, with homeward hopes belonging to it. And every man on board, waking or sleeping, good or bad, had had a kinder word for another on that day than on any day in the year; and had shared to some extent in its festivities; and had remembered those he cared for at a distance, and had known that they delighted to remember him. . . .

Much they saw, and far they went, and many homes they visited, but always with a happy end. The Spirit stood beside sick beds, and they were cheerful; on foreign lands, and they were close at home; by struggling men, and they were patient in their greater hope; by poverty, and it was rich. In almshouse, hospital, and jail, in misery's every refuge, where vain man in his little brief authority had not made fast the door, and barred the Spirit out, he left his blessing, and taught Scrooge his precepts. ❆

At Christmas Be Merry

Thomas Tusser

At Christmas be merry, and thankful withal,
And feast thy poor neighbours, the great with
   the small.

Christmas Time

From an 18th-Century Ballad

Oh, Christmas time is drawing near,
   And then I shall have money;
I'll save it up, and, box and all,
   I'll give it to my honey.

The Christmas Miracle

Robert Keith Leavitt

On the morning before the Christmas that fell when I was six, my father took my brother and me for a walk in the woods of the Old Colony town where we lived. Three times as we walked he stopped, and cut a small balsam tree. There was a very tiny one, hardly more than a seedling; a small one a foot or so high; and a youthful one of perhaps four feet. So we each had a tree to bear, flaglike, back to the house. It didn't occur to us single-minded larvae that this had the least connection with Christmas. Our father was a botanist Ph.D., given to plucking all manner of specimens whenever we walked, with the offhand explanation, "A fine *Tsuga canadensis*," or whatever it was. By nightfall we had forgotten all about the walk.

For this was Christmas Eve, and we were suddenly in a panic. Where was The Tree? On experience, we knew that it was usually delivered in the morning, that Father set it up in the afternoon and that Mother trimmed it at night, letting us help with the ornaments before she put us to bed in a fever of anticipation. But this year we had seen no tree arrive; look where we would, we could not find one; and even Mother turned aside our questions. Would there be no Tree? Would there, perhaps, be no Christmas at all for us? How we wished now, that we had not put the cat in the milk-pail!

But after supper Father and Mother took us into the sitting-room. In a cleared corner over by the big closet stood a jar of earth. "Christmas," said Father, "is a day of miracles, to remind us of the greatest Miracle of all. Perhaps we shall see one."

Then Mother led us out, closing the door on Father and the jar of earth—and the closet.

"We can help," she said, "by learning this song." And she began, softly but very true, "O Little Town of Bethlehem." We tried hard in our shrill way. But even Mother had to admit it was only a good try. Yet when the door opened and we went again into the sitting-room, behold! A tiny Tree had appeared in the jar of earth! Hardly more than a seedling, to be sure, and not old enough yet to bear ornaments, but indubitably a Tree. Marveling, we went out again.

This time we did better—on the words, if not the tune. And when we re-entered the sitting-room, the Tree had grown—to perhaps a foot or so in height! A blaze of hope flashed upon us. We went out and tried harder on that song. And sure enough, this time the Tree was taller than either boy. Terrific! We could hardly wait to get outside and sing some more with Mother. For now hope was a rapture of certainty.

To this day I cannot hear "O Little Town of Bethlehem," from however cracked a curbside organ, without hearing through and beyond it the clear, true voice of my mother. Nor hear that long-vanished sweetness without knowing that presently, somewhere, somehow a great door is going to open and disclose unearthly beauty. It is more than sixty years since our sitting-room door swung back for the fourth time, that night in the Old Colony of Massachusetts. But I can still see, sharp as life, the splendor of the Tree that towered to the ceiling in its glossy dark green, sparkling with silver tinsel, glowing with candles and half hiding in its crisp, fragrant needles, the incomparable perfection of spheres that shone like far-off other worlds, red and blue and green and gold . . .

Cynics say that miracles are all man-made—

contrived, like a Christmas tree hidden in a closet and flashed upon wondering kids. That even the Christmas spirit is only a spell we work up to bemuse one another—and then fall for, ourselves, like so many simple children. What of it? So much the better! If mankind, by its own devoted labor, can induce in itself—if only for a day—an all-pervading spirit of friendship and cheer and good will and loving kindness, that alone is a very great miracle. It is the kind of miracle that must please above all others Him who knows how miracles are wrought. ❄

A Christmas Eve Thought

Harriet Brewer Sterling

If Santa Claus should stumble,
    As he climbs the chimney tall
With all this ice upon it,
    I'm afraid he'd get a fall
And smash himself to pieces—
    To say nothing of the toys!
Dear me, what sorrow that would bring
    To all the girls and boys!
So I am going to write a note
    And pin it to the gate,—
I'll write it large, so he can see,
    No matter if it's late,—
And say, "Dear Santa Claus, don't try
    To climb the roof to-night,
But walk right in, the door's unlocked,
    The nursery's on the right!"

The Night Before Christmas

Clement C. Moore

'Twas the night before Christmas, when all through
   the house
Not a creature was stirring, not even a mouse;
The stockings were hung by the chimney with care,
In hopes that ST. NICHOLAS soon would be there;

The children were nestled all snug in their beds,
While visions of sugar-plums danced through their
   heads;
And Mamma in her 'kerchief, and I in my cap,
Had just settled our brains for a long winter's nap,—

When out on the lawn there arose such a clatter,
I sprang from my bed to see what was the matter;
Away to the window I flew like a flash,
Tore open the shutters and threw up the sash.

The moon on the breast of the new-fallen snow
Gave the lustre of midday to objects below;
When, what to my wondering eyes should appear,
But a miniature sleigh, and eight tiny reindeer,

With a little old driver, so lively and quick,
I knew in a moment it must be Saint Nick.
More rapid than eagles his coursers they came,
And he whistled, and shouted, and called them by
   name:

"Now, *Dasher!* now, *Dancer!* now, *Prancer* and *Vixen!*
On, *Comet!* on, *Cupid!* on, *Donder* and *Blitzen!*
To the top of the porch! to the top of the wall!
Now, dash away! dash away! dash away all!"

As dry leaves that before the wild hurricane fly,
When they meet with an obstacle, mount to the sky,
So up to the house-top the coursers they flew,
With a sleigh full of toys—and St. Nicholas too!

And then, in a twinkling, I heard on the roof,
The prancing and pawing of each little hoof.
As I drew in my head, and was turning around,
Down the chimney St. Nicholas came with a bound.

He was dressed all in fur, from his head to his foot,
And his clothes were all tarnished with ashes and
   soot!
A bundle of toys he had flung on his back,
And he looked like a pedlar just opening his pack;

His eyes—how they twinkled! his dimples, how
   merry!
His cheeks were like roses, his nose like a cherry!
His droll little mouth was drawn up like a bow,
And the beard of his chin was as white as the snow.

The stump of a pipe he held tight in his teeth,
And the smoke, it encircled his head like a wreath.
He had a broad face, and a little round belly,
That shook, when he laugh'd, like a bowlful of jelly.

He was chubby and plump; a right jolly old elf;
And I laughed, when I saw him, in spite of myself.
A wink of his eye, and a twist of his head,
Soon gave me to know I had nothing to dread.

He spoke not a word, but went straight to his work,
And filled all the stockings—then turned with a jerk,
And laying his finger aside of his nose,
And giving a nod, up the chimney he rose.

He sprang to his sleigh, to his team gave a whistle,
And away they all flew, like the down off a thistle.
But I heard him exclaim, ere he drove out of sight,
"Happy Christmas to all! and to all a good night!"

Is There a Santa Claus?

Francis P. Church

In 1897, eight-year-old Virginia O'Hanlon asked her father if Santa Claus was real. He suggested she write to the New York Sun. *Here is the Sun's response, which it reprinted every Christmas Eve for nearly fifty years.*

WE TAKE PLEASURE in answering at once and thus prominently the communication below, expressing at the same time our great gratification that its faithful author is numbered among the friends of *The Sun*:

> *Dear Editor, I am 8 years old.*
> *Some of my little friends say there is no Santa Claus.*
> *Papa says "If you see it in The Sun it's so."*
> *Please tell me the truth. Is there a Santa Claus?*
>
> > *Virginia O'Hanlon*
> > *115 West Ninety-fifth Street*

Virginia, your little friends are wrong. They have been affected by the skepticism of a skeptical age. They do not believe except they see. They think that nothing can be which is not comprehensible by their little minds. All minds, Virginia, whether they be men's or children's, are little. In this great universe of ours man is a mere insect, an ant, in his intellect, as compared with the boundless world about him, as measured by the intelligence capable of grasping the whole of truth and knowledge.

Yes, Virginia, there is a Santa Claus. He exists as certainly as love and generosity and devotion exist, and you know that they abound and give to your life its highest beauty and joy. Alas! how dreary would be the world if there were no Santa Claus! It would be as dreary as if there were no Virginias. There would be no childlike faith then, no poetry, no romance to make tolerable this existence. We should have no enjoyment, except in sense and sight. The eternal light with which childhood fills the world would be extinguished.

Not believe in Santa Claus! You might as well not believe in fairies! You might get your papa to hire men to watch in all the chimneys on Christmas Eve to catch Santa Claus, but even if they did not see Santa Claus coming down what would that prove? Nobody sees Santa Claus but that is no sign that there is no Santa Claus. The most real things in the world are those that neither children nor men can see. Did you ever see fairies dancing on the lawn? Of course not, but that's no proof that they are not there. Nobody can conceive or imagine all the wonders there are unseen and unseeable in the world.

You tear apart the baby's rattle and see what makes the noise inside, but there is a veil covering the unseen world which not the strongest man, not even the united strength of all the strongest men that ever lived, could tear apart. Only faith, fancy, poetry, love, romance, can push aside that curtain and view and picture the supernal beauty and glory beyond. Is it all real? Ah, Virginia, in all this world there is nothing else real and abiding.

No Santa Claus! Thank God! he lives, and he lives forever. A thousand years from now, Virginia, nay, ten times ten thousand years from now, he will continue to make glad the heart of childhood. ✱

INDEX OF TITLES

All Are Vocal with His Name, 153
Ancient Prophets Speak—The Coming of Our
    Lord, 3
Are You Ready for Christmas?, 93
As Joseph Was A-Walking, 34
At Christmas Be Merry, 203

Brightest and Best of the Sons of the Morning, 161

Charity Christmas, 103
Christmas at Sea, 186
Christmas Carol, A, 34
Christmas Carol, A, 164
Christmas Eve Thought, A, 205
Christmas Every Day, 195
Christmas Hymn, A, 84
Christmas Is for Sharing, 74
Christmas Legends, 153
Christmas Letter, The, 134
Christmas Miracle, The, 204
Christmas Peace, The, 173
Christmas Reminiscences, 180
Christmas, Second Time Around, 145
Christmas Thought, A, 121
Christmas Time, 203
Christmas We Gave Away, The, 131

Dividers of the Stars, 62

Earth Has Grown Old, The, 172
Ever 'gainst That Season, 174

Family Affair, A, 182
Food for Santa, 73
For All Mankind, 16
For Them, 94
Friend to Friend, 161
From a Far Country, 67

Ghost of Christmas Present, The, 200
Gift of the Magi, The, 147
Gift, The, 75
Gifts for the Poor, 86
God Is Born, A, 10
Good Tidings of Great Joy, 61

Harry's Carol, 97
His Gift, 28
Holiday on the Bus, 174
Holy Night, The, 69
How Simple, 62
Hymn on the Nativity of My Saviour, A, 66

I Think You Have a Fire at Your Store, 84
In Temptation, 42
In the Bleak Mid-Winter, 160
Is There a Santa Claus?, 207

Joy They Shared, The, 144
Joy of Giving, The, 96
Joy of Christmas, The, 164
Joys of Christmas, The, 154

Keeping Christ in Christmas, 30

Keeping Christmas, 128

Let Every Heart Keep, 40
Little Match Girl, The, 51
Looking for a King, 33
Loving Father, Help Us, 90

Mary and Her Son, 33
Mary-Song, The, 28
Miracle, The, 60
Mom's Vacation, 136
Most Gentle Love, 73
My Gift, 172

Nearest and Dearest, 117
Night Before Christmas, The, 206

O Holy Child, 40
Old Blue Bike, The, 179
On Another Street, 99
On the Morning of Christ's Nativity, 17
On the Night of the Nativity, 96
Our Pickle-Jar Christmas, 125
Oxen, The, 163

Pilgrimage to Christmas, 50

Remembering Jesus, 18

Shepherds and the Magi, The, 65
Snow Is on the Land, The, 110

Song of a Shepherd-boy at Bethlehem, The, 68
Special Christmas, A, 143

That Holy Star, 40
"The Birth of Jesus Christ Was on This Wise," 19
There's a Song in the Air, 160
Thou Whose Birth, 173
Thoughts on Christmas, 29
Three Christmas Gifts, 95
Three Levels of Christmas, 54
Three Kings, The, 59
Time for Hope, 41
To Springvale for Christmas, 112
Trouble at the Inn, 88

Uncle Kees' Christmas Rebellion, 162
Unto the Least of These, 111

Visit of the King, The, 78

Warm and Gracious Christmas, A, 165
We Three Kings of Orient Are, 66
When the Wise Man Appeared, 63
Winter Quarters, 53
Wonder of the Story, The, 27
Wondrous Gift, The, 37

Year of the Flexible Flyers, The, 129
Year We Discovered Tradition, The, 188
You, Simeon, Spirit-filled, 27
Yuletide in a Younger World, 54

INDEX OF AUTHORS

Alder, Elaine Reiser, 75
Andersen, Hans Christian, 51
Anderson, William Ashley, 63

Bell, Ruth Moench, 117
Benson, Ezra Taft, 30, 154
Boyer, Claire S., 60
Brooks, Phillips, 40, 153, 172
Brown, Marilyn McMeen Miller, 111
Brown, Hugh B., 29
Browning, Elizabeth Barrett, 69
Bryan, Joel R., 179
Bryant, William Cullen, 40

Carroll, Elsie C., 136
Chatterton, Aney B., 129
Chesterton, Gilbert K., 34
Christensen, Berta Huish, 53, 99
Church, Francis P., 207
Crawford, Vesta P., 62, 67

Dahlgren, Lisa, 97
Dickens, Charles, 164, 200
Donohue, Dina, 88

Farjeon, Eleanor, 94
Field, Eugene, 172
Finlinson, Shirley G., 86
Florence, Giles H., Jr., 28

Gabbott, Mabel Jones, 16
Gale, Zona, 112

Goff, Mildred, 95

Hanks, Marion D., 165
Hanson, Steve D., 145
Hardy, Thomas, 54, 163
Henry, O., 147
Holland, Josiah G., 160
Hopkins, John Henry, Jr., 66
Howells, William Dean, 195

Irvine, Bertha, 78

Jonson, Ben, 66
Junkin, Charles Irvin, 27

Kimball, Spencer W., 37

Leavitt, Robert Keith, 204
Lee, Harold B., 18, 93
Longfellow, Henry Wadsworth, 59
Lowell, James Russell, 121
Lund, Gerald N., 19
Lyon, Jack M., 73

MacDonald, George, 33
Madsen, Betty W., 28
Manwaring, Charles M., 134
McCarthy, Denis A., 153
McConkie, Bruce R., 10
McGrath, Joann Jensen, 41
McKay, David O., 61
Milton, John, 17

Moore, Clement C., 206

Parkinson, Tracine Hales, 174
Parr, Lucy, 182
Parry, Jay A., 27, 188
Peabody, Josephine Preston, 68

Rich, Wilma M., 125
Roberts, Dorothy J., 50
Romney, Marion G., 18
Rossetti, Christina Georgina, 84, 160, 164

Sadler, Juanita, 144
Scow, Anna Marie, 73
Shakespeare, William, 174
Silesius, Angelus, 62
Smart, William B., 54
Smith, Joseph F., 180
Smyth, A. C., 161
Soelberg, LaRue H., 84

Sterling, Harriet Brewer, 205
Stevenson, Robert Louis, 90, 186
Stewart, Margery S., 33
Sweet, F. H., 173
Swinburne, A. C., 173
Swinyard, Marilyn Ellsworth, 131

Tanner, N. Eldon, 18
Thayne, Emma Lou Warner, 74
Tusser, Thomas, 203

Van Dyke, Henry, 128
Van Paassen, Pierre, 162

Warner, Richard, 74
Wenig, Weiss, 42
Whittier, John Greenleaf, 96

Yates, Alma J., 103
Young, S. Dilworth, 110, 143, 161